LANA

By the Same Authors

JUDY: THE FILMS AND CAREER OF JUDY GARLAND

REBELS: THE REBEL HERO IN FILMS

Joe Morella & Edward Z. Epstein

LANA

The Public and Private Lives of Miss Turner

The Citadel Press   *New York*

Special thanks to:

"BUDDY," PATRICK B. CLARK, AND DAVID C. L'HEUREUX

First edition
Copyright © 1971 by Joe Morella & Edward Z. Epstein
All rights reserved
Published by Citadel Press, Inc.
A subsidiary of Lyle Stuart, Inc.
222 Park Avenue South, New York, N. Y. 10003
In Canada: George J. McLeod Limited
73 Bathurst St., Toronto 2B, Ontario
Manufactured in the United States of America
by The Colonial Press Inc., Clinton, Mass.
Library of Congress catalog card number: 73-175829
ISBN 0-8065-0226-6

*To our families
and the folks on Grove Street*

*Our sincere appreciation to the many
individuals who granted us interviews
in connection with this book.
In certain instances their names
have been withheld at their request.*

"My life has been a series of emergencies. . . ."
LANA TURNER

1

Men. Sex. Materialism. A tremendous career drive. These have dominated and engulfed the incredible life and image of Lana Turner.

She has survived what surely would have been insurmountable setbacks for even the most extraordinary career woman:

The fatal stabbing of Johnny Stompanato—

Seven unsuccessful marriages to date—

Dozens of headline-making love affairs and hundreds of less-publicized ones—

The public censure and private pain connected with the upbringing of her daughter, Cheryl Crane, a girl who in the minds of many is the classic example of Hollywood's mixed-up children.

Still, for almost thirty-five years, Lana Turner has remained a star. Her psyche, not to mention her career, has survived all this and more—the murder of her father, an impoverished childhood, at least one abortion, several miscarriages, bad scripts, suspected suicide attempts, lawsuits and sexual escapades that shocked even Hollywood.

She has had to share with the public the most intimate aspects of her life via a press which eventually turned against her. Yet, despite everything, Lana Turner has consistently excited the public's interest and, generally, she has won its sympathy.

To appreciate fully anything written about Lana Turner, the astute reader has had to read between and beyond the printed lines. The Lana Turner story, undoubtedly the classic Hollywood story, has been one of fact mixed with fantasy, fiction, half-truths, and outright lies.

Lana Turner wasn't discovered sipping a soda at Schwab's—the *New York Times, Esquire* and hundreds of other newspaper and magazine articles to the contrary.

Lana Turner wasn't an overnight success. She didn't bounce from soda stool to movie screen to every magazine cover in the country as the Sweater Girl quite as quickly as the myth would have you believe.

Most of the key men in Lana Turner's life have had several attributes in common. They have all been dashing. Charming. Fast-talking. Promoters. Many have had either gangster connections, mysterious backgrounds, or dealings on the shady side of the law.

Billy Wilkerson was a powerful man in show-business circles. In the early thirties he established and edited the influential motion-picture trade paper, *The Hollywood Reporter.*

The accepted facts are that in Los Angeles, on a balmy January day in 1936, Wilkerson sauntered over to Currie's Ice Cream Parlor on the corner of Highland Avenue and Sunset Boulevard, a few blocks from his office.

Across the street at Hollywood High School, restless fifteen-year-

2

old Judy Turner, as usual, wasn't looking forward to her next class. She decided to cut and go across to Currie's for a Coke.

She cut often and was a regular at Currie's, the "in" place for the sophisticated Hollywood High crowd. When there with her friends, the beautiful youngster was usually the center of attention. She was friendly and open, and even the girls liked her, despite the fact that she was very popular with the boys. It was at Currie's that she met the second-most-important man in her life.

Many men were attracted to the sweet, poised, well-stacked auburn-haired teen-ager. Wilkerson was obviously persevering enough, wealthy enough, and influential enough to be worth talking back to.

It must be more than coincidence that through the years many of Judy's friends were also warm friends of Wilkerson. Lawyer Greg Bautzer, close to Wilkerson, would be Judy's first serious Hollywood affair. (In addition, the much-married Wilkerson was not without gangster connections. He was later closely associated with Ben "Bugsy" Siegel and Mickey Cohen, the latter an underworld figure that would reappear in Judy's future. In the forties, both Wilkerson and Bautzer were involved in one of Siegel's Las Vegas business deals.)

In 1936, with *The Hollywood Reporter*, Wilkerson wielded a great deal of influence among movie men and agents. Judy's own version of their historic meeting, told years later, was that she was introduced to Wilkerson by the manager of Currie's, a close friend of hers, with dialogue to the effect: "Mr. Wilkerson is a close friend of mine, Judy. He's all right. He wants to be introduced."

According to Judy, she responded to several such overtures with polite refusals to meet him, but Wilkerson sauntered over anyway and presented his card. His line was, "How would you like to be in pictures?" Even in 1936 a kid from Wallace, Idaho, knew that one. Especially a sophisticated kid. But Wilkerson was persistent, and Judy has said it was when he told her to call with her mother that she took him seriously.

3

Supposedly Mildred Turner, after checking Wilkerson's credentials, took the girl to the publisher's office. The soda-shop meeting has, through the years, been questioned but never disproven. Whichever way Wilkerson and Judy actually met, it is a fact that Wilkerson arranged an interview for her with the Zeppo Marx Agency. (Zeppo, one of the four Marx Brothers, had retired from pictures in the early thirties to become an agent.)

Judy did not meet with Marx personally but was interviewed by Henry Willson, then twenty-one and the youngest vice president of a talent agency.

The classic version of the Turner success story is that just a few days later Judy was taken to Warner Brothers and signed by Mervyn LeRoy.

"It didn't happen quite that way," recalls Willson. The agency had signed her, and Judy was pretty, but the studios weren't interested. Willson first took her to the Selznick Studios and got her a job as an extra in the 1937 version of *A Star Is Born.* "I think she was in a scene set around a swimming pool," says Willson. "She had no lines. She got $25 for it," he remembers, "but Selznick turned her down for a contract."

Willson took her to RKO next, where they were filming *New Faces,* but they turned her down too. And he remembers distinctly that when he took her to 20th Century-Fox and they turned her down, the casting director telephoned and bawled him out for wasting their time because the drama coach at 20th said the girl couldn't act. Willson retorted, "I didn't say she could act. I said she could be a movie star."

These early rejections at other studios and being an extra are facts which, though not denied, have been ignored, altered, and kept hidden through the years—first by Warner Brothers, then by MGM and even now by Miss Turner, in the interest of maintaining The Legend.

Willson remembers taking Judy to the Trocadero one night, along with clients Anne Shirley and James Ellison. He recalls that at least five producers came over to ask who Judy was. And he also recollects that "none of the kids drank." His memory of Judy is that she was "a likable girl, a wonderful dancer, a sweet and quiet person."

But there were thousands of pretty faces in Hollywood. Judy had absolutely no acting experience or training. Surely she could expect to be in for a "long haul."

Judy and her mother lived in a modest little apartment off Highland Avenue, above Hollywood Boulevard, a residential area made up mostly of small and inexpensive apartment houses that cater to transient trade. Mildred was working and Judy was going to (but hating) school.

Although they were mother and daughter, Mildred was only seventeen years older than Judy. At times, friends remember, they appeared like girl friends, as they watched escape-oriented movies of the day.

Directors who later worked with Miss Turner remarked that if she hadn't become a star making movies she would have spent many of her waking hours watching them, since she was basically fantasy-oriented.

That spring of 1936 couldn't have been unpleasant. Judy was uncommonly pretty and sought-after, and she had Wilkerson and Willson who believed in her potential—if not as an actress certainly as a star.

Though rejected by Selznick, RKO and 20th, Judy had a trait then which she has carried through to the present—the ability to look ahead, not behind. Breaking into movies was tough, but the Turner women had faced and endured far tougher ordeals than this.

Billy Wilkerson was a key man in Judy's young life. But the first important man in her life—the man who had taught her to be positive and look ahead to what life has to offer—had been brutally murdered when Judy was ten years old.

5

"C'mon, Tex, roll 'em!"

"Hurry up, *shoot*, for Christ sake!"

The man they called "Tex" had been a loser all his life, but he had a feeling that at tonight's crap game he would be lucky. It was San Francisco, December 14, 1930. The basement of the San Francisco Chronicle Building. John Virgil Madison Turner, who often used names like Brown, Jones, Smith, was going under the name Tex Johnson that night. It was one of his favorite names, though it's likely he had never been to Texas.

Turner and his family had just moved to the Bay City area from the mining town of Wallace, Idaho. The itinerant worker was an inveterate gambler. He *was* lucky that night. He stuffed the money he won, as was his well-known custom, into his left sock.

The following morning, near the corner of Mariposa and Minnesota streets, in a district known as Butchertown, a man lay slumped against the wall. His coat was pulled over his head. His body was bent back at an awkward angle. He had been hit on the head and died of a fractured skull. His left shoe had been removed, and his left sock was gone.

There were no headlines, no flash bulletins. Just another gambler knocked off by one of his own crowd. In fact, to this day the murder of Lana Turner's father has never been solved.

A friendly, good-looking, genial man with a soft southern accent, Virgil Turner was thirty-six when he died. But he had lived long enough to have a profound effect on his ten-year-old daughter. From Alabama, he was one of a family of twelve, descended from old English and southern stock. Of modest means, like most of his brothers and sisters, he moved from Alabama to settle in the Midwest.

After serving in World War I, Turner moved further west to Wallace, Idaho, a small mining town of about 3,000 people on the northwestern tip of the state.

The man had great personal magnetism and sex appeal. Women were attracted to him immediately. Men liked him. He was a lusty miner who liked good times, with a shrug-of-the-shoulders damn-it-all devil-may-care attitude that was ingratiating rather than obnoxious. He worked as a mine foreman, but his first love was gambling. In Wallace, at a dance, he met Mildred Frances Cowan. Her father, an engineer, Henry Cowan, forbade Mildred to see Turner. She was only fourteen. But Wallace was a very small town, and there were few single girls as vivacious and pretty as Mildred Cowan. She had light-brown hair and blue eyes and shared Turner's love of dancing.

They eloped when Mildred was fifteen and traveled to Missouri, where Turner was a miner. But eventually they returned to Wallace. Mildred was pregnant. Their only child, Julia Jean Mildred Frances, was born there on a blustering winter night, February 8, 1920. (This date, corroborated in early official data, was never questioned until decades later, when Julia Jean swore she was born in 1921.)

The baby girl was baptized in the Protestant church.

In the twenties, the Turner family migrated often. They led a nomadic existence, moving from small mining town to small mining town in the Northwest. If even small-time operators were making money in the stock market, the boom wasn't rubbing off on the Turners. Virgil Turner tried his hand at a number of jobs. He usually worked in the mines. He tried to sell insurance. And he was a bootlegger.

He was a man always trying to make it big, always failing and forced to return to hard physical labor, in the mines or on the docks. Although it must have been a dismal existence, he was a positive, genial person, convinced that good times were just around the corner and probably able, for the most part, to keep this hope alive in his young wife and daughter. Mildred undoubtedly spent as much time as she could (with Judy at her side) at the movies. People in the movies never had any troubles. That fairy-tale world seemed perfect.

Judy has commented that the only secure times of her childhood

7

were when her father worked steadily in the mines. But Turner, it seems, was not the kind of man to be satisfied with this kind of drudgery. He became a casual bootlegger, always in small towns. He probably picked up the art of bootlegging from "friends" he met at crap games. When things got hot, the family moved and changed its name.

As a child Judy was often confused by this constant changing of names. "What are we this week?" the youngster might ask her mother. "Brown," Mildred might reply, or "Smith." They apparently chose easy names so the baby could remember. "I'd rather be Johnson," Judy has remembered saying, "like we were on Tuesday. But I like Turner best of all. Why can't we be Turner?"

"Turner next week," Mildred might have replied.

Virgil Turner had imagination and vitality. Even after a day of working in the mines, he would arrive home and, though exhausted, switch on the phonograph and whirl around the room with his wife.

Years later his daughter remembered that Turner loved music and dancing and singing. "He was an amusing mimic," she said, and felt it easily possible that, if he had had the luck, opportunity and training, "he might have been an actor, perhaps a fine one."

Turner had a wide repertoire of songs, mostly from the South, where he was born—cakewalks, hoedowns, spirituals, jigs. Whatever future studio biographies might say about Judy (and they'd come up with some far-fetched stories), the dancing that she learned in childhood—and she was an excellent dancer—she learned from her father.

The impact her father had on her was evidenced by comments she made decades later. "He was a grand fellow to know, my father, and I adored him. I resemble him, not only in looks—a rather unusual resemblance as a matter of fact—but in temperament and aptitude. He had a certain kind of devil-may-care gaiety combined with a hard kind of willingness to take the consequences. He would fight."

8

Despite Virgil's positive outlook on life, conditions got worse, not better. The Turners migrated to California, Mildred and Judy anticipating the "better life" that Virgil promised was waiting for them in San Francisco. But by now, Mildred probably knew better.

They drove to California in a secondhand Star, the only automobile of the day cheaper than a Model-T. It was a grueling trip across the mountains of the upper Northwest and down into San Francisco. This trip is one of the earliest and most vivid memories Judy has of her childhood. She has remembered one incident in particular during that trip. Her father had fallen asleep at the wheel one hot afternoon while her mother dozed in the back seat. Judy reached over and took the wheel and guided the Star for what seemed like more than ten miles before her father woke up. Judy was proud of her accomplishment. "I believe that such incidents in early childhood have a great bearing on what you are like and how you behave in later life," she has said. "I was applauded for taking over in an emergency. I learned that was the thing to do. Well, almost from that day my life has been a series of emergencies in which I have had to take the wheel without knowing where I was going or how to run the machine."

The great hopes with which the small family set forth were dashed upon arrival in the Bay City. The fabled Golden Gate Bridge which Turner had described to his wife and daughter as a glittering Arch of Triumph seemed to their eyes another crowded thoroughfare. The Turners couldn't afford to stay in San Francisco proper. They drove to a suburb, Daly City, and stayed at a small auto court. Later they moved into a factory district, and times got harder. Turner's luck was running bad at gambling. His occasional jobs as a stevedore were not enough to keep the family fed and clothed.

Somehow they managed. Whatever their lack of money, Judy has remembered that in her childhood she always had good clothes and doesn't ever remember feeling shabby in comparison with the

9

other children. But surely she must have been aware of the struggle to survive.

Despite his chronic troubles, by dint of his personality Turner was able for the most part to keep the family jovial and hopeful. At least Judy thought that was the case, until one day her mother had to have a little talk with her. She has a vivid memory of the conversation, her mother explaining the hard time they were having. "Your daddy can't get work," Mildred told her. "I'll have to find something to do to earn some money, so it means that for a little while we have to be separated." Mildred had some good friends in Modesto. "They want you to come visit them and play with their little girl and go to school. You'll have a wonderful time, dear, and I'll come to see you often and we'll all be together again soon."

Mildred and Virgil did not tell the child they were separating. Perhaps there was hope of a reconciliation. But more likely, they wanted to spare her.

For almost two years, Judy lived with these "friends" in Modesto. This was both before and after her father's murder. Around Christmas, 1930, she was called into the kitchen and told that her mother wanted her at once in San Francisco. The child had a foreboding that the news was bad, and her immediate thought was that her mother was ill. When Judy reached Daly City, she found her mother in good health, but she sensed a strange feeling of tragedy. Her mother said nothing.

The following morning, the child said: "You don't have to tell me. I already know. Father is dead." Mildred told her the whole story—the separation, the crap game, the murder. It was a shock, the kind of shock that makes kids grow up fast.

Years later, the little girl who became Lana Turner said, somewhat prophetically, "Since my life has been wayward and impulsive, always a search for something that is not there, and then disillusionment, I believe I need all the excuses I can make. The shock I suffered then," she said referring to her father's death, "may be a valid excuse for me now. It may explain things I do not myself un-

10

derstand. I know that my father's sweetness and gaiety, his warmth and his tragedy, have never been far from me—that, and a sense of loss and of growing up too fast."

Mildred had been working in a small beauty parlor when Virgil was murdered. She had to continue at her job, so she took Judy back to Modesto. Mildred paid board for Judy, with the arrangement that the girl was to be treated as a member of the family. She was to go to school and church with the other children and enjoy normal holidays.

The Modesto couple had a red-headed daughter, Valentine. But, unknown to Mildred, it was Judy who did all of the work. It would be hard for Judy to forget her years in this household—impossible, in fact. She has said, "I was treated as a servant. Servant is not the right word. I was a scullery maid. Every morning I had to get breakfast and make preparations for dinner before starting to school. On Saturdays I did the family wash, on Sundays I ironed."

Looking back twenty years later, Judy remembered how her mother discovered she was being maltreated. One day Valentine failed to do a small chore according to instructions. Judy was blamed and beaten with a stick until her back was bruised and bleeding.

"The next day I was sore and limping," she has remembered, "hardly able to stand up straight, but I did stand straight because my mother arrived for one of her infrequent visits." They had told the girl her mother was coming, and Judy was instructed to "Keep your mouth shut."

"I knew my lesson well by then. I kept it shut," she has remembered. "I kept it shut so well that but for a happy accident mother would never have known the truth."

During her visit Mildred told Judy that she thought the girl needed new underwear.

Fear of discovery quelled any desire the youngster had for new underthings. "Oh no, mother, mine are perfect. I have plenty."

"But you must need new things," her mother insisted. "Let me see what you have on."

She pulled off Judy's dress. Cuts and bruises were easy to see.

"Did she beat you?" Mildred asked in a stifled voice.

Judy told the truth.

"You are going home with me—after I settle with that woman." And Mildred settled things "in her own quiet way."

Back in San Francisco, the Turner women underwent hard times. It was the beginning of the Depression, and Mildred continued working as a hairdresser. At one point the two moved from San Francisco to Sacramento but found things no better there and moved back.

While in Sacramento, Judy attended a Catholic school run by the Dominican Sisters. Concerning her youth in the convent schools, she has said she plagued the sisters with demands that she be made a nun. "I don't know what foreknowledge they had," she has recalled, "but they smiled and discouraged me."

Judy's publicity as a young starlet often mentioned her early desire to become a nun, but went on to say that she changed her mind and decided to become a fashion designer when she learned that nuns had to cut off their hair.

In San Francisco Judy also attended Catholic school, the Convent of the Immaculate Conception, and later San Francisco Junior High. She was a poor student but had a perceptive mind and the capacity to learn if she wanted to, according to one of the sisters. And around this time Judy became more than interested in boys.

Mildred was working as a beautician at a small shop in the Richmond district. For a while the Turners lived with the lady who owned the shop, a woman named Meadows who had a daughter Hazel, three years older than Judy.

Judy was developing into a very beautiful young girl. Discounting the suggestion that the reason the Turners then moved to Los

Angeles was to get her into films, Judy has said: "My mother had a wonderful friend named Gladys Heath, who made a suggestion that abruptly and spectacularly changed the course of our lives." Mildred was suffering from a cough, and Gladys, with whom she remained lifelong friends, suggested the Turners move to Los Angeles with her, where the weather would be better for Mildred's health. The Turner family had long been used to quick moves like this.

"We did things like that," Judy said. "Moving to another city, starting something new was nothing to us. We had nothing to leave behind and darned little to take with us, so we moved to Los Angeles as casually as we might have moved across the street. We might just as readily have gone to San Diego or to Portland, Maine, depending on the carfare, but we went to Los Angeles, and this shift of scene changed our lives as fantastically as if we'd been transported to a mythical kingdom."

A few years later when Judy was signed to a Hollywood studio contract, the Turner background underwent an abrupt and amusing "mythical-kingdom" transformation. As she has said, "In studio biographies written by press agents who had the prestige of both their and their bosses' star in mind, it was always reported that my father was a mining engineer (a neat bit of snobbery!)."

It wasn't snobbery, of course. It was the job of that corps of skilled technicians in the publicity department of the world's greatest dream factory—MGM of the thirties and forties—to create an appropriate background for America's future Dream Girl. Judy went on to say that the biographies told "that we were prosperous —even well-to-do—before my father died in an accident; and that as a girl I was sent to the best dancing schools. It is assumed, naturally, that I displayed great talent.

"The fact is that all I ever knew about dancing I learned from my father before I was nine years old. I never went to dancing school. We were poor and harassed and no one thought I had talent."

13

These tough formative years were deemed totally unsuitable for public consumption when the image-makers took over Judy's life. Press releases and news stories early in her career carried such colorful and fanciful accounts of the lean Wallace years as:

"There wasn't much chance for dramatics in Wallace, although the town boasted an amateur theatrical group, country club and the 'young crowd.' Mildred and Virgil Turner were a part of this young set. They liked to dance, go to shows, play bridge and have a good time. The coming of the baby in no way stopped them. They just bundled her up, put her in a bassinet and took her along.

"Asked to be a model at the season's society fashion show, Mrs. Turner brought her little girl with her. Sitting in the audience was fun, but not as much fun as walking across the platform and hearing people applaud you. That's what three-year-old Julia Jean thought, and thinking and doing were as one with the youngster. Clutching her blue flannel coat tightly around her she slipped from the audience onto the stage and crossed the platform in a perfect imitation of a model's exaggerated walk. She was the hit of the show!"

The public learned that during her childhood: "Clothes were nothing new to Julia Jean. As soon as she could, Mrs. Turner took her out of ugly flannel night robes and put on crisp white batiste, fragile lace and other pretties. There was nothing unusual about the baby wearing three, four, even five different dresses in one day. Yes," rhapsodized the press releases, "Lana comes by her love of clothes naturally.

"Her debut as a dancer was just as natural. The Elks were putting on a large benefit. Virgil Turner, although an engineer by profession, had always hankered to be an actor. Here was his chance. He and another chap had a song-and-dance routine. But they had no sooner started than his young daughter ran out on the stage and danced with them. Once again she was the hit of the show."

This was typical of the pieces that would be written about Judy and accepted as gospel by the myth-believing populace of the thirties. In those years, the press was very much influenced by the major motion picture studios. Sometimes the same story would be reported four different ways, with different dates, places, facts, in different papers and wire services.

With so much written about one person—with so many press releases and press agents, interviews, conjecturings on the part of interviewers and journalists—the myths and misconceptions were magnified . . . repeated . . . accepted as truth.

Even people involved in the stories began to believe they were true.

In the beginning, although the publicists kept Judy's background relatively "humble," it was strong on fairy-tale qualities. One press release stated that she was dissatisfied with her dress when she was graduated from grammar school, and at that moment she decided to learn designing. Her paternal grandmother was reported to live in Chicago, and the girl supposedly visited her while living in Wallace. Another release said that, after moving to San Francisco, she visited her grandmother in Webb City, Missouri, and that she visited "all the Turner relatives from Missouri down to Mexico City."

While one news story said that it was her grandmother's attic in Chicago, another said it was her grandmother's attic in Webb City which was bulging with the best French fashion magazines that led her to an interest in designing. Articles were run saying that, though Mildred Turner had a difficult time supporting herself and her daughter, she always "managed to find time to keep the icebox well stocked. Their home was still the after-school 'spot.'"

The fantasylike feature stories continued, "Soon there was a tiny amount left over for a few luxuries. The first went for violin lessons for Judy. In order to encourage her daughter to practice, Mrs. Turner started lessons on the banjo! When neighbors asked about the queer noises emanating from the Turner apartment, she didn't bother to explain that Judy was practicing in one room—she in another. 'Turkey in the Straw' was the extent of their joint musical education."

It is doubtful that the Turners could have afforded a violin, a banjo or, for that matter, a two-room apartment of their own when they first moved to Los Angeles. But from the onset of her career, publicity like this would lay the foundation for the legend of Julia Jean Mildred Frances Turner. And it is important to report it, because it was typical of the Hollywood Dream Factory's approach to the manufacturing of a commercial human product.

The truth was that, when they arrived in Los Angeles, the Turners lived with Gladys Heath. Mildred got a job in a local beauty shop (The Lois Williams Beauty Salon) and Judy was enrolled in Hollywood High School. Up to this point, Judy's education had been sporadic, since the family had moved so often. But her physical development was striking. At fifteen she was 5'3", well developed and had brown-auburn hair, enormous blue-gray eyes, magnificent skin and a beautiful dimpled smile. She made an impact even on her sophisticated classmates. Nanette Fabray once remembered, "She was the most incredibly beautiful girl we had ever seen. Even the teachers stared at her. She'd walk down the hall, her back straight, looking straight ahead while all the other kids gawked at her. She was only fifteen but even then she had the bearing of a princess. We all knew she would be a movie star."

Judy's good looks were more than appreciated by her enthusiastic young classmate, Mickey Rooney. He has described Judy Turner as a warm, lovely girl with poise, a superb figure, a beautiful, innocent but know-it-all face. Rooney has said many times that she had "class." He dated Judy for three or four months, having taken her away from Jackie Cooper. Rooney has said that Cooper claims Judy switched her attentions because Rooney got a driver's license first. Rooney liked to believe it was because he himself had the quality he admired in Judy—class. But he conceded that he must have run out of class, because Judy quickly moved on to others.

If one is to believe Judy, she and her mother didn't consider her the great beauty everyone else did. Looking back after a decade as a major star, she claimed: "We did not go to Hollywood with the

16

slightest notion of putting me in motion pictures. I had no such dream. It would have seemed absurd. I had never acted, I had never danced, or tried to do either even semiprofessionally. People didn't stop me on the street and say, 'Ah! What a pretty girl! You ought to be in pictures!' ' "

True, she displayed no abilities. She couldn't act, dance professionally or sing. However, her beauty *was* dazzling and it obviously did make people stop and say, "You ought to be in pictures." Surely Judy, especially living in Hollywood, like all pretty fifteen-year-olds, *must* have dreamt of becoming a movie star.

It was Christmas, 1936, almost a year since her initial discovery by Wilkerson at Currie's. Judy was still with the Zeppo Marx Agency.

Solly Baiano, a former California State tennis champion, was Willson's assistant at the agency. Solly recalls that the first time he saw Judy Turner was in a dress shop on Hollywood Boulevard, where she was working as a salesgirl during Christmas vacation. He had seen her picture at the agency, and he stopped in at the store to see her and set up a time when he could take her out to Warner Brothers. He remembers her as being rather plump.

Judy was one of a group of girls that Baiano was taking around to meet casting directors. The group consisted of types varying from girls-next-door to femmes fatales. Judy somehow combined both types. All Judy has remembered of this period was the disinterested casting directors at studio after studio with directions like, "Walk, turn around, lift your skirt, don't call us we'll call you."

Baiano, however, had a close friend at Warner Brothers, Baron Polan, an assistant to Mervyn LeRoy. Polan saw in Judy something he felt the director wanted for his new picture.

LeRoy, a dark-haired, good-looking, short man who smoked a big cigar and burned up a lot of energy, had made quite a name for himself at Warner Brothers. An astute and talented producer-director, he had promoted the film careers of young Ginger Rogers and

Loretta Young and had unsuccessfully attempted to get Warners to sign Clark Gable in the early thirties. LeRoy had started as an actor himself but switched to directing in the late twenties and producing-directing in the thirties. He had directed such Warner Brothers hits as *Little Caesar*, *I Was a Fugitive from a Chain Gang* and *Anthony Adverse*.

Currently LeRoy was directing a sociological drama, one of many produced by Warner Brothers in the thirties. Claude Rains headed the cast of LeRoy's tentatively titled *Murder in the Deep South*, a tale of a southern trial of Blacks accused of rape and murder.

LeRoy had already interviewed dozens of girls for a pivotal part in the film. "In casting the role, I was looking for a very sexy but very clean—wholesome—young girl," says LeRoy. "One day Solly Baiano brought her in. The minute she walked through the door I knew she was the girl for the part."

He had her walk across the room several times. "I made tests of her. She had terrible hair—dark and all bunched up. So I changed it." He signed her to a personal contract at $50 a week. To the Turners at that time it was a fortune, since Mildred averaged ten to twelve dollars a week at the beauty shop.

LeRoy liked everything about the girl except her hair and her name. Over the years there have been many versions of how she was renamed. Judy has told some interviewers that she named herself and told others that LeRoy picked her unusual new name.

"I named her Lana because I used to go with a girl named Lana years ago at school," says LeRoy. "The soda-fountain discovery story? It might have been true, I don't know," says LeRoy today. "I always thought it was a publicity stunt."

2

The Hollywood that young Lana Turner was christened into in 1936 was a glittering, fast-paced town. In comparison with the rest of the depressed nation, it was, to many people, Utopia. While the average family man fortunate enough to have a job earned about twenty dollars a week (and felt damned lucky to be making it), newcomer Lana Turner had a starting salary of $50 a week, and it would soon be upped to $75.

The studios were in their heyday. The Burbank studios of Warner Brothers were among the most productive, grinding out dozens of pictures annually. The top box-office stars in the nation included Shirley Temple, Gary Cooper, Clark Gable, Ginger Rogers and Fred Astaire, Joan Crawford, James Cagney, Claudette Colbert.

Warners was not noted as the studio of the stars, although they certainly had their share (Bette Davis, Cagney, Edward G. Robinson). Warners was the story studio. And *Murder in the Deep South*, retitled before its release as *They Won't Forget*, was strong on story. A hard-hitting social drama, it had no stars of great box-office power. But the theme of the film was then extremely controversial, and LeRoy's punchy direction would make the most of it.

"Getta load of that kid! Whatta pair of tits!" were the descriptive phrases, accompanied by low whistles, that greeted Lana Turner's appearance on the set, a crew member recalls. The usually blasé crew had seen sweaters before, but obviously Lana's measurements brought a new dimension to the garment—a portent of things to come. This reaction by the hard-bitten crew could not have been lost on LeRoy.

"She was scared to death in her first scene," remembers the director. "She was always a little nervous but she loved her work and she tried to do her best. She *wanted* to be in movies."

LeRoy had given her the role in *They Won't Forget* after some preliminary tests. She had two key scenes: First, she sat at a soda fountain sipping a Coke with her girl friend. Then she left the shop and bounced down a thoroughfare with the camera following her.

"I knew she'd make an impression," says LeRoy, but he admits, "I didn't know she was going to make such an impression."

Her breasts in a tight sweater bounced as she walked. When she turned, the camera, in a long seventy-five-foot tracking shot, followed her bouncing buttocks down the street. "I scored the music to match the up and down of that sweater," says LeRoy.

Cameraman Arthur Edelson and Director LeRoy had seventeen-year-old Lana walk "from here to there" about a dozen times. The crew couldn't have been happier. One onlooker remembers, "Usually crews get bored with constant retakes. It sounds phony to say they weren't bored in this case, but it's true."

Lana didn't have a single scene with the principal players. But she was the character on which hinged the effectiveness of the

20

drama. She had to be a believable, sexy girl-next-door whose rape and murder would evoke the proper emotional response from the townspeople in the story, as well as the audience.

That was all there was to the part. No acting ability required. Just screen impact.

Before the film was released, Lana spent weeks doing publicity layouts for the studio. Sometimes she was photographed with other aspiring starlets at Warners, like Ann Sheridan and Jane Wyman.

Publicity man Bob Taplinger took Lana's photos, plus a new slogan, and promoted her to the press before the film's release. Newspapers and wire services recognized a great gimmick, and Lana Turner became "The Sweater Girl." And, as Lana became part of the lore that America weaves around its Hollywood stars, the term Sweater Girl became an American idiom.

They Won't Forget was released in June, 1937. It was previewed at the Warner Brothers Hollywood Theatre. LeRoy hadn't let her see any of the daily rushes, and Lana has recalled that she and her mother had to wait until the preview. Then, "A girl came on screen. A Thing came on screen. She moved," Lana has remembered, "sinuously, undulating fore and aft. But with a kind of young, coltish grace. Mother and I scrooched in our seats, and my mother said 'My Lord,'" Lana remembered too that, "someone in the audience whistled. There were also some gasps. Then the Thing was gone."

According to Lana's recollection, "Mother and I crept out of the theatre and stumbled into a cab, not knowing what to say to each other. I held myself very self-consciously, trying not to bounce."

Henry Willson says he took her to the preview of *They Won't Forget*. Willson recalls, "After the film, she said, 'I hope I don't look like that.' And I said, 'Fortunately, you do.'"

"Of course I knew I had a bosom," Lana said years later, "but I had assumed that it was stock equipment for girls. All the girls I knew were adequately supplied. I knew I had a rear, too, but it had

21

certainly not occurred to me that my derrière (a word I did not know then) was anything a $2,500-a-week Hollywood cameraman would want to train his lens on."

However, the photos Lana posed for during this period, sweater and all, would seem to indicate that she was quite aware of her physical assets and knowledgeable in displaying them.

The film was well received by critics and was a commercial success. But what is most remembered about *They Won't Forget* is the two-minute bit by the teen-age kid in a tight sweater, skirt and beret. The film launched the career of Lana Turner.

The publicity she received, both prior to and after the film's release, made her if not an overnight star at least an overnight celebrity. The public was interested.

Lana was lucky. She not only possessed physical qualities which had in-person impact, she was also gifted with the indefinable quality of being photogenic.

Mervyn LeRoy was instrumental in furthering her career. "She was fantastically beautiful, and she had *great* screen impact," says LeRoy. He was in a position to give her a lot of help.

Lana, at seventeen, was "merely" a beautiful face and beautiful body, but she had the ability to follow direction. And luckily for her, she had the potential to become a good actress, and would be allowed the opportunity to develop in a series of small roles.

Although her big break was being signed for films initially, she served a three-year apprenticeship and wasn't cast in a really important role until 1941. But during this "apprentice" period, the publicity she received and the life style she set for herself in the late thirties (and continuing throughout the forties, fifties and even nineteen-sixties) made the name Lana Turner synonymous, for better or worse, with the town of Hollywood and the label Movie Star.

Like her father, Lana had a strong will. She was malleable, but only to a point. She was determined to be a success and was, understandably, very materialistic. But she was also determined to have a good time. Her flair for high living had been curtailed by her extreme youth, her lack of funds and also because (according to one of her ex-husbands) of her equally strong-willed mother.

Though Mildred may have been strong-willed with that particular husband, most people remember her as a warm, sweet woman, "not a stage mother." In fact many say that, had Mildred been a stage mother, "Lana would never have stood for it."

But with a taste of success, and LeRoy's belief that Lana would make the big time, the girl started to live it up. She went nightclubbing at every possible opportunity and was dubbed "The Night-Club Queen" in less than a year. She dated her friends Mickey Rooney, Jackie Cooper, Don Barry and all other eligible young (and not so young) men around town.

"It was different in those days," remembers Henry Willson. "People used to meet people easily." Willson referred to the fact that the Hollywood night-club circuit then was one big friendly family constantly welcoming new members, especially beautiful ones like Lana Turner.

She was sophisticated beyond her seventeen years, and knew how to cope with her equally sophisticated suitors. ("She was as warm as she was beautiful," Mickey Rooney has remembered.) The parade may have passed by mother Mildred, but Lana obviously had no intention of letting it pass her by.

Mervyn LeRoy saw to it that in newspaper advertising of *They Won't Forget* Lana received major star billing right alongside of the other, experienced cast members. And Billy Wilkerson made sure that Lana's appearance in the film received major coverage in *The Hollywood Reporter.* The review for her short bit read, in part, "[Lana Turner is] worthy of more than passing note. This young lady has vivid beauty, personality and charm."

Lana would always receive major coverage in the *Reporter.* This trade-paper publicity (the *Reporter* was read daily by every important producer, director and other influential person in Hollywood) was invaluable to her career during these pre-stardom years.

Still under personal contract to LeRoy, Lana went casually to

23

school during this period. But now she was a celebrity. And naturally, thanks to the publicity, she was getting a reputation as a swinger.

LeRoy was now paying her $75 a week. "Sam Goldwyn called me," recalls LeRoy, "and said, 'Mervyn, you have a girl under contract . . . Lily, Lani, Looni . . .'—you know Goldwyn. He knew what her name was. So I said, 'You mean Lana Turner.' I lent her to him."

It was for a bit part in Goldwyn's Gary Cooper vehicle, *Marco Polo*. It literally had "a cast of thousands," and Lana was cast as a Eurasian girl. It was her first experience with a grand-scale Hollywood production. She wore a black wig and scanty outfit and was totally overlooked.

She was unhappy filming *Marco Polo*. ("Anytime Lana isn't the center of attention, she's unhappy," observed one of her friends.) She was embarrassed, felt undressed, didn't know how to play a siren and didn't have Mervyn LeRoy to direct her. One of the stars of the film, Alan Hale, consoled her. "He didn't tease me," Lana has said, "he assured me that 'this too shall pass.' " That philosophy, echoing Virgil Turner's credo, obviously made an indelible impression on Lana. It would see her through many crises in her life.

The most significant aspect of *Marco Polo*, from Lana's point of view, was that the make-up people shaved off her eyebrows. They have never grown back. Many times in later years in candid shots, Lana, minus make-up and eyebrows, would be unrecognizable.

After *Marco Polo* she returned to Warner Brothers for a bit as a scullery maid ("A part I knew how to play!") in LeRoy's *The Great Garrick.*

Garrick went into release first, and five months later, in February, 1938, *Marco Polo* was released. That month Lana celebrated her eighteenth birthday. At Warners, she also played a bit part, almost an extra, in a forgotten film, *Four's a Crowd*.

Years later, recalling LeRoy and her days at Warners, Lana said: "I can't say I ever thought of Mervyn as a father. No matter what writers say, if I have a father complex I don't know about it. But Mervyn certainly was there to counsel me."

Lana has told a story of being at a party where she wore a huge ring, "imitation glass with rhinestones." LeRoy looked at the ring but said little.

"The next day he called me into his office," Lana has recalled. "I still had that ring on. Mervyn was so gentle. He said, 'Lana, you're just starting now, and I believe you're going to be a big star. One day you'll thank me for giving you this tip. Never use anything that's imitation, because you don't need to imitate or pretend, as you're doing with that ring.'

"I can remember the blush, if that's possible, starting from my toes," Lana recalled years later. "I had been seeing all those women with their beautiful jewels, and I did so want to be like them."

Lana was still in her teens. She saved the ring for years and looked at it many times to remind herself of that lesson.

"I wonder," she later speculated, "if that experience could have been partly responsible for the fact that, when I hit my stride, I spent the money faster than it came in, mostly buying jewels."

In 1938, LeRoy, although married to one of the Warner sisters, had been wooed from Warner Brothers to MGM, at that time the largest and most prestigious motion-picture studio in the world. Lana, under personal contract to LeRoy, also made the move.

"When I left Warners," says LeRoy, "Jack Warner said, 'You take her. I don't think she'll amount to anything.'"

This was another fortuitous move for Lana. Not only had she come to Metro as the protégé of the most favored and highly paid producer-director on the lot (LeRoy was making $6,000 a week—twice as much as any other producer and more than any of the studio's stars except Gable), but MGM was noted for building stars. Jean Harlow had been an MGM commodity. Her recent death left a vacancy for a new sex symbol.

"I sold Lana to Metro in a deal with Benny Thau," says LeRoy. Ben Thau was one of Louis B. Mayer's most trusted lieutenants; his recommendations to the front office regarding talent were invaluable. Hollywood tales over the years have pointed to Thau's importance at Metro. Supposedly the starlets who never made it at the studio were those who "wouldn't play ball with Benny." Ava Gardner was said to be one who became successful despite Thau's lack of help, but it took her years to do it.

When she switched to MGM, Lana was enrolled in school on the lot with Mickey Rooney, Judy Garland, Freddie Bartholomew and others. They attended school in a fantasylike Little Red Schoolhouse presided over by a special teacher who was part of the Los Angeles school system.

Rarely has a less-interested group of students been assembled. Lana's indifference to school was greater than ever. Judy Garland, who became one of Lana's best friends at MGM, remembered that Lana always used to raise her hand to be excused, and she would go outside to smoke.

Lana has been a heavy smoker for much of her life. She smoked incessantly on the sets of her films, but any photos taken had cigarettes airbrushed out before the photos were released to the press, by specific order of Louis B. Mayer.

Lana has said of these years, "I spent most of my time fending off learning and fending off Mickey Rooney."

But she was learning the business. Her first Metro picture was *Love Finds Andy Hardy*. It wasn't a Mervyn LeRoy film, "But everyone went into the Hardy films," chuckles LeRoy. It was Louis B. Mayer who personally determined what shape these films would take. This was the third Hardy picture, and a special one, because it utilized the talents of three performers in whom the shrewd Mayer sensed big profits: Rooney, already well on his way; Arthur Freed's protégé, Judy Garland; and Mervyn LeRoy's protégé, Lana.

Rooney was very helpful to Lana during filming. He taught her how to make sure the camera caught her face, even in shots where another actor would be the focal point of the scene. If she wasn't too bright with schoolbooks, Lana was a scholar of genius proportions when it came to the camera. A fellow actor has described her mind as "a steel trap" when it comes to being photographed and playing a scene.

LeRoy and almost every director she has worked with concur that she learns fast, is a quick study and a real pro. A person who has worked on many Turner films agrees. "She's quick on pickup," the friend says. "When it comes to knowing how she's coming across, she never misses the mark. Never. Because wherever her key light is she hits it to perfection. She's the cameraman's dream when it comes to that. He never has to worry about focusing. He gets it in rehearsal and he knows exactly what to do in the take because she won't vary a fraction."

In *Love Finds Andy Hardy*, they used Lana as the story's sex symbol, but in a toned-down, Middle-America, Andy Hardy-series way. No bouncing buttocks or bouncing breasts were in evidence here. Her hair was still red and photographed brown. She did, however, manage to convey a certain sophistication—especially in contrast to Garland's Betsy Booth character and Ann Rutherford's Polly Benedict. And naturally she was sexy enough to overwhelm gullible little Andy Hardy.

Lana Turner and Sex—synonymous even in an Andy Hardy picture. She did wear a bathing suit in one scene, and again they capitalized on her highly publicized drugstore discovery by inserting a scene with her, Judy and Mickey in Carvel's local Malt Shop. Years later Mickey Rooney remembered that after their innocuous kissing scene where "we smacked like a couple of aging virgins," he would run to his dressing room to play the horses and Lana would run to the telephone to talk with men ten times more sophisticated than Andy Hardy.

MGM's publicity department found in Lana a willing and highly promotable subject. Their public-relations people were the best in the business. They were able to generate news and press interest in uncooperative stars who wouldn't succumb to Hollywood-type socializing or reveal facts of their personal lives—stars like Greta

Garbo, Luise Rainer, Spencer Tracy. With someone like Lana Turner, the publicity people found it difficult to keep just one step ahead of her. She was making news without their help. In fact, in ensuing years, their job in many cases would be to keep her name out of the papers.

Many ex-MGM publicity department employees claim that Howard Strickling, head of the studio's publicity operations, came to loathe both Turner and Garland because of the problems they created.

Laszlo Willinger was one of Metro's top still photographers, brought over from Europe in the thirties. He spent many hours photographing and working with the young talent at MGM. He says, "Lana was just another little girl who happened to have a good figure, so she was elected to do leg art. Don't forget, there were 350 people under contract to the studio, so the amount of exposure you got was due to cooperation with the publicity department. Part of the publicity department's job was to do internal selling—they had to sell the stars not only to the public but to the studio's staff of producers and directors. Lana and LeRoy helped each other. I think she was one of LeRoy's biggest assets."

Lana's secret, according to Willinger, was that she was never too tired for the publicity department. "She had an absolute understanding of the value of publicity and knew that whatever she did she had to be up and looking beautiful at 9:00 a.m.

"She moved up from man to man," says Willinger. "I always thought her acting was sort of a sideline and she showed no development. I think her approach was even then old-fashioned because she was so out of touch with outside life at that point. She practically lived at the studio and was a total product of publicity. What's more, she believed in her image. When she was seventeen or eighteen and making about $100 a week [Willinger was making over $300 a week], I got annoyed with her at one sitting and raised my voice and she said, 'How dare you talk to a star like that!' "

Lana obviously didn't captivate Willinger, who admits that she had a certain radiance whenever she walked into a room. And he recalls that she was pleasant while rising to the top, very popular with crews. "She never developed airs, and was like Gable in that respect. That's why they liked each other." But he also thinks that her work was all, she had no other interests. "The only thing real to her was the camera," says Willinger.

Lana fell into tinsel town's social whirl as though born into it. She made the transition from abject poverty to conspicuous consumption in almost record time.

Lana's mother had long since quit the beauty shop (when Lana's salary hit $100 a week after *The Great Garrick*) and before long Lana was earning almost triple that figure. They had moved into a better apartment and Lana bought herself a fire-engine-red roadster. Lana willingly believed all her publicity ("It was heaven on earth," she said years later, "which isn't bad") and was happy to be the sexy sweater girl incarnate and a member of the giant MGM family. Father-figure Louis B. Mayer willingly spoiled his star children and put up with their antics as long as their box-office power remained strong. While Lana was not a big box-office draw yet, her fan mail was heavy and she was improving as an actress. And Mayer's fair-haired boy, LeRoy, believed in her. "It was all politics at MGM in those days," remembers a director on the lot. "If you were in with the right people, doors would open for you. Turner was LeRoy's pet, Ben Thau liked her too and LeRoy and Thau were Mayer's favorites. This relationship gave Lana time to learn the business. She was a damned good politician herself."

In discussing the men she knew at MGM, it was Willinger's opinion that, compared with the "gangsters and riffraff" she came to run around with on the outside, the men that she associated with at the studio who furthered her career were cultured gentlemen.

At the time, MGM's drama coach was Lillian Burns, and she agreed with LeRoy and Mayer that Lana's potential as an actress was greater than anyone initially supposed. If Lana wouldn't burn

29

the candle at both ends, she could make it. Lana and Lillian (who later became the wife of director George Sidney) became close friends and have maintained a lifelong friendship.

But although her acting potential was yet to be fulfilled, Lana was fulfilling her potential as a newsmaker in Hollywood's young set at an alarming rate. She and others of her crowd, which included Mickey Rooney, Judy Garland, Linda Darnell, Bonita Granville, Gene Tierney, Ann Rutherford, Robert Stack, Mary Beth Hughes, and Jackie Cooper, were described as "the current leaders of the new Hollywood social scene."

As "The Night-Club Queen," Lana lived up to her reputation. She has said, "I liked the boys and the boys liked me. I think men are exciting, and the gal who denies that men are exciting is either a lady with no corpuscles or a statue."

Lana's corpuscles were getting a workout. She was a regular at Charlie Morrison's Mocambo and at Ciro's. The Beverly Hills Tropics Restaurant invented a drink for her, and named it "Untamed." She was named by Walter Winchell, America's most powerful columnist of the day, as "America's Sweater Sweetheart." Whether promoted or not, she received all sorts of attention as the sweetheart of college fraternities, the Queen of the Dartmouth Winter Carnival and honored guest at Princeton house parties.

Lana Turner was Happening. *Life* magazine tagged her America's idea of what a motion-picture starlet ought to be. Young girls across the nation started to idolize her. She was living the life all of them yearned to lead. Though a budding sex symbol she wasn't resented by female fans, and in later years women would make up the bulk of her following.

Her love life was so hectic and obviously fulfilling that it started to take precedence over her career. Lana has said of this period, "Oh I did some pictures and went casually to school, but that was incidental to being in Hollywood and being part of Hollywood. Mother fretted. She thought a working girl should be in by 11 o'clock. She actually thought I ought to work. What odd ideas parents have."

L. B. Mayer obviously agreed with Mildred Turner. Several times he found it necessary to reprimand Lana. There were tears and promises. And, according to Lana, a while later she'd "play hooky" again. Her mother tried to control her. But Lana had a strong will of her own. And she was the breadwinner.

She was a swinger with style. She did it with a flair matched by few. She had (and has) an instinct for making an entrance, for getting the spotlight.

Men have always gravitated around her. And a man's looks were what interested her right away. "Let's face it, it's the physical that attracts me first. If you get to know a man's heart and soul, that's icing on the cake." She was, according to one of her ex-husbands, "basically a romantic. She wanted her love life to play like a scene from a romantic Hollywood film. Only with lots of sex. Sex is very important to her. She can't seem to get enough of it. She's like two people. She's a purring baby doll on one hand, and almost animal in her appetites at the same time."

Lana's first highly publicized affair in Hollywood was with young, sophisticated attorney Gregson Bautzer. Bautzer, then as today, handled the affairs of many of Hollywood's elite. By 1939, even though her date list included George Raft and even Bentley Ryan, Bautzer's law partner, MGM reported she had "narrowed her attentions to Greg." The Metro executives were happy with her choice of Bautzer. Perhaps he could keep her in check. Bautzer was a charming, good-looking man, experienced in the ways of Hollywood courtships. He had entertained many of Hollywood's sophisticated stars.

Although no formal engagement was announced, it was assumed by their friends and the press of the day that the couple was engaged.

Later Lana said, "I was engaged to Greg Bautzer. That is, if any-

one can claim actually to be engaged to this astute escape artist."
The astute-escape-artist tag was picked up by the press, and Bautzer
remained one of Hollywood's most eligible bachelors for several
years. Though he had a brief marriage to Buff Cobb in the middle
forties, he and Lana remained good friends. In fact, Bautzer handled her first divorce case and advised her on many subsequent sep-
arations.

They attended Hollywood openings and frequented all the
nightspots, many times staying until closing. While Mildred Turner didn't approve of Lana's nightclubbing till dawn, she did approve of Greg Bautzer. He was everything a mother could want for
her daughter—a lawyer, wealthy, successful. And Lana apparently
respected him.

Nightclubbing and entertaining Greg did not prevent her from
continuing her career, although even at nineteen it would seem she
couldn't go to bed at 3:00 a.m., be at the studio by 6:00 a.m., and
look her best for the all-seeing eye of the camera. "She didn't stay
up too much when she was working—that *I* know of," says LeRoy.

Laszlo Willinger, who worked with Lana often in recreating certain scenes from her films for poster art (in those days still photographers were not permitted to photograph actual shooting), says,
"She was always on time, always sober and always extremely patient." But he regarded her patience as indicative of a lack of intel-
ligence. "She was no trouble, but then again she was never any in-
spiration either," he says.

"Despite her heavy make-up and rotten diet [she drank Coke all
the time and ate chocolate bars, according to Willinger], she did
have magnificent skin. I loved to photograph her in close-up because of her flawless complexion."

Willinger's favorite photograph of Lana was never released. The
Hays Office killed it as being too suggestive. It was a closely
cropped portrait of Lana's face—including only her forehead to her
chin, even excluding her hairline. The Hays Office killed it because
there wasn't any evidence she had clothes on.

"In the early days," according to Willinger, "Lana sometimes had to wear wigs, since her hair color changed so often. One day she even came in with green hair." Her mother dyed her hair then and Willinger remembers Lana saying, "I can't tell my mother she doesn't know what she's doing." She wore a wig for that photo session.

In her next film, *Rich Man, Poor Girl*, Lana was billed as "The Kissing Bug from the Andy Hardy film." Then came Mervyn LeRoy's production of *Dramatic School*. In this Lana played Mado, described in the ads as "the girl who traded her career for jewels." The film played Radio City Music Hall, and MGM publicists contributed new lore to the legend of Lana Turner with misinformation that read, "A talent scout saw her at lunch at school, suggested a screen test which won her an MGM contract and she made her film debut in *Love Finds Andy Hardy*."

Both these films were released in 1938, and that same year Lana screen-tested for the role of Scarlett O'Hara. Every actress under fifty in Hollywood was mentioned for the role. Lana's test wasn't the worst of the lot, but it proved she wasn't remotely ready to undertake such a part. However, in real life Lana, like Scarlett, had a "damn the consequences" and "I'll think about that tomorrow" philosophy. That year she also lost out on a role in MGM's Clark Gable-Norma Shearer starrer, *Idiot's Delight*. She had to relinquish that one because of her poor grades at school.

But in 1939, with school behind her, Lana made three films. In *Calling Dr. Kildare*, she played a "bad girl," but with sympathetic overtones. She did a good job, and was believable. Her acting was improving. This time her studio publicity read, "[Lana] was educated in San Francisco and was a model and designer before being discovered by Mervyn LeRoy."

In *These Glamour Girls*, there were other bigger stars in the picture who had their own dressing rooms. Lana wanted a private dressing room, but was told she wasn't a star. She came in the following morning with a little dog on a leash, followed by a Black maid. She said now she *was* a star and should be treated like one. Lana got her dressing room. She also got star billing with Lew Ayres. Her build-up continued: "Lana Turner, the red-headed sensation who brought 'It' back to the screen."

Onlookers remember that Lana was always "a lady" on the set. "She demands respect and she treats people in kind, the way they treat her."

In the summer of 1939, she was given the starring role in *Dancing Coed*, a property originally purchased for Eleanor Powell. The film was notable for two reasons. First, although all of Lana's films at Metro up to this time were "B" films, the studio recognized her improvement as an actress, and *Coed* gave her a title role assignment for the first time. Secondly, the picture co-starred bandleader Artie Shaw. It was his first picture, but he was already established as a famous musician, composer and dance-band leader. He was also touted as one of the most intelligent and learned of show-business personalities, held several degrees and was a writer as well. He was billed as a "King of Swing," but didn't keep it a secret that he "hated jitterbugs."

While they filmed *Dancing Coed*, it was hardly love at first sight. Lana was involved with Bautzer (although he was dating others, including "Bugsy" Siegel's girl, actress Wendy Barrie). Making the movie was a routine assignment as far as Lana's attitude toward leading man Shaw was concerned. She and Shaw usually sat at opposite ends of the set.

Today Artie Shaw talks freely of his relationship with Lana. He remembers that Lana was gorgeous, but not very communicative. On a day during *Dancing Coed* when a camera setup was taking a particularly long time, he made a "verbal grab" for her.

"Say," Shaw kidded Lana, "if you don't talk to me I won't play your music right."

Lana took the remark completely seriously. "You wouldn't dare," she shot back.

Shaw, surprised, explained that he was only kidding and was

trying to break the ice between them. "You might have said something nicer," she said, not at all placated.

Shaw hadn't endeared himself to anyone in the Hollywood group. He came to the town already famous and took a dim view of the movie business. It has been reported that on the set of *Dancing Coed* the lighting crews spent time planning how to "accidentally" drop a sun arc lamp on the musician's head.

After she and Shaw completed the film, Lana remarked: "He was the most egotistical thing. He hogged the camera all the time and he spent more time with the hairdresser and the make-up man than any actor on the lot. That was funny, because he wasn't any too good-looking to begin with."

Shaw says he had good reason to be unhappy with *Dancing Coed.* In it he played himself, Artie Shaw, placed in a fictional situation. He had signed for the role with the understanding that, if he were playing himself, he could write his own lines. "I would have been happy to speak the inane lines in the script if I were playing a character with any other name, as long as he wasn't supposed to be me," he says. The studio agreed, but when production started it was obvious that they meant him to read the script as written. He was unhappy, and didn't try to hide it.

According to Lana, Shaw's opinion of her was no higher than his opinion of Hollywood. "He regarded me as an untutored blonde savage, and took no pains to conceal his opinion," she has said. (She was, in fact, a redhead at the time.)

The picture was completed without incident and released in October, 1939. It did well commercially, and Lana's star was rising. She was the cover girl of *Look* magazine, and a few months later she would be on the cover of *Life.* Metro put "America's Blonde Bonfire" into *Two Girls on Broadway* and gave her billing over established stars Joan Blondell and George Murphy. The studio claimed it was Lana's "hottest, most daring role." During this period, while she was still dating Bautzer, it was reported that Lana was hospitalized for "an emergency appendectomy."

Shaw saw no more of Lana after *Dancing Coed* was completed. One day, a short while later, Phil Silvers paid a visit to his friend Shaw.

"There's somebody who wants to see you," Silvers said.

"Who?" asked Shaw. "Do I know her?"

"Just come with me."

Silvers took him to MGM, where the guard wouldn't let Silvers through the gate until he spotted Shaw with him. Silvers took Shaw to an enormous sound stage. On one end of the stage, in a pool of light, a group of actors were doing a scene. At the top of the staircase set was a girl Shaw remembers as "a knockout, incredible. She was literally sewn into a green satin gown. You could see every pore, even the outline of her nipples. It was quite a sight. I didn't know who it was, but I was interested."

Finally, the scene for *Two Girls on Broadway* was shot, and the girl in green satin made her way over to Silvers and his friend.

"Hi," she said to Shaw. "Remember me?"

Shaw remembered, and, alongside beaming Phil Silvers, engaged in about five minutes of meaningless banter with Lana. "She was like a different person. She was sweet, charming and available. She said to me, 'Let's go to dinner sometime.' I said, 'Fine. How about tonight?' 'Okay,' " she answered.

MGM publicity described their meeting much more romantically. According to it, the meeting occurred in the Metro commissary. Lana was having lunch one day, and a waitress handed her a rose. It was from Artie Shaw, who bowed and smiled from across the room. Then, the fablelike story continued, "Shaw and Turner became friends, sort of."

The Lana Turner and Artie Shaw of 1939 had at least one volatile trait in common. They were impulsive. Although Lana later said, "He could be one of the most amusing and charming persons in the world when he wanted to be," Lana's friends thought she hated Shaw and were startled by the Turner-Shaw elopement.

"She had gone to her agent and L. B. Mayer
when she found out she was pregnant
and the three of them decided on the abortion."
ARTIE SHAW

3

Artie Shaw wasn't always charming—at least according to Lana. There are, of course, two sides to every story and a half-dozen versions of each side. Lana has admitted that her elopement with Shaw was a spur-of-the-moment decision made at a time when she was angry with Greg Bautzer.

On her twentieth birthday, February 8, 1940, Lana had a special evening planned. She was looking forward to a date with Greg, who was supposed to take her and Mildred out to celebrate. Friends felt she wanted to—was ready to—marry Greg. But was he ready—or willing—to marry her?

Early in the evening on her birthday he called to cancel the date because of a stomach problem. Lana was not convinced that it was the reason. She was furious. She has said that she had barely hung up on Bautzer when Artie called. (According to Shaw, Lana broke the date with Bautzer in favor of *him*.)

"Okay, feller, let's go for a ride," she said.

"There we were in the car," remembers Shaw. "That face of Lana's. It really was The American Dream. Unbelievably beautiful. Yet she seemed genuinely concerned about other things. She wanted children, a home, she said. I'm sure she actually *believed* the things she said when she was saying them.

"Hell, why not, I thought. The marriage just might work."

Lana's version, given years later: "I'd hated that man—oh how I'd hated him—and the awful things I'd said about him in print!" But it was a lovely night and Lana said that *Shaw* began telling *her* that all he wanted was the little house, the picket fence, lots of kids. "All the things I dreamed of having with Greg. Only Greg wasn't going to marry me."

Shaw had been married twice before. If Lana was psychologically ready to marry at the moment, she could not have selected a less suitable mate. To Shaw, marriage was, he says, "a legal way of going to bed with someone. If that's what it took, I'd get married."

Life magazine later reported that Herbert Radden, whom *Life* described as "an informed commentator" but whom Shaw doesn't remember at all, said: "Artie was in rare form. He gave forth first with the 'I'm sick of it all' routine, followed by the 'futility of it all' barrage, then the 'chaos of the world, desire for the tranquility of the home and family.' "

Life also quipped that "at the end of the campaign, Miss Turner . . . gave her consent with a brevity almost Lincolnian.

" 'Let's go,' she said."

Shaw jerked his car around and rushed back to his house in Hollywood, where he telephoned Paul Mantz. Mantz was known as "The Honeymoon Pilot."

"I can still see Lana's face looking up at me," recalls Shaw. "She was committed."

Lana's recollection of the event was that they moved faster than a chase sequence in a Keystone comedy. At the time Mantz ran a plush Honeymoon Special. It was a small plane for movie stars and other celebrities who might want to take a short trip to Las Vegas (then rather a hick town) or Reno (then the "in" place) to get married or just spend the weekend.

He piloted Shaw and Lana to Las Vegas, where a sleepy justice of the peace, Judge George E. Marshall, dressed in a polka-dot dressing gown, performed a simple ceremony. And, according to Lana, "It was then I kissed Mr. Shaw for the first time."

She wired her mother a cryptic, GOT MARRIED IN LAS VEGAS. LOVE, LANA. The elated girl forgot to say whom she married. When Mildred received the telegram, she was delighted. She, of course, assumed Lana had married Bautzer. However, well aware of Hollywood mores and her daughter's impulsive nature, she decided to check. She called Bautzer and was shocked when he answered the phone. She related the message in the telegram, and Bautzer asked whom she went out with. He guessed that she had married Shaw, but told Mildred he would check and call her back. Mildred hadn't made a secret of the fact she didn't like Shaw.

Even Lana has said, "My elopement with Artie Shaw was typical of Hollywood at that time." It was indeed typical. On screen, the sequence might have been played by Claudette Colbert and Ralph Bellamy. "The sudden marriage, the chase by reporters, the whim, the dashing action, that was the style in 1940, so I lived up to it."

On their way from the airport back to his house, Shaw and Lana passed reporters but made it home free of their pestering.

It hadn't occurred to the newshounds that night to check Shaw's residence, but the press located the couple the following morning. Shaw says he will never forget that morning. The hilltop, as seen through their window, was crawling with people—reporters, fans, curiosity seekers. They were all over the place.

"The whole business had an unreal feeling about it. Even Lana, lying there next to me, seemed unreal. It had all happened so fast."

Lana and Shaw posed for impromptu pictures in which Lana

wore Shaw's pajamas and dressing gown. She had drawn on eyebrows with a lead pencil. Urged on by Shaw, she called the studio, told them she had gotten married and wouldn't be in for work.

For the next few days, Artie and Lana were front-page news. The deserted Bautzer was called on for a statement. From the man whose ring Lana said she had worn "so long it's almost covered with skin" came the following: "My God, I'm really heartbroken. This came as a complete surprise to me. I can't really put it in words how much I cared for Baby."

Betty Grable, Shaw's most recent girl friend, was located in New York, presumably "grieving furiously." Asked if she were brokenhearted, Betty remarked, "No, I wouldn't say that exactly." What she would say was, "It must have come on him very suddenly."

MGM officials gave out statements of surprise and shock at news of Lana's elopement. Although they didn't state it publicly, they were particularly upset that Lana had tied herself up with a very independent thinker who might disturb her relationship with the studio.

However, two months later, Metro cashed in on all the publicity with the release of *Two Girls on Broadway*, and Lana and Artie's much-publicized cross-country trip to New York concurrent with the film's opening at the Capitol Theatre. The trip was paid for by Shaw, since Metro wanted Lana to stay put.

The studio was genuinely concerned over her impulsive behavior. They didn't want a potential gold mine to run out on them. Louella Parsons, in those days a tremendously powerful public-opinion-making force, often used her column, at the urging of friendly studio officials, to castigate stars who weren't behaving themselves.

Louella reported that Lana would have walked out on her MGM contract rather than forego the trip to New York with Shaw. In a column dated April 27, 1940, Miss Parsons said prophetically: "If Lana Turner will behave herself and not go completely berserk she is headed for a top spot in motion pictures. She is the most glamorous actress since Jean Harlow." She compared Lana to Clara Bow as being emotional rather than practical. "Both of them, trusting and lovable, use their hearts instead of their heads. Lana, of course, has never been in any scandal, but she has always acted hastily and been guided more by her own ideas than by any advice any studio gave her."

Louella continued, "However, she is very young and perhaps one day will realize that, although the breaks may come easily, it takes real effort to stay on top."

Louis B. Mayer paid a personal visit to Artie Shaw. "He told me not to get Lana pregnant," remembers Shaw. Since Shaw wasn't under contract to MGM, and was making a fortune from his other endeavors, he was in the enviable position of being able to tell Mayer to go to hell.

During this period, Lana was hospitalized for what was described as "exhaustion."

"I believed her," says Shaw, "until someone told me that Lana had had an abortion. I couldn't believe it. I confronted her with it, but she denied it. But I kept after her and finally she admitted it. She had gone to Johnny Hyde, her agent, and L. B. Mayer when she found out she was pregnant, and the three of them decided on the abortion.

"I didn't know what my feelings would have been. I may not have wanted the kid myself. But I felt I should at least have been consulted, since I was paying the rent."

In Shaw's opinion, Lana was like a horse with blinders when it came to her career. She saw straight ahead to her goal, ignoring everything else. And she certainly wasn't interested in having a baby. She was having too good a time. Shaw feels that this was the point in their marriage where things turned sour.

In early 1940, it was taking all of Lana's efforts to concentrate on her marriage to Shaw. Mildred was not at all happy with the alliance, and it was reported it took her weeks to get over the "shock."

"Mildred was a hard-assed man-eater," Shaw says. "She was a

stage mother. I recognized the breed. I had one. She wanted very much to control Lana's private life, but she couldn't. Lana was strong-willed. Mildred kept popping in on us unannounced, and I figured out a way to take care of that," Shaw remembers.

"I asked Lana if she would mind if I stopped Mildred from dropping in unexpectedly. Lana giggled and said of course she wouldn't mind, which should give you an insight into the relationship they had. So I told our valet that the next time Mildred came to the door to let me know, but keep her outside. It happened, and I dismissed the valet for the evening while Mildred was waiting outside the front door. Then I stripped, completely, to the buff. I went to the door, stark naked, and flung it open. I pretended to be startled to see Mildred. She was genuinely shocked to see me—bone naked. She gasped. 'Oh,' I said, pretending to be surprised, 'I thought it was someone else.' That was the last time she ever paid us an unexpected visit."

While married to Shaw Lana completed an innocuous MGM drama, *We Who Are Young*. Some of the reviewers noted in her performance a potential for drama. Her trip to New York with Shaw in April, via the famed 20th Century-Limited, was touted as her first trip to Gotham, and the press welcomed them with open arms and flash bulbs. Shaw didn't like New York any more than he had liked Hollywood. He said he had brought Lana to New York to see the Lower East Side, the ghetto in which he had grown up.

Lana seemed to have a good time on the trip.

Back home they went to a sneak preview of *We Who Are Young*. In one sequence, Lana was gowned in a negligee. "It had tremendous impact up there on the screen," remembers Shaw. "It was very sensual and there were whistles in the audience and excited mumbling. I didn't like her parading herself like that for everyone to see. But she loved it, of course."

In 1940 *Newsweek* reported—in an article with a picture of Lana—"Sweaters have become a glamour garment and the Breen Office (formerly the Hays Office) has sent a letter to producers that any sweater shots in which breasts are clearly outlined will be rejected." Still, sweater sales in 1939 were 22 percent ahead of 1929.

In Hollywood, Shaw supposedly expected Lana to cook and keep house. Since she was then earning close to $1,000 a week and he reportedly was earning in the neighborhood of $150,000 a year, these chores were hardly necessary. Many of the stories were planted by MGM to build sympathy for their budding star so that if and when the marriage collapsed the blame would fall on Shaw, at least in the minds of the ticket-buying public.

Judy Garland had had a crush on Artie, and Shaw's mother had wanted him to marry her. When he married Lana, Judy stopped visiting him. "I asked her why," says Shaw. "I knew she had had a crush on me, but it never went beyond that. And I knew that she liked Lana, and Lana was fond of her. But Judy said, 'Artie, she's a nice girl, but it's like sitting in a room with a beautiful vase.' "

The honeymoon didn't last very long. Lana has called her marriage to Shaw "my college education." She said Shaw told her she was ignorant, which she admitted. She claimed he found fault with everything about her . . . her make-up, clothes and desires to go nightclubbing and dancing. Magazines of the day reported that she made "a desperate effort to conceal a secret passion for the music of Clyde McCoy" ("a pathetic lie which irked me," says Shaw), and that there was an explosive argument over her desire to attend Guy Lombardo's opening at the Coconut Grove.

Years later, Lana's version of how it went between them: " 'Get rid of those ridiculous high heels. Wear low heels,' commanded Mr. Shaw. 'Also that damn lipstick. Wipe it off your mouth.'

"Shaw muttered a quotation one day, 'From Nietzsche, *Thus Spake Zarathustra,*' he said impatiently.

" 'Zara-who?' I asked.

"Shaw stalked out, disgusted."

Shaw denies all this and calls it nonsense. He points out that they had a servant and Lana wasn't required to do any domestic chores. In addition, he says he made no attempt to improve her mind. He calls "that college education quote" sarcastic, "unlike Ava Gardner, who meant it when she called me her college education. Ava was a much deeper person than Lana. She had other dimensions to her personality. Lana was dumb."

Lana also said she was supposed to iron Shaw's shirts after having washed them herself in the bathroom sink. And she didn't like his musician friends or her hausfrau duties. One night, she claimed, when she tried to entertain guests at a dinner she had cooked, Shaw disgustedly threw the plates on the floor. That was Lana's last attempt at dinner. On another occasion, he reportedly hit her.

The final straw in their relationship, according to her, was when he threw a pair of shoes at her and said, "And don't forget to have those cleaned." Then he slammed the door. Lana ran. She knew the telephone number. She called it, crying. "Greg, I've had it," she whimpered. "What do I do?"

"Get out, baby, get out," Lana has remembered Bautzer saying. "I'll take care of everything."

She began to pack her things as soon as Shaw departed, "in a frothy burst of angry genius." She called her business manager and told him she was leaving Shaw, so that certain arrangements could be made, and Shaw learned of her impending departure from him.

Lana was dating Tony Martin by now. "Tony and I were doing a show at the same radio network at about the time that Lana and I had decided to split but before the split was made public," says Shaw.

"One day, in the men's room, Martin ambled in and started using the urinal next to me. 'Hi, Artie,' he said. 'Say, would you mind if I started dating Lana? She told me that you two were finished, but I wanted to ask your permission anyway.'

"I didn't like him asking me like that over the latrine nor did I like his attitude, and I said, 'Sure, do anything you like. It doesn't make any difference to me.' I was bugged that he knew about it, since he must have heard it from her."

An interesting sidelight is how the press learned of the Shaw-Turner split-up. According to Lana, the following day Artie phoned and asked her to come to a radio station where he was working to pose for newspaper stills he had promised. She agreed, and the two spent the morning in affectionate attitudes and embraces while the cameras photographed them.

One of the newspapermen got wind of the unannounced separation and he asked Lana about it. "That is correct," she is reported to have said as she disengaged herself from Shaw's arms. "We're through for keeps."

The marriage had lasted a few days more than four months. It was Lana's first marriage, Shaw's third. They would go on to become two of the most-married personalities in the history of show business.

The separation was obviously amicable, strengthening the suspicion that Lana's dramatic stories of Shaw's mistreating her were inspired by the MGM public-relations brains.

"I really like Lana," says Shaw. "She wasn't a malicious person. After we split up, she kept in touch with me." As a matter of fact, Shaw recalls, they remained on occasionally intimate terms.

Lana was supposedly emotionally exhausted by the whole Shaw ordeal, at least according to stories given to the press. She checked into Santa Monica hospital and, while Greg Bautzer took care of the details of her divorce, she had what was reported as "a nervous breakdown."

"Lana's not the type for a nervous breakdown," laughs Shaw. "She may have been despondent for a few days, which I doubt, but that's all. It was all part of a public-relations campaign by the studio to make her the innocent victim. To get sympathy on her side. I didn't care. I was involved in other things."

The studio took care of everything—a procedure which would set the pattern for Lana's adult life. Legal problems, marital problems, any kind of problems—tell the studio, they'll take care of everything. Tell Benny Thau, he'll take care of it. Some have said that Lana's emotional development did not progress beyond these years and that even today, although an astute career woman, she remains emotionally a willful, spoiled teen-ager.

"She's probably MGM's greatest product," says Laszlo Willinger. "She is totally artificial, was controlled like a puppet, a studio property."

After checking her out of the hospital, Metro decided that a trip was called for before returning her to work. They decided to send her on a cruise to Honolulu, and she was accompanied by MGM troubleshooter Betty Asher, assigned to keep Lana company and "make sure she doesn't dance with the wrong people."

Betty Asher, an indispensable employee at MGM, was later assigned to watch over Judy Garland after Judy's divorce from David Rose. Betty was Judy's maid of honor at her wedding to Vincente Minnelli in 1945, but was later denounced by the volatile singing star as "just another hateful MGM spy." Shaw remembers Betty Asher. "She was Lana's witness at our divorce. Before the trial she paid me a little visit and stayed three days."

According to Shaw, he and Lana remained on friendly terms. "One Christmas, after I returned home from a performance, I was dead tired," he remembers. "I was living alone, and I was lonely. I came into the house and switched on the light. There were wrapped presents sprinkled all over, with a Christmas tree in the middle of the living room. A minute later, Lana popped up from behind a couch, and giggled 'Merry Christmas.' She did things like that, sometimes. She was basically a nice sweet girl. A victim of her own dreams." Shaw says that they spent that night together and their relationship continued on and off for some time. She dated him openly, and in November, 1941, there were even published rumors of their remarriage. Shaw admits, "There was a time I did consider remarrying her. But suddenly a crazy thought came to mind. It was those one hundred pairs of shoes she had. I just couldn't bear that."

Lana confided in him, according to Shaw, and let him know whom she was dating, what she thought of the date and the romantic escapades that followed. "I wasn't interested in who she was sleeping with," says Shaw, "but she gave me all the details anyway.

"One of her boyfriends at the time was a well-known radio crooner. Lana called me one night, after they had 'done it'—that was how she described lovemaking, 'doing it'—and she was very happy. 'He says the sweetest things,' she told me. 'Like what?' I asked her. 'Well, after we did it, we were lying there, and he said, "Boy, can you imagine how many guys out there would like to be in my place right now?" Wasn't that sweet?'

"That tells you a lot about Lana," continues Shaw. "Obviously the guy had gone to bed not with Julia Jean but with Lana Turner Sex Symbol, and she was flattered by it.

"As a matter of fact," Shaw comments, "I even inadvertently suggested playmates for her. I would tell her I just saw a film with so-and-so and he was terrific in it, and a few days later Lana would phone me to tell me she and so-and-so had 'done it' and then I'd get all the details."

Shaw remembers that Lana had a distinctive habit which he found amusing. It was her own private radar system. She would straighten her back, thereby thrusting out her breasts "like a pouter pigeon" when somebody who interested her entered a room. "It became involuntary," says Shaw. "I would often know who she was going to sleep with before she did. Once at a party," Shaw recalls, "Victor Mature entered the room and Lana 'straightened up.' I knew she'd make it with him and I was right."

Lana's Honolulu cruise went smoothly, and according to columnists from this point on instead of saying "before I was married" and "after my divorce," Lana used the terms "Before Honolulu" and "After Honolulu."

In the fall, after Honolulu, Lana went up to San Francisco to be maid of honor at Hazel Meadows' wedding. There was an ASCAP convention in town, which she attended. According to newspapers and magazines, it was there she "ran into" Tony Martin. This was the first public announcement of her "romance" with the sexy radio crooner, then recently divorced from his wife Alice Faye. Tony was Lana's kind of man—good-looking, successful, fun-loving and adept at showing her a good time.

The studio was anxious for her to return to work. They felt she was ready for an important picture. They were preparing *Ziegfeld Girl*, an "A" film originally touted for Joan Crawford. Although Lana wasn't highly regarded as a dramatic actress, she seemed right for what in the original script was one of the featured but not leading roles. The part was that of Sheila Regan, a dazzlingly beautiful and ambitious showgirl who loses her sense of values, deserts the only person who truly loves her and, unable to cope with success, becomes an alcoholic. Realistically, the character dies at the end. It was not a large role, and Robert Z. Leonard, who had directed *The Great Ziegfeld* a few years earlier, felt Lana could handle it.

In those days decisions about production and casting were made by committee. Louis B. Mayer, of course, headed the committee, which consisted of his trusted lieutenants, including Benny Thau and Eddie Mannix. Lana was well liked by the influential members of the committee. They undoubtedly felt the time was right to give her a "push."

Lana has said, "They cast me in *Ziegfeld Girl* to wear plumes and satins, to walk down grand staircases, to be looked at and to say as little as possible. No one considered me an actress.

"For once I studied my part long and faithfully. It's interesting that as I worked on my part the part expanded. With each day of added dialogue and action, she began to be important. In the end, I think she was a believable character."

Ziegfeld Girl was the turning point in Lana Turner's career. She received fourth billing but star billing with James Stewart, Judy Garland and Hedy Lamarr. (Lana and Stewart were both fun-loving and got along famously, off the set as well as on. Mr. Stewart was keeping many famous Hollywood beauties happy, but he avoided marriage with all of them.) *Ziegfeld Girl* enabled Lana to cross the threshold from sweater-girl-gimmick celebrity to authentic leading lady. Her salary was upped to $1,500 a week.

Lana's new build-up, begun before the film's release, stressed her new stature as a star. The publicity said: "The public will soon see Lana Turner in the best role of the biggest picture to be released by the industry's biggest company within the next few months."

For *A Star Is Born*-type article he was writing about Lana for *Life* magazine, writer Niven Busch sent a memo to the home office correcting misinformation in his original story, replacing it with fresh misinformation. His memo said to change "Owl Drugstore to Top-Hat Malt Shop. Also all reference to drugstore should now read malt shop."

Life then did another article on Lana and the navy. A poll had been taken of sailors on the *S.S. Idaho*, and Lana Turner was voted their favorite star. A series of confidential memorandums from *Life*'s staff illustrates the influence that MGM wielded over mass circulation magazines thirty years ago:

10/8/40—Confidential Memo from *Life*'s Dick Pollard to Mary Fraser re Lana Turner/navy story. . . .

". . . I had trouble with MGM, who were very much afraid that Lana would be tagged as the Sweetheart of the Navy. Also they were afraid of what 50 sailors might do to Lana.

"My obligations are these. Can we say that *Life* gave the party and introduced Lana to the sailors or at least not say that Lana gave the party?" He also added, "You will probably wonder why we didn't have this party at Lana's house. She lives in a two-room apartment and not a very glamorous apartment at that."

10/10/40—Memo from Pollard to Helen Robinson re party: "We aren't kidding about not saying that Lana gave the party. MGM wouldn't go for it on the basis of Lana inviting 50 sailors. Would much prefer the angle of *Life*'s party. I don't understand it either but you know MGM."

Later that year Lana and Mildred were "reunited" and moved

from the apartment where Mildred had been living to a new Medi-
terranean-style house off Benedict Canyon in Beverly Hills. (It was
at the bottom of the hill from where Shaw was living.) It was a
Movie Star mansion, and for the first time the Turners had servants. Lana was living the role of Movie Queen, and the money was
being spent as fast it it came in.

"She was irresponsible with money and always in debt," says
Laszlo Willinger. Louis B. Mayer used to lend stars money, to be
used as a wedge during contract negotiations.

Ziegfeld Girl was released in April, 1941, and was one of the
biggest hits of the year.

But even before its release, from *Ziegfeld Girl*'s rushes, MGM
knew Lana was ready. She immediately went into *Dr. Jekyll and
Mr. Hyde*, opposite Spencer Tracy and Ingrid Bergman. The studio
had originally cast Lana in the bigger, dramatic role of "the girl of
the streets." But Tracy wanted Ingrid Bergman for that part and,
according to Hollywood observers, was interested in the possibility
of co-starring with Bergman offscreen as well. Ingrid had to test for
the role, and after her scene it was evident to Tracy and director
Victor Fleming (fresh from *Gone With The Wind*) that she was
perfect for the part. The smaller ingenue role went to Lana, but her
billing was equal to that of Tracy and Bergman.

Metro gave her the star part opposite box-office-king Gable in
Honky-Tonk. She was at the top. She got equal billing with him,
and their on-screen chemistry was explosive. Gable and Turner
shared the cover of *Life* as the screen's "hottest new team."

Stagehands from the crew of *Honky-Tonk* remember that Gable's wife, Carole Lombard, visited the set far more frequently than
she had for any of the King's other films. While beautiful, blonde
Mrs. Gable, a top star in her own right but much older than Lana,
may not have felt that brunettes Joan Crawford or Hedy Lamarr
were threats, she was aware of Gable's penchant for blondes.

Lombard spoke to L. B. Mayer and less than subtly made her

50

point that Lana be told that Gable was off-limits. Lombard said that, if "conditions didn't improve," Gable "might become ill" and cause costly production delays on his next picture. Reportedly Lana had set her mind on Gable but was cautioned by the film mogul. Filming of *Honky-Tonk* was completed without further incidents.

Then Lana was given the coveted role of the society beauty who falls in love with unscrupulous gangster *Johnny Eager,* played by heartthrob Robert Taylor. The film was directed by Mervyn LeRoy. The man who had given Lana her first break now directed her in one of her best roles. Under his guidance she delivered an excellent performance. The photography presented her at a peak of physical beauty and sensuality. The ads for *Johnny Eager* are still remembered: TAYLOR AND TURNER . . . THEY'RE HOTTER 'N T-N-T . . . THEY'RE DYNAMITE IN JOHNNY EAGER.

All four films were released before the end of 1941. Every one was a smash hit. Lana Turner was twenty-one and a full-fledged leading lady opposite the screen's top actors. It had been a fast four years.

Lana quickly learned the ropes, as she recalled years later. "When you hope to hold your own against men with such impact as these, you had better know all the tricks of the trade, little girl."

She was a sharp, fast learner. Decades later the training was still very much in evidence. Even in the late 1960s, fellow actors recalled an attempt by an actor to upstage Lana. She stopped the scene cold and said, "Don't ever try that with me again because I'll walk right out of here and leave you standing with egg on your face."

Other fellow actors remarked she knew exactly how and when to flub a line if the scene wasn't going to her best advantage and she wanted it shot over.

She learned all the techniques of movie-making from the top pros at MGM.

In September, 1941, her divorce from Artie Shaw became final. She was a free agent. In November she was in New York and did personal appearances for *Honky-Tonk*.

After another quick trip to New York in January, Lana and Gable were re-teamed in *Somewhere I'll Find You*, a romantic drama in which she had the unlikely role of a war correspondent. It was during production of this film that Carole Lombard was killed in a plane crash. After only three days of shooting, the picture was halted for several weeks because of Lombard's death. Observers on the set recall that Lana, usually full of laughs and clowning around, refrained from any frivolity in deference to Gable's grief. She usually had a phonograph in her dressing room and music playing constantly, and she stopped that too. She was sweet and kind without being maudlin.

Although Gable and Turner had made only their second film together, after *Somewhere I'll Find You* the reviewers were calling Gable and Turner "the screen's most provocative lovers."

After Carole Lombard's death, Gable was fair game for many Hollywood blondes. But he decided to escape them and Hollywood and join the army.

It was 1942, and after Pearl Harbor, Hollywood, like the rest of the country, was on a wartime footing. Lana was toned down for her role in *Somewhere I'll Find You*—much less the glamour girl and sexpot. Her long blonde hair had been bobbed short, and her wardrobe was decidedly un-movie star. The women of America could identify with her.

Lana was working hard, and again she was playing hard too. And by now she was quenching her thirst with stronger nectar than lemonade. She has recalled that around this time she rebelled against her mother's steadying influence. Their mansion was constructed so that Mildred had her own wing and Lana's "friends" could come and go without "disturbing" Mildred.

"When we arrived in Hollywood, mother was naturally inexperienced. She did not know how to cope with Hollywood people and did not know how to cope with me as I became a Hollywood person. She tried to keep me from staying out all night, from having too many dates with too many playboys," Lana has said of this period.

Lana revolted. She said her mother was critical, fault-finding and old-fashioned. They bickered, quarreled and finally separated.

Years later Lana said, "Fortunately, our separation did not last long. But it was while we were apart that I made most of my notorious mistakes."

"For the sake of the child. . . ."
LANA TURNER, 1943

Although Tony Martin was a perfect playmate for Lana, the relationship soon cooled, and later Martin was taken out of circulation when he enlisted in the navy. But there were others on the Hollywood circuit to keep Lana happy.

She dated bandleader Tommy Dorsey, also under contract to Metro, actor Robert Stack and multimillionaire Howard Hughes, not the playboy he was in the thirties but not yet a recluse. He was in a financial position to show Lana the town the way she liked to see it. Columnists said their marriage was imminent, but Hughes wasn't the marrying kind.

Drummers Buddy Rich and Gene Krupa dated Lana frequently. "He wants to *marry* me!" it was reported Lana exclaimed to a friend about Buddy. "He wants to drive to Mexico tonight and get married. What am I going to do?"

"Tell him you don't want to get married," advised the friend.

"Oh I couldn't do that," replied Lana, "he'd be hurt." Whatever the reason she gave Buddy, they were never married.

Lana dated many others during this period, but it was the big names linked with hers which made the news.

Sources at the studio revealed that Lana had been given a verbal spanking by L. B. Mayer for being seen too often with "various orchestra boys in local dance halls."

The late Billie Holiday once remembered that, when she was performing at Billy Berg's night club in the valley in the forties, many Hollywood stars would visit the club, including Clark Gable, Judy Garland and Bette Davis. According to Miss Holiday, Lana was a regular at the club, came in every Tuesday and Thursday and "could really dance." Lana would always ask Billie to sing "Strange Fruit" and "Gloomy Sunday." These are two woeful ballads and, even though Lana contends she never had a father complex, it's interesting to note that "Strange Fruit," written by Miss Holiday, concerned her feelings about her own father and his tragic death.

About this time reports were that Lana's bosses at MGM were fretting over an unscheduled New York jaunt she made. Years later, a scandal magazine reported: "Broadway insiders still whisper about Lana's visit to Gotham in the early days of her stardom, when she used to don slacks and dark glasses and scurry off on nightly trips to the 'Red Rooster,' an intimate little joint in Harlem. The magnet that drew her there was a then virtually unknown singer who also owned the place, Billy Daniels. When MGM biggies saw that Lana could not be dissuaded from these late-hour jaunts uptown, they resignedly assigned Johnny Meyer, who later became Howard Hughes' handyman, to accompany her, just to protect their investment."

Back on the west coast, after dating the cream of the Hollywood crop, Lana shocked her studio, the industry and her fans by suddenly marrying an unknown and unemployed young man, Josef

Stephen Crane, in July, 1942, less than a year after her divorce from Shaw became final.

She had just returned to Hollywood from a west coast bond-selling tour. In cities like San Francisco, Seattle, Portland, Spokane and Tacoma, Lana did her bit for the war effort by distributing kisses to purchasers of $50,000 bonds.

"No kiss is worth that much money," she laughed. However, she sold over $5 million worth of bonds.

Back in Hollywood, Lana repeated almost exactly her elopement with Shaw. She had known Crane for at most slightly over a month —some people say only nine days. The studio said she didn't know him at all, but Lana said they had been serious for four months.

According to Lana, when in Mocambo one night, the good-looking and charming Crane came over and introduced himself, and she asked him to join her party.

They danced all evening and Crane took her home. The eternal romantic, she has concurred, "What happened happened instantly with no more premeditation than a pistol bang. I was heels-over-chin, pinwheels-on-fire in love."

All she really knew about Crane was that he was from Indiana, supposedly had some sort of business there, that he danced superbly and was fantastically charming. She later said the fact that he had been married before was never brought to her attention.

His financial status didn't concern her. First of all, he appeared to have money. But in any case, Lana was making thousands of dollars a week. For most of her adult life, Lana never worried about money. A friend says, "Lana had a business manager. She didn't get her check, the manager did. She didn't go to the bank. You don't stop to think how much you put in or take out. You think the income is inexhaustible. Especially at Metro.

"It took a lot of money to keep up that image, and the studio expected it. But Lana also enjoyed it. My God, yes. She'd see something and she'd buy it. She didn't give it any thought or call her manager or ask . . . she'd just do it. Listen, that's half of being

Lana Turner. Just living on impulse. Everything was an experience to her. . . ."

The "mysterious" Mr. Crane was subsequently identified as a Hollywood business executive, a former New York and Chicago broker (presumably a stockbroker), a junior executive with a Los Angeles beverage company, a young actor, a tobacco heir. All that was really known was his age, twenty-seven, and his hometown, Crawfordsville, Indiana, and that he had been graduated from Butler University in 1936. Snide comments were that Steve's only relationship to tobacco was via a pack of cigarettes. Someone said his father owned a cigar store in Crawfordsville.

If it's true that Lana didn't know of Steve's previous marriage when they eloped, she certainly learned soon enough. Although regular news stories carried no mention of Crane's first marriage, the fact was subsequently revealed by fan magazines that summer and fall. They described Crane as "handsome, very likable and ambitious" and noted, erroneously, that he was "divorced two years ago."

Important fan magazines such as *Photoplay* and *Modern Screen* started giving Lana a tremendous amount of coverage after the Crane marriage. She had, of course, been mentioned in the fan books since 1938 but generally she had been used just as a pretty starlet to promote her films. In 1940 when *Photoplay* did an article on glamour girls, they didn't even include Lana.

Occasionally there would be a picture of her and Greg Bautzer at one of the Hollywood nightspots or Lana would be photographed at a premiere.

Although it cannot be denied that fan magazines were manipulated and used by the studios and that they often gave fanciful accounts of the stars' lives, it must be pointed out that the fan publications of the thirties and forties did not rely on sensationalism and misrepresenting facts as they do today. If they lied, it was in a positive way to help the studios build the stars' images rather than in a negative way to create a sensational story. They had close connec-

tions with the studios, access to the stars and widely read and reliable writers such as Adela Rogers St. Johns, Hedda Hopper, Dorothy Kilgallen, Erle Stanley Gardner, James Hilton and others. In
addition, the fan magazines were extremely important because of
their popularity and ability to build a star's following.

Lana's marriage to Shaw had taken the fan journals by surprise,
but they managed to cover it and the subsequent divorce and ran
blurbs such as, "Lana Turner may have a no-marriage clause in her
new MGM contract."

In June, 1941, *Photoplay* had run its first full-color portrait of
Lana after the success of *Ziegfeld Girl*. In November it ran a shot
of her in a dress with a cut-to-the-navel neckline, obviously bra-less,
with the caption: LANA IS KNOWN AS ONE OF THE MOST DARINGLY
DRESSED WOMEN IN HOLLYWOOD. In May of 1942, prior to her marriage to Crane, there was a picture of Lana with Mildred at a night
club on the same page as a picture of Tony Martin with his new
flame Carole Landis, the implication being that he had found a
new steady but Lana hadn't.

Once again the fan magazines were caught off guard when Crane
eloped with Lana, but they caught up quickly.

Whether or not Crane worked before marrying Lana, he didn't
work after. Lana's wedding gift to Steve, it was reported, was a gold
watch with all sorts of gadgets on it. And it was rumored that Steve
was to have an MGM contract, too.

The marriage was another Hollywood story. They flew to Las
Vegas, where Judge George E. Marshall, who had married Lana to
Shaw in her first elopement, again performed the double-ring cere-
mony. The judge supposedly said, "Welcome back, Lana," and
Lana supposedly retorted, "Tie it tighter this time."

It was still not the church-bridesmaids-guests wedding that Lana
had always dreamed of. But there was a touch of glamour in that
beautiful, raven-haired actress Linda Darnell was Lana's maid of
honor. Linda's fiancé, publicist Allen Gordon, was best man.

Julia Jean Mildred Frances Turner Shaw became Julia Jean

Mildred Frances Turner Shaw Crane. "There is nobody so charming as Steve Crane when he wants to be charming," Lana has said. "I am lonely unless I have someone to love—and there was Steve. I married him. Of course," she conceded later, "I married him without enough thought and, if I had pondered for a long time, for ten or fifteen minutes even, I'd have married him anyway."

Judy Garland and her husband David Rose (they had angered MGM by getting married the previous year) hosted a small reception for the Cranes when they returned from their elopement.

As a way of celebration, Crane also took Lana to his hometown of Crawfordsville, where they visited his dad's cigar store. The local folks jammed the lobby of the movie house to glimpse Lana ("She was cute as a bug") as she came out after viewing a war picture. Students from nearby Wabash College drove back and forth in front of the Crane house hoping to spot the Sweater Girl.

The Sigma Chi House at the college, where Steve's brother was a member, threw a big party honoring the happy couple, and Lana told reporters she hoped she'd have lots and lots of babies.

Returning to Hollywood, the Cranes settled down in (according to Lana) a big new house (but according to the Associated Press, his $150-a-month apartment) and she returned, amidst rumblings that all was not well with the hasty marriage, to work at MGM.

The fact that Lana had married Crane was greeted with astonishment in the Hollywood community. She was, after all, the epitome of beauty and success. At twenty-two she had everything: striking good looks, money, a movie contract and a more than bright future.

She surely didn't marry Crane for his money, but in all probability she thought he had money. What else was she to think—when they met he didn't work but he lived in high style. Although she certainly didn't expect to retire and live off his income, it must have been a shock for her to realize that he couldn't even support himself in the style in which they were living, let alone support both of them.

If Lana's great gift was her beauty, Crane's was his charm. Even today, after a series of marriages to young women, and over two decades as a successful restaurateur, Crane is still noted as one of the most charming men in Hollywood, the man with "the million-dollar smile." His skill at dealing with people has won him many friends in the movie colony.

But Lana was *the* important first link.

Metro put Lana into a light comedy programmer with Robert Young. Originally titled *Nothing Ventured*, it was retitled *Slightly Dangerous* for Lana. Her myth-like drugstore discovery was again exploited in the script and subsequently in the ads. In the opening sequence, she was a brunette waitress at a soda fountain, unhappy with her lot and ambitious to get somewhere in life. She bleached her hair blonde and things started happening.

Steve was still not working, but Lana later said, "This was incidental and cast no shadow on our sunshine." In September, 1942, she again denied a family rift.

Questions were buzzing around Hollywood concerning Lana's career, and it was reported that impulsive Lana was no longer as close to the people at Metro as she had been prior to the Crane marriage.

Friends said, "Lana and her husband are happy in night clubs only when others are looking at them. Left alone, they look bored and miserable." Still others said Crane was just right for Lana.

Hollywood was now on a wartime footing. Lana did her bit for the Hollywood Canteen and danced with the servicemen on Monday nights. Steve did his bit and busboyed, and Mildred was back at the snack bar with the other movie mothers.

Lana spiked all rumors of discord between her and Steve with an announcement on December 8, 1942, that she was pregnant. Asked whether the baby would arrive early or late in July, she replied: "Never mind that late or early stuff. July is good enough." Louella Parsons reported that Lana said she wanted a son.

60

The studio had been afraid that Lana's image would be damaged by impending motherhood. It wasn't. Her fan mail increased 20 percent, and she gained new fans among women. In addition, although she was a pinup during the war, motherhood only helped cement in the minds of the GIs the fact that Lana Turner was *real* . . . the typical, beautiful girl they had left behind.

"Having a baby was probably the biggest shock of her life," concluded Artie Shaw years later.

But before the birth of her baby Lana was in for a bigger shock and the first public scandal to mar—some say it helped—her career. After Lana's announcement of pregnancy, Carol Kurtz, vaguely described by newspapermen and magazines as a society girl from Indianapolis, disclosed that she was still married to Steve Crane because her divorce from Crane would not become final until January, 1943.

Lana was at least saved the embarrassment of the newspapers' finding out first. It was she herself, and MGM, who made the announcement in January, 1943, which shocked the movie colony and her fans. The announcement very simply said that she was suing Steve Crane for an annulment on the grounds that she had discovered that Crane's divorce from his first wife was not final at the time she and Crane eloped.

Crane, always the gentleman, issued the following statement when Lana and the studio issued their statement about seeking the annulment: "I deeply regret the unhappiness which this misunderstanding has brought about. It is exceedingly unfortunate that Miss Turner should be the innocent sufferer through a legal circumstance of which she had no knowledge.

"Naturally, I feel Miss Turner should do everything legally necessary for the protection of her child soon to be born as well as for her own protection."

Some thought it odd that he referred to the unborn baby as "her child" rather than "our child."

Years later, Lana gave her account of learning "the shocking news." Her recollection of the confrontation with Crane went something like this:

Lana: "Why didn't you tell me? How could you do this to me?" She has remembered she sat with tight fists and dry eyes, more baffled and frustrated by this turn of events than by anything before in her life. "How would you dare do such an awful, horrible thing? What are you? What kind of man are you?"

She remembered that Steve tried to explain. "Darling," he said, "this is just an awful mistake. Sure, Carol and I were married and it didn't work out. We got a divorce in Mexico. At least, I thought we did. It seemed no good to mention it to you when I thought it was all over. . . ."

With this dialogue, Lana implied that she was unaware of Crane's first marriage. This is very likely false, since she regularly read the fan magazines, which had carried information on Crane's first marriage only weeks after he had married Lana.

In all probability the argument wasn't about her knowledge of his first marriage but that she suspected and accused him of knowing when he eloped with her that his divorce wasn't final.

There was speculation among Hollywood sharks that Crane had to marry Lana while she was in a marrying mood. He was afraid, they thought, that her ardor would cool in the months-long wait for that final decree. No pun intended, they added, but Crane had to strike while the iron was hot.

Further speculation was that Crane had then planned for the child and persuaded Lana to have it. These rumors and suppositions were given some credence by the fact that Lana, hurt and upset over the turn of events, absolutely refused to remarry Crane when his divorce did become final even though she was pregnant by him. If Lana had not been pregnant, she almost certainly would *not* have remarried Crane.

It's interesting to note that in 1951 when Lana discussed her marriages in a national magazine article she altered the facts not only

62

about her first knowledge of Crane's previous marriage but also regarding the dates of the annulment and pregnancy. Her version was that *after* finding out about Crane's first marriage and having their marriage annulled she *then* discovered she was pregnant. Facts are that she announced her pregnancy in December, the annulment in January.

Lana's 1951 version was: "It seemed, finally, like a reasonable idea to share this news [of the pregnancy] with my annulled husband. I asked him to come to the house. And I hurried home weakly to tell a man something that should have made us the happiest two people in the world."

Before she had a chance to tell him, Steve told Lana he had been drafted. At that point Lana said she laughed. "I guess it was rude of me," Lana recalled. "I too have a bit of news," she said she replied.

"Then I told him. And then we played a big scene, actor and actress."

Lana was known to be a pro at delivering epithets in ultracolorful and descriptive language. She undoubtedly made good use of this expressive vocabulary while arguing with Crane about the entire situation.

But in her polite recollection she continued, "Steve was noble, I was somewhat less than noble. The scene went on for hours—an argument which I have not the heart or the memory to repeat. Its theme was: 'For the sake of the child.'

" 'We have to think of him first,' was Steve's point. 'That means we must get married again, at once. Don't you see?'

"I saw. Of course it was the only possible thing to do—if we could. We decided to start all over again, forget the past and try to make a happy life as mother and father for our child. Steve's divorce from Carol had now become legal and proper. We could get married again, and we did."

However, Lana and Steve's remarriage wasn't quite as uncomplicated as Lana has remembered it.

Crane had married Miss Kurtz in 1937. They parted in 1941 and

63

she obtained her interlocutory decree on January 19, 1942. Later, Crane said he thought the interlocutory decree had been granted in February of 1941 when a separation agreement and property settlement were made.

Supposedly Crane then came to the coast with $10,000 in cash and big ideas. It hadn't taken him long to make the front pages of every newspaper in the country. Hollywood speculated that he talked Lana into a quick elopement to avoid an engagement announcement which would give Miss Kurtz an opportunity to notify Lana of the situation in time for Lana to change her mind.

The Turner-Crane annulment, of course, was only a legal whitewash. Obviously the marriage never existed under California law and therefore could not be annulled. But the entire affair with Crane had to be made to appear legal and unsordid, with Lana the innocent victim—as, of course, in this instance she really was.

The case was not without precedent. In the late thirties a similar episode had concerned Ruth Etting, the torch singer, and her second husband, accompanist Merle Alderman. While the public was used to sensational news about Ruth Etting, such stories about twenty-two-year-old Lana Turner, "The American Dream Girl," were, to put it mildly, bewildering. MGM's image-makers had done their job well, and this dissonant chord in her private life clashed with the rest of the public image. The studio was frantically pulling strings behind the scenes to be sure the embarrassing situation was reported to Lana's best advantage.

On February 4, with eyes and nose red from crying and a cold, Lana told Superior Court Judge Roy B. Rhodes the circumstances of her marriage. She told him she and Crane had separated immediately after she discovered he was still married, and she had the locks changed on the doors of her home. (Later newspaper reports said that, when Lana learned of her predicament, she moved in with her mother.)

Judge Rhodes, in addition to granting the annulment and giving custody to Lana, said the annulment would protect the legitimacy of the unborn child. However, he declined to elaborate on how this would be the case.

At the time of the annulment, when asked if she intended to re-marry Crane, whose divorce had now become final, she hastily replied, "Oh, don't ask me that. I have nothing to say on that subject."

The bewildered fans were shocked when they learned that, although Crane was now legally free to marry the pregnant Lana, she did not seem interested in remarrying him and legitimizing their child. The tabloid press had a field day. It was a change of pace from serious war news.

Lana's discovery for films, her whirlwind social life, quick marriage and divorce from Shaw, elopement and legal problems with Crane had already set a pattern of tornadolike living which Lana would continue for years to come.

Sources at the studio said L. B. Mayer had all the persuasive public-relations forces at the mammoth studio's disposal working on the project of getting Lana remarried.

A Mayer confidante remembers Mayer's anger. "Whatever L. B. did in his private life, and whatever his stars did in theirs, was okay as long as it was never made public. Mayer was a puritannical moralist when it came to MGM films and the public image of MGM personalities." That one of MGM's leading stars was about to have a baby out of wedlock was incredible.

Although the press of 1943 didn't phrase it as forthrightly as they would today, the innuendos were obvious and Mayer was furious.

Lana, one of Mayer's spoiled children but one of his biggest moneymakers, had to be made to realize the seriousness of the situation.

Soon afterward, according to observers at the Mocambo, Lana and Crane seemed about to re-enter marital paradise.

Ten days after the annulment, Hollywood columnist Florabel Muir reported that Crane and Lana were celebrating Valentine's Day together at the Mocambo.

"Both wearing the wedding rings they exchanged at the Las Vegas ceremony last July 17th, Lana and Steve staged their reunion at the Mocambo Club, which was almost as effective as broadcasting it over a national hookup," said Florabel.

Steve told Florabel, "I haven't much to say now, but time may bring a happy ending for us both."

The war was raging all over the world, and even in Hollywood its effects were felt. Florabel reported that Lana and Crane discussed plans for their baby. "Even the matter of a baby buggy was discussed," Florabel related. "Lana happily accepted a friend's offer of one after disclosing that war shortages had thwarted all of her attempts to buy one."

However, that blissful Valentine's Day reunion had a tragic aftermath a few days later.

Since the annulment, Crane had been trying to persuade Lana to remarry him. "For the sake of the child" was his strongest argument. She was reluctant and undoubtedly even ignored the advice of the studio.

That Valentine's Day weekend seemed to be going well. From Saturday night to Monday morning she was "constantly in his company." And he seemingly had finally talked her into remarrying him. They drove to her home to pick up some clothes. But Lana reportedly came back out and said, "Sorry, darling, I just can't do it now." Crane charged that her mother had influenced her, and they argued violently.

Another version of this story quoted friends who said that Crane and Lana were at the Mocambo and Lana definitely refused to remarry him. Steve had demanded a definite answer to his latest marriage proposal, they said, and Lana retorted that if he insisted on a yes or no she'd say no.

Whichever story is true, Lana hadn't been won over by Valentine's Day. Steve was determined to convince her of his sincerity and it seemed he was being driven to desperate measures.

The reports of what happened during the next few days in the

Turner-Crane situation, if written in scenario form, would have produced a script which even the "B" unit at Monogram Pictures might have turned down as being too far-fetched.

Newspapers said that on the night of February 15, after his ill-fated reunion with Lana, Crane tried to drive his car over a cliff and into the bedroom of Lana's house. Thick underbrush supposedly stopped the car, but no reports recalled the height of the cliff or the exact location of the suicide attempt.

Crane tried another route. He took an overdose of sleeping pills. No one reported who discovered the overdose or who notified the police but it is a fact that during the night of February 15 he was admitted to Cedars of Lebanon Hospital in critical condition due to an overdose of barbiturates.

Lana was called. When she learned that Crane wanted to kill himself, she rushed to the hospital and collapsed. She refused to leave until Crane was pronounced out of danger.

In her emotional state, her doctor said he feared for the safety of her unborn child. When Lana left the hospital she still refused to disclose her intentions. "How do I know what I am going to do?" she said. "It's all so terrible and everybody is so unhappy."

Later her doctor and close friend, William Branch, reported that Lana was resting at home. "Her child is alive and she will be all right," he said.

In addition to Crane's ordeal over Lana's refusal to remarry him, he was being faced with induction into the army.

On February 20 Lana issued a formal statement: "I had hoped that it would not be necessary for me to make a statement at this time," she said. "However, because of recent events and specula-tion as to my plans, I can only say that I have no intention of remarrying."

But, with all the pressures, including her own physical condition (she had to have several blood transfusions during the pregnancy), Lana finally capitulated and agreed to remarry Crane. However, it took almost another month, for they weren't married until March

14. They were in Tijuana, Mexico, and it was only one day before Crane was to be inducted into the army.

Lana has recalled, "Six months with child, in as drab and shabby a ceremony as was ever performed, in the heat and squalor of Tijuana, I stood before a little man whose office sign said, 'Legal Matters Adjusted,' and again became Steve Crane's wife. We called a Mexican off the street for a peso or two and made him a witness."

It was easily the most unromantic of Turner weddings. There was no press coverage at all. (It's interesting to note that when the studios really wanted to keep an item out of the newspapers, they could.) In fact, there was speculation late in March that the Cranes hadn't yet remarried. News stories of Lana and Steve nightclubbing at Mocambo appeared on March 27, with Crane in uniform as a private. He told friends that "everything was going to be all right."

It's amazing, in retrospect, to think that Lana stood alone for so long in her refusal to remarry Crane. This was 1943. This kind of adverse publicity for a young star on the rise could have ended her career. Surely she must have been deeply hurt and embarrassed by the whole affair. She undoubtedly resented what she must have felt was trickery and deceit on Crane's part.

However, remarrying him was inevitable. He was about to enter the army. By now sympathy was on his side. Whatever Lana's hurts, all that the public knew was that Steve was professing his deep love for her and eagerness to remarry her and legitimize their baby. That she didn't seem so eager had not put her in a flattering light.

Not coincidentally, MGM released *Slightly Dangerous* the same month Lana remarried Crane. Although a light programmer (critics said Lana and Robert Young were above the level of material), the film was a success. And it set a pattern in that Lana's career was in fact furthered by the kind of publicity that might have destroyed other personalities.

"Lana Turner typifies modern allure," wrote Anita Loos. "She is the vamp of today as Theda Bara was of yesterday. However," con-

68

cluded Miss Loos, "she doesn't look like a vamp. She is far more deadly because she lets her audience relax."

The next property in the works for Lana was aptly titled *Marriage Is a Private Affair*, and newspapers of the day jested that the studio might combine titles for Lana's next vehicle, and call it *Marriage Is a Slightly Dangerous Private Affair*.

The day after their remarriage, Crane left for Fort MacArthur, outside of Los Angeles. During his tenure in the army (and this was at the height of World War II) he never left the States. Lana has said, "I'm not under the impression that he fought an uncomfortable war. He was able to bring captains and lieutenants home for dinner almost every night."

Cheryl Christine Crane was born on July 25, 1943, at 5:15 a.m. in Hollywood Hospital. She weighed seven pounds fourteen ounces, but she was an RH baby. Lana had gone into premature labor and drugs had been injected into her spine to end the contractions. Later when the baby was full term, labor was normal but went on for eighteen hours. The memory of childbirth is still vivid in Lana's mind. She has recalled, "I'll never forget that mass of black, wet curls and the absolutely *ivory-white* baby. My doctor, thank God, noticing how pale she was and knowing that after all those hours of labor she should have come out fiery red, had a blood test made right away. The child was almost dead."

In 1943 many hospitals were not prepared for the blood transfusions necessary to save RH-negative-factor babies. The baby girl was taken from Lana and transferred from Hollywood Hospital to Los Angeles Children's Hospital.

Cheryl's birth had been duly reported. The press waited outside the delivery room and rushed to the phones to report that the trials and tribulations of Mr. and Mrs. Steve Crane had culminated in a happy seven pound-fourteen ounce ending.

The public was not informed of the baby's fight for survival. In fact the usual communiqué that "Mother and child are doing well"

69

was issued by Lana's mother. The only hints of trouble that appeared in the press were reports that the newborn baby was suffering from anemia, had been given a blood transfusion and "was responding to treatment."

Years later, Lana recalled the ordeal: "I was told the truth as soon as I was strong enough to know, but it was nine days before I was even allowed to see my baby. Then I walked to an enormous crib and looked down on a tiny little girl fighting for her life. She was not the healthy pink and white of newborn babies. She had a sickly yellowish color, as in jaundice.

"RH factor," the doctor explained. "We have to give her transfusions every four hours. You see, the father's blood and the mother's blood don't mix. Positives and negatives. We have to change the whole bloodstream."

One specific and harrowing incident occurred when Lana made an unscheduled visit to the baby. She usually was allowed visits at times when transfusions had been completed. But this time, she arrived unexpectedly. As she and Mildred walked down the hospital corridor, they noticed a great deal of activity in the infants' ward. A nurse with a bloodstained uniform rushed by. Then another nurse came near, carrying a baby whose head was smeared with blood. Lana screamed as she recognized the child as Cheryl. The nurse hurried on, and Mildred led her hysterical daughter into another room. Both women were reassured that nothing serious had occurred, that the baby's kicking had merely dislodged the transfusion needle and made things messy. The doctors assured her that Cheryl would be completely normal and healthy, eventually.

But the image of her baby bleeding would remain vivid in Lana's mind, recurring in nightmares.

Cheryl had to stay at the hospital many months after Lana had recovered and been dismissed.

Lana and Steve fell back into the Hollywood social whirl. Young Frank Sinatra was photographed with Lana and Crane. Sinatra, new to Hollywood, was obviously dazzled by Mrs. Crane.

The Cranes found they had money problems. After paying all their bills, night club as well as hospital, they were broke. It was summer and Lana was off salary between pictures. She and Crane headed for New York, where Lana agreed to do some radio programs for quick cash. The going rate for star talent on radio in 1943 was about $5,000 per appearance.

Back in Hollywood, she and Crane again were having serious marital problems. He had been released from the army on a medical discharge after Cheryl's birth. Since this was the middle of World War II, the news of Crane's discharge wasn't publicized, but it still incited some bitter talk that the studio had used its influence. Years later it would be revealed that Louis B. Mayer had indeed been able to keep top stars out of the service. James Stewart and a few others at MGM were appalled when they learned of Mayer's interference on their behalf, and to the mogul's chagrin they enlisted.

Lana has remembered, "Steve was unhappy. Nothing had gone right for him. He had no work and he undoubtedly resented my carrying the whole load. Often I would be starting to the studio at 6:00 a.m. when he would be coming home from a late night. Obviously, being remarried in desperation, having no life together, this was an alliance that couldn't last."

A clear interpretation of this: She was working. He wasn't. He was partying. They saw little of each other and, although she had remarried "for the sake of the child," she was quickly and bitterly disillusioned.

But there were other versions. Crane was reportedly furious with Lana for *her* partying and late hours with others. In or out of marriage, Lana was maintaining her reputation as filmdom's Number One Party Girl. It was said that Crane found it hard to keep up with Lana's unbridled urges for high living, liquor, love and late hours.

It's doubtful that Crane couldn't keep up—perhaps he didn't want to—or perhaps she'd lost interest in him. Of course Lana was paying the bills, so it was difficult for Crane to argue. Some of the late-night parties then attended by Lana were the subject of local gossip. It was no secret that Lana was uninhibited in her choice of playmates and frequented parties and night clubs where guests were, in the jargon of the day, "mixed."

It has been printed that Crane found out about a particular party Lana attended on Central Avenue, the Harlem of Hollywood, and he threatened to sue for divorce. Lana then supposedly went running to her bosses at MGM, and the studio "convinced" Crane to at least let Lana divorce him.

This, too, is highly doubtful. But their marriage *was* definitely over, and the divorce was conducted with what she and the studio hoped would be a minimum of fuss.

After her final separation from Crane, Lana "confided" in Louella Parsons (and her several million readers): "Steve and I sat down and talked the whole thing over. We had no quarrel but the separation seemed the best for all concerned. Steve is welcome to see Cheryl anytime he wishes and I don't feel our trouble is any more his fault than mine."

Louella said that Steve was eager to make a career for himself apart from being Lana Turner's husband, and had refused a contract at MGM. "He told me at the time," said Louella, "that he came to Hollywood to get into the movies but he wanted to get in on his own merit." She then said that Crane had a contract at Columbia and he had told their publicity people that in his publicity his wife's name was not to be mentioned since he didn't want to be "Mr. Turner" for the rest of his life.

At Columbia he made at least one picture, *Mark of the Whistler*, with Nina Foch.

When Lana sued Crane for divorce and custody of the child, in April, 1944, he filed a countersuit and asked for complete custody of Cheryl. Lana won the divorce and, without any fuss at all, custody of the child.

The actual divorce took about seven minutes. Lana told the

judge the whole marriage had been a mistake. She said it made her extremely nervous, irritable, caused her to lose weight and catch colds, and furthermore the work on one of her pictures had to be halted because she was feeling so poorly.

Steve yelled at her, that's what did it all, she explained.

Mildred said that the couple had lived with her during the marriage and she corroborated Lana's testimony.

Lana has remembered, "I know, of course, that my love affair with Crane, my quick remarriage because of my child, and then a divorce—I know that these matters were treated hilariously in the press and that to many people they must have seemed hilariously funny, the irresponsible antics of Hollywood people of no character. I can blame no one."

In that agonizing period, the Turner resiliency again asserted itself. Summing up the experience, Lana later said: "So that was that, and back to work."

"I have never in my life broken up a home."
LANA TURNER, 1946

5

Although her marriage to Steve Crane was stormy, short-lived and some thought image-damaging, it might have been quickly forgotten and glossed over like the Shaw marriage but for one human factor which will link Lana and Steve together for the rest of their lives—Cheryl Crane.

Despite their legal imbroglios, and the fact that he had made a fool of her, Lana wasn't one to hold a grudge. She may have divorced Crane, but, just as she remained friendly with Shaw, she continued to date Crane while she played the field.

Through the forties Crane made news by dating actresses such as Sonja Henie and Sheila Ryan. He also dated Virginia Hill and other starlets. Virginia, "Bugsy" Siegel's girl friend, had a brief contract at Columbia. She was innaccurately described in fan magazines as "a socialite."

In addition to Crane, Lana dated a bevy of other admirers. By now, magazine articles were appearing with titles like LANA TURNER'S SENSATIONAL LOVES and similarly angled stories. Lana's reputation was growing, not only as an offscreen sex symbol but also as a young woman who could more than hold her own with the hard-drinking Hollywood crowd and match their expletive-peppered vocabulary word for word.

Lana, like many Hollywood personalities, was living the life of the image she was projecting. It was the life, as she envisioned it, a star should live. And the studio encouraged her to live it and live extravagantly.

Friends said her roles and her personal life became intertwined. But her offscreen self did in fact help reinforce in the public mind her onscreen image.

A danger in show business is that people begin believing their publicity. One true story to illustrate this concerns a successful producer. Years ago, when he was the production head of a studio, his studio biography incorrectly reported that while on the UCLA football team he made All-Amrican. Now, twenty years later, after this "fact" has been reiterated in hundreds of newspaper and magazine interviews, the producer actually believes it so vehemently that he would swear on his eyes that he *was* an All-American.

In the case of Lana and other glamour girls, believing their own publicity was not only dangerous but could eventually prove personally destructive. Still, at twenty-four, when you're young and beautiful, the fact that youth and beauty won't last forever can hardly concern you. Lana was the most desirable woman in the world, according to her publicity, and in 1944 she had no reason to doubt it.

After her divorce from Crane, Lana sold her Bel-Air mansion and moved to a rented house. Along with her movie salary she picked up additional thousands by doing guest stints on radio. She appeared on Frank Sinatra's network show and with Victor Mature on the Lux Radio Theatre.

She dated Peter Lawford, record executive Manny Sachs, and was briefly involved with John Hodiak, her *Marriage Is a Private Affair* co-star. Their first date was originally for publicity but it soon went beyond that stage, according to magazines. Insiders at the studio remember, however, that Hodiak was one of the few stars at MGM who wouldn't give in to Lana's charms, and this infuriated her. But snide reports were that he was her *only* holdout.

It was during this period that Lana began building her offscreen reputation. "Lana had the morals and the attitudes of a man," opines an ex-MGM executive. "If she saw something she wanted, she took it. But most of us at MGM never thought of her as immoral. She was amoral. If she saw a muscular stage hand with tight pants and she liked him, she'd invite him into her dressing room."

Over the years studio executives and many of Lana's directors have contended that her publicized private life and these unpublicized but widely circulated stories about her made it difficult for people in the industry to consider her as a serious acting talent, although she was a gifted actress.

She had been a big enough star by 1943 to be included in *Current Biography*. The story recounted the soda fountain myth, the sweater-girl image and detailed her life through her marriage to Crane. Her biographer remarked, "It is said that she 'has dated, conservatively, some 150 members of the opposite sex,' that she has been 'reported engaged to marry five different men at the same time, and actually was on the verge of going to the altar with a dozen.'"

Baby Cheryl was getting the build-up in fan magazines as "Lana's Little Dividend, 'Cherie.'" Lana called Cheryl "Baby" or "Cherie," which she pronounced Cherry. Although she loved the little girl ("She's the only thing Lana really loves besides herself," says one of Lana's later husbands), Lana was a busy movie star and didn't have much time for the baby. "Cherie" was usually in the care of nannies and Grandma Mildred.

A respected Hollywood writer recalls, "When I saw Lana and

Cheryl together, during Cheryl's young years—when anybody saw them together—they seemed very fond of each other. But Lana wasn't particularly maternal, either by nature, instinct (lots of women aren't) or by circumstances.

"Don't forget," continues the writer, who also considers herself Lana's friend, "when Lana was a young star, stars worked much harder, made more pictures than they do now. She had neither the time, nor money, nor husband-father assistance that Elizabeth Taylor has.

"I'd say Lana's attitude towards Cheryl was always sort of *surprised* and 'What do I do now?' It takes a remarkable character to be a young hot-pants top movie star and an adequate mother. Lana's sex life was always spinning; she had all those troubles, plus her career, plus her own never-very-sound character to cope with."

In 1944 Lana's face appeared in millions of magazines, endorsing products such as Woodbury Soap and plugging her latest movie. These endorsement ads were standard for the time, and they were important in helping make names like Lana Turner household words.

MGM wasn't above using its stars in "programmers." Although she had starred opposite Gable, Taylor, and Tracy, Lana also had to carry certain films. In *Keep Your Powder Dry*, she starred with Laraine Day and Susan Peters in a "timely" story of three girls in the WACS. Lana was the spoiled rich girl who was only in the service so she could collect an inheritance. Laraine portrayed a super-patriot. Lana and Laraine were supposed to hate each other in the film, and they hated each other on the set as well.

Obviously there was an ego problem over who was getting the star treatment. Laraine, it was reported, was annoyed whenever Lana was delayed in her dressing room playing the phonograph or entertaining.

"Of course," an observer recalls, "Laraine was always going around trying to convert people anyway. She was a real moralist."

An insider on *Powder* recalls that at one point in the shooting it was stiflingly hot on the set. Susan Peters collapsed and had to be taken to the hospital in an ambulance. Lana got on the phone to the front office. Lana always went directly to the front office when she wanted something.

"Look, they just carted Susan off in an ambulance," he remembers Lana saying, "and I feel kind of faint myself. If this studio isn't air-conditioned by Monday, I don't know if I'll be able to go on!" The set was air-conditioned over the weekend.

Lana visited Frank Sinatra on a nearby sound stage where he was in sailor uniform for *Anchors Aweigh* and she was in WAC uniform for *Powder*. Photos of them together in uniform were widely circulated.

Lana had seen MGM's film *Dragonseed*, and now its co-star, handsome Turkish actor Turhan Bey, had entered her life. As Artie Shaw said, she often discovered new boyfriends by seeing them in movies and then meeting them afterward. She wanted to meet Bey after *Dragonseed*, and later did at a party at Jean Pierre Aumont's house. By September, 1945, she revealed to friends that she planned to be married to Bey. She had even posed with him for publicity photos at his studio, Universal.

Although Steve Crane and Lana were divorced, Crane was obviously still infatuated with her. At a swank Saturday night party for over 150 guests at Ann Rutherford's home on North Canyon Drive, Crane and Bey fought over Lana.

Witnesses said the spark of the battle ignited when Crane objected to Lana attending the party with Bey and the two men went to the garden to "settle matters."

They traded several blows before friends pulled them apart. According to spectators, Crane had a black eye and Bey had scratches around the face. Lana, it was said, then tossed away a diamond ring in disgust and left the party with Bey.

Crane spent much time looking for the diamond ring. It was the one he had given Lana before their marriage.

By October, the Bey romance was at an end. The marriage never materialized. Friends said religious differences were to blame for the bust up. Other friends said the romance ended for a very simple reason: Lana was tired of him. Her newest escort was new young actor Rory Calhoun.

By this time, Frank Sinatra was busy making the Hollywood rounds. Rumors of Frank's romancing Lana began to circulate. "They used to smooch in his car parked on the lot," recalls an ex-MGM publicist. "It was kind of funny, considering they both had dressing rooms to go to, but I guess they thought it was romantic."

While Lana was "smooching" with Frank, soldiers, sailors and marines in the armed forces were dreaming of "smooching" with Lana. She was the servicemen's favorite pinup, according to Adela Rogers St. Johns. Adela interviewed many of the men, and quoted them: "Somehow it is better to be fighting for Lana Turner than it is to be fighting for the Greater Reich. Understand? Because she is all our girls rolled into one and we can get together and know how the other fellow feels."

The year 1945 was a busy time in Lana's life. She was now also dating Robert Hutton, the handsome Hollywood actor getting the big push from Warner Brothers. Winchell called him "Lana's biggest thrill yet" (that "biggest thrill" line was laughingly repeated throughout Hollywood by Lana's "friends") but the romance quickly died and Hutton married soon afterward. Other Turner dates were John Dall and Peter Shaw (Shaw later married Angela Lansbury).

That year, Lana got her best screen role since *Ziegfeld Girl* in *The Postman Always Rings Twice*, the last of James M. Cain's novels to be filmed. Director Tay Garnett remembers that, "*Postman* was considered a very daring picture for MGM. Metro wanted Lana in the film. They felt she'd leveled off, bogged down. The producer, Carey Wilson, convinced them this film would stimulate her career, give her a new image.

"I had a very insistent voice in choosing her. I didn't have the final say because at Metro at that time almost everything was done by committee. Producer Wilson and I were good friends and both agreed on Lana. Actually, it was a question of convincing Lana. There were several other units at Metro who wanted her for films. So I took her to lunch one day at Romanoff's. And I said, 'This is the best acting opportunity you've had.' She'd had some good acting opportunities that perhaps she wasn't quite ready for. But I was convinced she was ready for this and that it would be a giant step forward for her, which it proved to be.

"The temptation is great," says Garnett, "for a gal of that beauty of face and body—she had everything—to coast on that. The same holds true for actors. Bob Taylor had the same problem—to avoid being just a pretty face. Lana was a little late starting [as an actress]. She was rather ga-ga when she was picked up at a soda fountain and suddenly she was a movie star. It was almost that fast. She couldn't believe it. So for a long time Lana was inclined to do whatever the studio said.

"It didn't occur to her to argue. At that time there were several other projects besides *Postman*—all attractive—for which she was wanted."

Postman is one of the few Lana Turner films which has endured well. It is memorable for several reasons. It was stylistic and tense, much like the Cain novel. And Lana's appearance in that film has gone down in cinema folklore. Her hair was platinum white-blonde, her complexion tan, her clothes stark white. There was also an unmistakable chemistry between her and co-star John Garfield. They successfully projected an aura of uncontrolled passion, and Lana was the epitome of deadly beauty.

Garnett remembers, "She already had platinum hair. She'd been that color. So we left it for the film. The white clothing was something that Carey and I thought of. At that time there was a great problem of getting a story with that much sex past the censors. We figured that dressing Lana in white somehow made everything she did seem less sensuous. It was also attractive as hell. And it somehow took a little of the stigma off of everything that she did.

80

"They didn't have 'hot pants' then," kids Garnett, "but you couldn't tell it by looking at hers."

Discussing Lana's work habits, Garnett reiterates what almost all Turner directors have said. "She was always on time. A pro. Always knew her stuff. She takes direction beautifully. I think that Lana is capable probably of more than she ever did. She's easy to direct. She was eager. She had developed an instinct for acting. I think she might have gone a lot further after *Postman* if she had someone to guide her career. It's rather remarkable that she survived the scripts they gave her at all.

"There was some fairly raw kidding going on during production of *Postman*," Garnett recalls. "When we finished the picture, Lana gave me a fur-lined jockstrap. She'd bought a regular jockstrap and had it fur-lined, and she said, 'Don't let anyone say you don't go first class.' "

Garnett enjoyed working with Lana. "I was nuts about her. Everyone who worked with her was. She was a big favorite with crews. She was wonderful to them. There was never any star stuff as far as the company was concerned.

"Lana always looked at the rushes," says Garnett. "And looked at herself very critically. I think she was always making notes, saying 'I mustn't do that again.' "

Publicists on the set of *Postman* relate: "Whenever Lana got her period, she had a nurse in attendance and would take little mincing steps from her dressing room to the set. During this film it was particularly funny to see Lana in white followed by the nurse in white. Lana and Garfield had hit it off beautifully. They both had a fantastic sense of humor. One day when the nurse was on set, Garfield said to Lana, 'How about a quickie?' Lana scowled and shot back, 'You bastard.' "

By 1946 Lana was one of the ten most highly paid women in America. She was earning $226,000 a year, equivalent to half a million by today's standards. Although taxes took much of this, she lived like a millionaire.

Weekend at the Waldorf had been a huge hit for her the previous year. It was loosely based on *Grand Hotel*, and Lana played the stenographer portrayed by Joan Crawford in the original. *Postman* would be an even greater personal success for her in 1946 and her image as a femme fatale was strengthened by bold ad lines for the film—LANA TURNER—TEMPTING TO LOOK AT, DEADLY TO LOVE—IT STARTED WITH KISSES AND ENDED IN MURDER.

That year the most-talked-about best-seller was being made into a film, and the role of the heroine was the most sought-after since Scarlett O'Hara. Darryl F. Zanuck had bought *Forever Amber* for 20th Century-Fox and had cast an unknown British actress, Peggy Cummins, in the lead.

After investing $2 million in the film, Zanuck dumped the footage and the director. The project was assigned to Otto Preminger and, according to Preminger, Zanuck told him, "If you want to recast or rewrite it, you can do anything you want. But you've got to do this picture." Preminger didn't want to direct the film (he had hated the book) but he had no choice.

Otto wanted Lana for the part, and she wanted the role, but Zanuck had been insisting on Linda Darnell. Preminger tried the usual approach. "Very much in the Hollywood manner," recalled Otto, "I invited Lana and Zanuck to a dinner party so she could persuade him—and she was practically sitting in his lap. She wanted the part but she was at MGM and Zanuck wouldn't give it to anyone he didn't have under contract."

Zanuck's reasoning was very much in the Hollywood manner also. He told Preminger, "If you think Lana Turner is right, then we'll dye Linda Darnell's hair blonde and she'll be exactly like her."

As it turned out, losing the part was fortuitous for Lana. Neither Preminger nor Miss Darnell could save the film.

In February, Lana made a good-will trip to Buenos Aires, also stopping in Rio de Janeiro. It was her first trip out of the United

States since her Honolulu jaunt in 1940. On the trip to Rio, she stopped in New York and nightclubbed with old friend Greg Bautzer. Always the party-giver, Lana threw a farewell party before leaving for South America.

Upon her return, she said Latins "are all they were supposed to be." On the good-neighbor policy, she said, "There should be a lot more of it." Metro was glad to have her back in the United States where they could keep closer watch on her.

Lana was still dating Bautzer and Crane. But she was keeping the columnists dizzy trying to keep tabs on her latest love affairs.

In Hollywood in April, she revealed that New York radio executive Charles P. Jaeger, a vice president of the American Broadcasting Company, had asked her to marry him but she wasn't considering his proposal seriously. However, she was packing her bags to meet him in the East because "he is just what I want."

"He is tall and very handsome and very wonderful," Lana confided. "Yes, he has proposed but I don't know yet what will happen. I just met him a few weeks ago when I returned from South America," she said. "I am leaving for New York at the end of the week with my baby and her nurse."

She went on to explain that she had met Jaeger "at a party given by Martha Kemp's mother, Mrs. Helen Forester. I haven't turned him down yet but I hardly know him."

Jaeger, who had an eight-year-old son from his marriage to model Loretta White, was newly divorced. In New York, the executive denied Lana's statement that he had proposed to her. "That is just a lot of publicity magnifying a nice friendship," he said. "I have seen no such written statement from Miss Turner. She is a very wonderful girl."

It's interesting that Lana's sudden declaration of affection for Jaeger came only a few days after her name had again popped up in connection with Frank Sinatra. That was on April 4. There was trouble in the Sinatra household and he and Nancy separated. The rumor that Lana was the reason for the separation started when she and Frank had danced together all night at Sonja Henie's party.

It was reported on April 7 that Sinatra was in hiding at a desert resort after moving out on Nancy. Sinatra's press agent said, "There is no other woman involved, no matter what the gossip columnists say."

The studio wanted Lana out of town and away from the Sinatra hassle. On April 13 Lana flew east with Cheryl, now two years old, and the baby's nurse, reportedly to see Jaeger.

However, United Press reported that Jaeger had come to California to fly back with Lana on the same TWA flight. It was all very mysterious. He traveled under an assumed name. UP said, "Jaeger, according to a good source, got on the plane alone using the name of George Armstrong and posing as her [Lana's] business manager."

Lana had reserved three tickets for the flight, although she didn't need a ticket for baby Cheryl, and she had reserved three seats: one for the child, one for herself and one for the nurse. UP noted, "Jaeger boarded the plane on one of the three tickets reserved by Miss Turner."

When she got to New York, Lana checked into a suite at the Sherry-Netherland. She told reporters who called her at the hotel, "We're not even engaged. I have no ring. I have no definite idea of marriage. I'm not even engaged."

The newspapers noted that a little sleep apparently had accomplished a change of heart in Lana. Only twelve hours earlier, when she and Jaeger stepped off the plane at La Guardia, Lana had said the wedding might be "within a month."

Jaeger at the airport told reporters the marriage would take place "anytime from a week to five years. You see, we want to be sure."

When, at the Sherry, Lana was reminded of this quote, she snapped, "That doesn't sound like Mr. Jaeger."

The Jaeger affair ended as quickly as it began.

While in New York, Lana posed for photographs with United Nations big shots. She also dated A&P multimillionaire Huntington Hartford.

Back in Hollywood she was as usual not at a loss for men. Among others, she was again dating Howard Hughes. She had been seen at Catalina Island, Palm Springs and other vacation spots with the "handsome film producer and airline builder," as Hughes was referred to in those days. In July, when Hughes's newest plane had cracked up with him at the controls and he was almost killed, Lana tried without avail to reach his bedside. According to Associated Press, Lana arrived unannounced at Good Samaritan Hospital, asked permission to see Hughes and was told his condition was so critical that no visitors were permitted. She stayed on at the hospital for several hours and was upset and crying when she left for home. Some Hollywood reports said that she told friends she and Hughes might marry and that she had gone so far as to plan her trousseau.

But Hughes proved to be an even more elusive Hollywood bachelor for marriage-minded Lana than Greg Bautzer. It was after this nearly fatal accident that Hughes started his recluselike existence.

In 1947 Dorothy Kilgallen, never specifying exact dates but presumably discussing the Turner-Hughes relationship before his accident, wrote in the *New York Journal-American*: "The climax of Lana Turner's romance with Howard Hughes was like a scene out of a glamorous movie. One starlit night the flyer got word to his aide Johnny Meyer, who was on the coast, and ordered him to 'have reporters at the airport ready for a big announcement.' He confided to Johnny, 'We're going to be married.' Then he and Lana climbed into the plane and sped from New York to California. By the time they arrived they weren't speaking and the press got no pictures. No one ever found out what happened on the romantic moonlit ride but it ended the briefest betrothal in cinema history. Lana and Hughes made up their quarrel sometime afterward but still that old feeling was never the same."

Even today rumors circulate about a blonde actress who had had her linens initialed HH. When Hughes refused to marry her, he supposedly quipped: "Go marry Huntington Hartford."

By October of 1946, rumors of Lana's breaking up Sinatra's home had become so loud that she called Louella Parsons to seek her aid in denying them. Even *Newsweek* carried an item: "Rumors of a romance with Lana Turner were met by a silent Voice and a tearful Miss Turner: 'I have never in my life broken up a home.' "

It had been a busy year and Lana Turner had been in love with at least a half dozen men. But in the fall she fell in love with the one man who might have changed her life.

*"If I had to choose what was the
most important thing in Lana's life,
I would have to say it was
her relationship with Ty Power."*
HELEN YOUNG

In the fall of 1946, Lana Turner fell in love with Tyrone Power. He would be for Lana, according to a renowned and respected Hollywood writer and a close friend of Lana's, "the real thing. He was the *only* one for Lana, and she was totally in love with him."

Power had become a star in Hollywood shortly before fledgling Lana bounced across the screen in *They Won't Forget*. He came from a theatrical family and his father, Tyrone Power, Sr., had been an established stage and film actor.

Ty, Jr., was incredibly handsome, talented, intelligent, and gifted with charm. With his good looks and his success he was used to being sought after and playing the field. He was described as "a charming man but an incurable flirt."

Despite Power's absence from the screen while serving in the Air

Force during World War II, he easily recaptured his prominence after the war, with *The Razor's Edge.*

Prior to the war, Judy Garland had been in love with Power and he wanted to marry her, but MGM convinced Judy that she had only fallen in love "with the cover of *Photoplay.*"

Even if they had wanted to, neither MGM nor anyone else, for that matter, could have deterred Lana's pursuit of Ty. Although she and Power had traveled in the same social circles for years, they didn't "discover" each other until 1946.

"By the late fall there was hardly a weekend when Lana wasn't flying someplace to meet Ty or Ty wasn't flying someplace to meet Lana," a friend recalls.

Power had the dark and sexy good looks Lana was always attracted to, plus a sensitivity that was apparently often lacking in many of the other men Lana became involved with.

Lana and Power were on the same level, as far as careers were concerned. He wasn't using her to further himself. Power was about seven years older than Lana, mature but still young at thirty-three, and equally used to the flamboyant life of Hollywood.

Lana, at twenty-six, was the kind of woman Power was attracted to—glamorous, sensual and aggressive.

They were two of Hollywood's brightest luminaries and they appeared to be in love. That Christmas of 1946 was a special one. Lana was always generous. "She was generous to a fault," says an intimate of Lana's. "Someone would say, 'Gee, that's a pretty ring.' And I've seen her take it off and give it to them. She always remembered birthdays and things like that."

Lana was lavish that year in her Christmas gifts, and *Newsweek* reported that she was giving away five hundred presents: "There were two dozen cashmere sweaters (at $35 apiece) for her young men friends; and wallets with engraved gold plates ('Eddie from Lana') for her older men friends. There were jackets, purses, gloves and jewelry for her women friends.

"There were cases of bonded bourbon (at $120 per case) for the boys on the lot. The whole thing would simply be a production."

Newsweek didn't mention what Lana was giving Ty but they did report: "There was a diamond and sapphire clip for her mother and an ermine coat for her three-and-a-half-year-old daughter." (Years later Lana, accused of indulging Cheryl with furs at the age of three and a half, snapped: "No, she was *two*-and-a-half. And it had a matching ermine halo and she had handmade French glacé white gloves, because when this child was out of her pajamas she was *dressed.* She was my precious, my only child, and I wanted to see beauty.")

In a national magazine article in the early fifties, long after their liaison had ended, Lana gave a polite account of her torrid affair with Power. She said then, "I had serious discussions with Tyrone Power about our doing a picture together, if Louis B. Mayer and Darryl Zanuck could be brought around to letting us work. I found in him the kind of maturity and balance that I so sadly lacked. We were often seen together."

She added, "Shall I say that I was in love with Mr. Power? Hardly, nor was he in love with me. But companionship in Hollywood is always interpreted as romance."

However, in 1958, over a year after Power's death, Lana revealed her true feelings: "I wouldn't say it if he were still alive," she admitted, "but now somehow it's different. I loved Tyrone Power in a way that I never loved anyone else in my life."

Although Lana rescinded her earlier statements that *she* wasn't in love with Power, this time she made no mention of whether Power had been in love with her. He must have been—at least for a while—for from the fall of 1946 through December of 1947 their affair raged and their names were constantly in the news. Their respective studios might not have been happy with the alliance— Metro didn't want to lose Lana to 20th and Fox didn't want to give Ty up to MGM—but a source close to Lana remembers: "The movie colony was for them, and their fans were too. It would have been the perfect union."

But Power was still married to French star Annabella. They were separated, but not divorced.

Not long after Lana and Ty began their affair, Power's studio sent him on location to Mexico for *Captain from Castile*. As Lana has said, "I soon pulled off a Lana Turner stunt that vaulted us into the headlines." Her account of the story, told only several years later when she was still contending that their "companionship" had been mistakenly interpreted as a romance, was that: "Late in January of 1947 Ty was in Mexico on location. I was still making *Green Dolphin Street*. Suddenly, I had a day off and a weekend coming up. I was tired, bored. It struck me as entirely reasonable to fly down to Mexico to see Ty. I could fly back to Los Angeles without missing a scene from the *Dolphin*."

Lana's gesture wouldn't be received by her studio as "entirely reasonable." Metro had cast her in the multimillion-dollar spectacular, *Green Dolphin Street*. It was an important assignment for her in more ways than one. It was a heavy acting role originally intended for Katharine Hepburn, and Lana was playing a nonglamorous, aggressive woman. Quite a change of pace from the platinum blonde femme fatale in *The Postman Always Rings Twice*.

"I'm bold and scheming and sometimes I think I'm not quite nice," Lana says early in *Dolphin* to establish her character.

The film was winding up production when Lana's impulsive nature erupted. She defied the moguls at MGM by flying down to Mexico City, but it wasn't late January, as she has said, it was to spend New Year's Eve of 1946 with Power. She was due back on the set at 9:00 a.m. the day after New Year's. She hadn't reported in by noon. Then she called the troubleshooting talent executive at MGM and said, "This is Lana. I won't be in today. I'm still in Mexico City."

Columnist Florabel Muir reported that she cost MGM $100,000 in production delays (later this figure was more realistically reported as $35,000) and sent Louis B. Mayer's blood pressure up several points. An associate recalls Mayer's fury as he uttered an atypical, "Can't she find enough in LA?"

Lana has recalled the trip as a belated Christmas celebration: "I was no sooner on my plane and in the air, clutching my gift-wrapped presents, than I began to be doubtful about this adventure. I was badly frightened by the time I arrived in Mexico City and tried to call Ty by long-distance telephone. I had to use the phone because Mr. Power was not in Mexico City at all but eighty miles away on location, in a small town across the mountains.

" 'It's me,' I said in the small voice.

" 'Merry Christmas,' said Ty. 'How's everything in LA?'

" 'I'm in Mexico City.'

" 'Good Lord.'

" 'Aren't you glad to see me?'

" 'Of course. What are you doing in Mexico City?' "

Lana has said her thought at the time was, "How difficult can a man get?" Continuing her recollection, " 'I'm here because I came to eat a postponed Christmas dinner with you,' I said brightly. 'Now how do I reach your location?'

" 'Good Lord,' said Ty.' "

(It must be remembered that both Ty and Lana were used to language a bit stronger than "Good Lord.")

" 'Why? What's the matter? Don't you want to see me?'

" 'Of course I do! It's a swell idea but there's no train out of Mexico City for where we are. No bus. I guess I'll have to dig up a plane and send for you. You wait there. I'll let you know.' "

Even though many of her interviews have been equivalent to polite recollections, Lana does give insight into herself with lines such as: "There was I, the patsy all over again, trying to pull off a party with all the good will of a fifth grader and being a spoiled-brat nuisance.

"All I could do was wait at the Reforma Hotel, hiding behind newspapers, until from heaven-knows-where the efficient Mr. Power dug up a small plane and sent it for me."

Lana's next line, recalling this trip which would become one of the most publicized "events" of her private life, once again points to her ability to bounce back after disappointment. Although the trip obviously hadn't gone well up to this point, she has recalled that after she and Power were finally together, "Life picked up at once. We inspected a charming old town, visited the missions, had fun with cast and crew and Ty was his own fine self, not blaming me for a very silly thoughtless whim."

Lana recalled that inclement weather forced her to change her plans for her return flight. She remembered, "It rained. It roared. It stormed. I wept. I wept for two days." She has said that she finally left Mexico by dirt road, bumpy car and airplane and when she arrived at last in Los Angeles she immediately took a cab to the studio. She hurried to her dressing room. There was no message to see Mr. Mayer in his office. No one talked with her. No telephones rang. She noted a conspiracy of silence.

Lana was thirty hours late, and the studio was going to make a pointed reminder of her absence. When she reached the set there wasn't a soul in sight. Then, according to a report by Florabel Muir, suddenly from the wings came director Victor Saville and cameraman George Folsey, dressed up with serapes and sombreros and strumming guitars. They danced around Lana, singing "la, la, la, la," an old Mexican love song, then walked off the set without saying a word.

"In a few minutes everybody appeared and work resumed on *Green Dolphin Street*," concluded Florabel.

Seemingly all was forgiven, but it was definitely not forgotten. Lana was given specific orders to stay grounded while working.

Lana's version of the story is a little more colorful than Florabel's. She has said, "The entire sound stage—one of the biggest on the Metro lot—was dark and empty as far as I could see. One dim bulb glowed and a little man was sweeping up. I went on past him, wondering if Victor had called the whole show off because of my absence. Would you like to know what I felt like? I felt like a burbling idiot in a serape.

"Suddenly all the blazing lights went up and there they were, Saville and the whole cast—in serapes and sombreros just like mine! Someone hit a big note on the piano and they began to sing 'South of the Border.'

"Thus they welcomed the prodigal and gaily forgave me. I was never scolded."

She may not have been scolded (*Weekend at the Waldorf* and *Postman* were tremendous hits, so they couldn't complain that Lana was slipping at the box office) but the public Lana Turner image was getting another dent, thanks to her pursuit of Power.

Up to now, Lana had always been the pursued—the beautiful, innocent, chased victim. Now, in public, she was doing the chasing, and it placed her personality in quite a different light. While it had only been hinted at that she was "a home-wrecker" during the Sinatra affair, she was now providing her detractors with further ammunition to back up the charge.

But the war had sobered up American dreamers, and the Hollywood gods and goddesses could be less perfect than had been imagined and still not lose favor. And besides, Lana had always had a sex symbol-femme fatale image. It wasn't as if Shirley Temple was chasing Tyrone Power all over the world.

During Lana's sojourn in Mexico, reporters had called Annabella, then staying in New York, to ask her opinion of the Turner-Power affair. The French star was awakened at 11:00 a.m. and appeared more irked about being awakened at that indecent hour than at what was happening between her husband and Lana.

"We are separate," she declared. "You wake me up to tell me about heem weekending in Mexico with theese Lana Turner? Why don't you ask heem how ees theese with Lana Turner?"

Though Lana was back in Hollywood and working, newspapers kept the public alerted concerning her offscreen activities. They reported that Lana intended to fly to Mexico again to join Ty after she completed *Green Dolphin Street*. Power still had a month to go making *Captain from Castile*. It was expected that he would get a fast Mexican divorce from Annabella so he and Lana could marry.

Ironically, a dark-haired young beauty, Linda Christian, who was discovered and named for films by Errol Flynn, had a bit part as Lana's native maid in *Green Dolphin Street*. Linda was dating Lana's former lover, Turhan Bey, and it would be Miss Christian, and not Lana Turner, who would be the next Mrs. Tyrone Power (to Errol Flynn's astonishment: "He *married* her?!" Flynn exclaimed when he found out).

When Power and Annabella announced their separation, it was understood that it would be Power who would get the divorce. But Power seemed in no hurry. He did not get a Mexican divorce, and Lana did not visit him again while he finished *Castile*. But she almost did.

Lana's hair-stylist and close friend Helen Young vividly remembers the *Green Dolphin Street* days and Lana's trips to see Ty.

Helen Young was a pretty, spunky girl from a little town in upstate California. She had come to Hollywood to work as a hairdresser in the movies. After getting a job in a little beauty shop on Sunset Strip, through friends she wangled an introduction to the man who was in charge of security at MGM. He in turn got her a job interview.

"In those days, we worked six to six, six days a week. But the money was good. You always made more money in the studios than outside."

When Helen went to meet Lana, there was sort of a test period to see if their personalities were compatible. "I did some period hairdos and Lana could sense I was nervous. She was so dear. She said, 'Sit down, relax.' We talked a while, and then she said, 'Okay, are you ready now?'

94

"I remember she was very patient. She used to come in earlier than she had to."

After Lana's unscheduled jaunt to Mexico to meet Power, she planned another. Helen remembers, "We used to work on Saturday. But one week Lana told me and Del [Armstrong, Lana's long-time make-up man] she wasn't going to work that Saturday, since she wanted to go see Ty again. She told us, 'Plan on taking the day off.' I was delighted. At that time my parents lived in Madeira. Up near Fresno. That's about a seven-hour drive.

"I no sooner got there [Friday evening] when there was a phone call. It was Lana. She said, 'Helen, I couldn't do it.'

"It was a big set and they'd hired a lot of extras. Lana hadn't realized what was in mind for her that day. I couldn't find a bus back Friday night, so she said, 'I'll call you back.' She and Del got together and she called back and said, 'Del is going to come up and get you.'

"Del took Lana's limousine. And he and his wife arrived about 12:30 or so. Between his wife and me we kept him awake and arrived back just in time to drive through the studio gate and punch in on time the following morning.

"This is how Lana is. She always wanted to do these marvelous things, but she always protected us in case something went wrong.

"Lana gives everyone a love name or pet name," says Helen. "Mine is Bubble or B.B., which is short for Bubble-Butt. That's because I was a very healthy young girl when we met."

Lana and Helen have remained friends through the years. One reason is that they have many traits in common. Both are women of strong determination and both have a keen sense of humor.

Lana maintained close ties with Helen personally and professionally, even on films to which Helen wasn't assigned. "We're almost like sisters," Helen comments. "She asks me to break in her shoes."

Ty came back to Hollywood in February, 1947, and the Turner-Power affair continued to blaze. They were the town's most talked-about couple. Lana had often discussed the problems a man faced being "Mr. Lana Turner." With Ty, that problem wouldn't exist. Hollywood writers had visions of them as the new generation's Doug and Mary.

Lana was now making *Cass Timberlaine* with Spencer Tracy. Director George Sidney remembers that Power was on the set all the time.

Sidney says the studio hadn't wanted him to use Lana in the picture because they thought she wasn't "heavy" enough to carry the role. However, other Hollywood sources say that Metro had purchased the Sinclair Lewis novel because the roles were tailor-made for Tracy and Turner. And, in fact, that Tracy wanted Vincente Minnelli or George Cukor to direct and accepted Sidney, and the final script, reluctantly.

Many Turner devotees today like the film because it allowed Lana to be natural and appealing rather than a sex symbol. "At the time we thought we were making a good picture," says Sidney. "On television it comes over like a soap opera."

Lana worked well with Tracy (they hadn't co-starred together since 1941 in *Dr. Jekyll and Mr. Hyde*), and the picture was fun for her to make under easy-going director Sidney.

Sidney was, and is, an avid photographer and loved to take countless candid shots on the set. With this, and working with Tracy and seasoned actors like Zachary Scott and Mary Astor, and, of course, with Ty on the set most of the time, Lana was happy. There is a theory among her close friends that her happy mental states induced by being in love produced her most beautiful on-screen self.

"She had an inner glow when she was in love, and the camera picked it up."

Lana's friends knew that she was deeply involved emotionally with Power and it wasn't just "a physical thing." Generally it was assumed that Lana was interested in only one aspect of a man.

With Power, the feeling was that she loved the whole man. The question was: Did he feel the same way about her?

Along with his obvious attributes, Power appeared to be well bred and well educated. Had they married, he might have had a steadying effect on Lana and the raising of her young daughter, now almost four.

In addition to parties and the usual rounds of Hollywood's social life, Lana had even gone fishing with Power off the Mexican coast. Now the 210-pound swordfish he had helped her catch was stuffed and hanging over the mantel in her home.

Lana was at a peak in popularity. Amusingly during this sex-symbol period of her career, she was voted one of the "most glamorous mothers in the U.S.," along with Marlene Dietrich and Gene Tierney's mother Belle Taylor—both years older than Lana.

Renowned photographer Eliot Elisofon, for his series on movie queens for *Life* magazine in 1946, photographed Lana's face through smoke. The smoke was said to symbolize her smoldering sex appeal.

Columnists continued adding to the Lana Turner legend. Dorothy Kilgallen summed it up when she wrote: "Lana Turner is a super-star for many reasons but chiefly because she is the same off-screen as she is on. Some of the great stars are magnetic dazzlers on celluloid and ordinary, practical, polo-coated little things in private life. Not so Lana. No one who adored her in movies would be disappointed to meet her in the flesh. The flesh looks the same. The biography is as colorful as any plot she has ever romped through on the screen. The clothes she wears are just like the clothes you pay to see her in on Saturday night at the Bijou. The physical allure is just as heavy when she looks at a headwaiter as when she looks at the hero."

Like many in Hollywood, Lana by this time was surely caught up totally in the whirlpool of her own publicity. She said a few years later, "We are unconscious of what Hollywood may do to us. And at the same time it is unfair to blame this on Hollywood. It is due to everything that goes with big success, and sudden success. Such success is the most dangerous thing that can happen . . . there is nothing more devastating."

Cheryl began making news on her own. In January, 1947, when she was three and a half, *Newsweek* ran a photo of her with Rebecca Welles (Orson's daughter) and Becky's glamorous mother, Rita Hayworth, at Becky's second birthday party. Cheryl wasn't smiling.

Lana monopolized Tyrone Power's nonworking hours, and by the summer of 1947 there were reports that he was becoming irked by her possessiveness.

"He was giving Lana a rather bad time," says a friend.

Some people say she deserved the problems he gave her since she had fallen in love with the male version of herself. "Ty had so much charm it was illegal," says a friend. "But his tastes were varied. He could never be happy with just one person. Not even Lana." People say Ty had an insatiable desire to "be like the wind —go everywhere—do everything."

Lana, always a great party-giver and gift-giver, gave a party for Ty. The theme was Love. Every important star and producer in town was there. The decorations and favors all included hearts and flowers entwined. Many assumed it was an engagement party and that Lana and Ty would announce their marriage plans. No plans were announced other than Ty's upcoming good-will tour of Africa.

On September 1, Power took off on the two-month good-will vacation jaunt of the dark continent, also stopping in South America and Europe. Some people said the trip was to get away from Lana, since Power "needed a breath of free air."

In a converted DC-3 he was accompanied by his male secretary and a press agent, James Denton. Air-hopping on a vacation tour wasn't new with Ty. He had done it in the late thirties, and the previous year he had junketed around South America.

98

Although he hadn't yet divorced Annabella, the talk in Hollywood was that Lana wouldn't be able to bear being separated from Ty. But during his absence she did not once fly to join him.

During the next few months many startling events concerning both Lana and Ty would become front-page news.

Lana set the scene by arriving in New York in October, wearing a blue mink coat in what reporters described as "last year's length." She confided that she had let her skirts down an inch and a half in line with "The New Look," but said, "That's all. I won't wear that ugly new length."

Her affair with Power was about to come to an abrupt end. He had met Linda Christian in Rome, and although Lana wired him and telephoned him across the Atlantic, it seemed all in vain. Friends said that she was hurt, insulted, furious, miserable. But she still loved him.

Miss Christian later recalled an incident in Rome when she was with Power in his hotel room and he received a telephone call from New York. She recognized the "strident" voice at the other end of the line, which screeched: "I've been trying to get you all day! Where the hell have you been?"

According to Miss Christian, Power was uncomfortable and embarrassed at the tone of the conversation. Before it ended, the voice on the phone loudly commanded: "I want you to say, 'I love you.' Now, right now!"

Power told Linda that a solution would have to be found regarding the "girl I used to love." And in addition, before Power could marry Linda, a divorce settlement had to be finalized with Annabella.

While Lana was in New York, Ty flew back to the States and purposely avoided New York City, flying directly to Kansas City and then on to California. It is not certain whether he phoned her, as she has told magazine interviewers, or whether she phoned him. At any rate, Power was in Palm Springs and Lana was in New York, and she impulsively flew to meet him.

Power wrote to Linda concerning the meeting. He said that Lana had sensed immediately that "things were different" and an "Iron Curtain" came down between them. After she left, he mentally debated with himself whether he should call—or just leave things alone. He also said he mentioned "nothing specific" to Lana about a new woman in his life—"time will take care of that."

Lana's version, told after Power's death, was that Power told her he had been summoned home by his studio and he had been unable to stop in New York. But when Lana arrived in California, he wasn't waiting. He appeared an hour later, gave her a cool reception and they subsequently agreed to end their relationship.

Lana maintained that Power had been told lies about her by a woman she believed to be her friend. Lana didn't leave the airport. She hastily boarded a plane and headed back for New York.

Other versions claim that, as soon as she stepped out of the plane, Lana greeted him with, "Well, are we going to get married or not?" When he said no, she returned to New York.

Still another more colorful version claimed that Power was informed that during his absence Lana had been romancing a famous married crooner, even having rendezvous with him in his hospital room.

In any event, the split was a bitter disappointment for Lana. She would remember it always. Ty was enamoured of Linda Christian and eager to end his relationship with Lana. He was gentleman enough to let her make the announcement, and on December 1 Metro released the information that "Lana Turner and Tyrone Power have called it quits."

Throughout the years Lana has fondly remembered Tyrone Power as her one great love, even though their relationship ended on a sour note. Obviously the affair ended before Lana wanted it to and left her with certain romantic concepts of "what might have been."

Friends felt that the Power split was a turning point in her life,

100

that it would take her a long time to recover. Her ego must have been flattened, especially since the whole business was public knowledge. The man she loved, Tyrone Power, didn't want to marry her. Worse yet, he was going to marry another woman! Even Louella Parsons said, "I feel this is where Lana's self-destructive impulses took over."

Lana once said, "When a small-town girl makes a mistake, her family covers up for her. But me—nobody ever tries to cover up for me. My mistakes are magnified."

At the time of their split, Lana tried to save face by telling Hedda Hopper that she and Ty Power had discussed their problems like grownups and decided to go their separate ways. "We never discussed marriage," Lana told Hedda, "but the press did and that put us out on a limb."

Helen Young says: "If I had to choose what was the most important thing in Lana's life, I would have to say it was her relationship with Ty Power."

Whatever her personal hurt, Lana would not sit home to brood about it. After her breakup with Ty, her quest for diversion appeared considerably heightened.

Events of the next few weeks moved at lightning speed. Even the hardiest of reporters covering the Hollywood beat found it difficult to keep up with Lana's feverish pace.

Even before the public announcement of her break with Ty, in late November Lana dated Bernard Baruch's nephew, Perry Belmont Frank, Jr. With Frank at El Morocco on November 26 she met handsome socialite John Alden Talbot, Jr., who was with his wife, Nancy Rheem Talbot. The Talbots had only been married since April.

Lana, as always, was the center of attention. And her attention was caught by Talbot. It didn't take long. At the Stork Club Talbot danced cheek-to-cheek with Lana while his lovely wife sat at ringside trying to look nonchalant.

Lana returned to California, and on December 4, Talbot told his pals that he and Nancy had agreed to a trial separation and his wife was "going home to mama" in Washington, D.C.

Before marrying Nancy, Talbot had been voted one of Society's ten leading playboy-bachelors. Columnists were now touting, "There is some talk about John Alden speaking for himself in Hollywood pictures," leading to speculation that Lana Turner was telling him, "You oughta be in pictures. . . ."

On December 5, Lana, Cheryl and Talbot were caught by reporters as they disembarked at Grand Central Station in New York after their arrival from Chicago. Headlines screamed, LANA AND YALE MAN ARRIVE. And the copy said, "Lana Turner, whose love life has been cluttered up with the men most gals dream of, it says in her scrapbooks, arrived in town on the 20th Century-Limited yesterday with her small daughter and a brand new escort in tow. The escort was handsome as a collar ad and as inarticulate.

"Not that Lana contributed any nifties to the press interview dialogue. It went like this:

"Q. Is this the new flame?

"A. I wouldn't know.

"Q. Well, a couple of weeks ago you said you and Ty were . . .

"A. (interrupting): I have nothing to say about any romance of any kind.

"And so Lana betook herself to the Plaza to put her daughter, 4, who is suffering from a cold, to bed. Talbot was on trial separation from his wife."

But Lana was playing the field. On December 21 she was seen at the Stork Club with millionaire Bob Topping. Talbot was there too and, according to observers, "looked very happy as he and his date tripped the light fantastic as close as possible to Lana and Topping.

"The explanation for the Talbot grin was as transparent as the headache Lana said she had when she asked Bob to put her in a cab in front of the Stork and showed up later that same evening at El Morocco with Johnny."

A little over a month later, Mrs. Talbot was awarded $200-a-month temporary alimony in her suit against Talbot. To MGM's horror and dismay, she named Lana Turner corespondent in a subsequent separation action, even though Talbot was by then well out of Lana's orbit.

By the end of December, Lana, her mother and Cheryl would be spending the holidays with Henry J. "Bob" Topping and Topping's family at his estate at Round Hill, Connecticut.

"Who's to say why the sudden switch to Talbot and Topping?" asks a close friend. "I know Lana was deeply in love with Ty. No one knows what her deep hurts and feelings are. All we know is she's able to erase them and go on."

"I did it! I did it!"
LANA TURNER, 1948

7

Christmas in Connecticut was hardly what Lana could have had in mind a few months earlier. Friends noted that she was bitter and dejected over the Tyrone Power debacle. She has said that the farthest thing from her mind after that was a serious involvement with another man.

But Bob Topping was no mere "other man." He possessed the two most respected commodities in Hollywood: money and social position. He had background and breeding—at least by Hollywood standards—and if his physical characteristics didn't place him in a league with Tyrone Power, his finances put him in a league far above almost every other man Lana had known, except Howard Hughes.

Topping wasn't new to Hollywood circles. At the time he met Lana, he was separated from his third wife, actress Arline Judge.

104

That marriage had generated a great deal of gossip, since Miss Judge had been married five times and her second husband had been Dan Topping, Bob's brother. By marrying Arline, Bob Topping became stepfather to his nephew Dan Topping, Jr., and Miss Judge became a sister-in-law to her ex-husband.

Bob Topping's marriage to Miss Judge was short-lived (less than a year). Topping apparently had a habit of courting the lady who would be the next Mrs. Topping before bothering to divorce her predecessor.

His two previous marriages had lasted longer than his marriage to Miss Judge, but they were equally "glamorous." Topping's first wife had been actress Jayne Shattuck. His second wife was Gloria "Mimi" Baker. Mimi, the half-sister of George and Alfred Gwynne Vanderbilt, had been the glamour girl of café society in 1937. With Mimi, Topping had two children, Sandra and Henry J., Jr.

The Topping brothers, Dan, Henry J. (Bob) and John, were heirs to a huge (over $140 million) fortune which was amassed by their grandfather, Daniel G. Reid. Reid made the fortune mostly in tin-plate but then went into tobacco, steel, finance and railroads. Nevertheless, the Topping brothers were constantly referred to in newspapers as "the tin-plate heirs."

From his early youth, Topping was characterized as a playboy. He spent much of his youth in traveling and big-game hunting. He was attracted to women who had a penchant for making news. His brother Dan, then part owner of the New York Yankees, had similar leanings. In addition to Arline Judge, one of Dan's ex-wives was skating star Sonja Henie.

Lana entered this complicated marital picture in January, 1948.

Topping had been in Hollywood in 1947, and Lana has said that, although he was still married to Arline Judge, he began an ardent telephone campaign to get a date with "L.T." and sent lavish gifts of flowers and candy to the set of *Green Dolphin Street*.

However, Miss Turner's memory appears faulty, since Topping didn't marry Arline until May of 1947, and *Green Dolphin Street* had completed production by that time. In all likelihood, Lana first encountered Topping while she was shooting Mervyn LeRoy's *Homecoming*, her third of four films with Clark Gable.

Lana has said that during this period her friends were urging her to date other men. Obviously this was a reference to the fact that Tyrone Power was trying to ease her out of his life. Lana has said that, when Greg Bautzer joined Lana's friends in urging her to date his pal Topping, "I listened with more attention."

Topping was enterprising (and determined) and "managed" to get her telephone number. It was after this that he began sending gifts to her set. She was furious, she has said, and told him to cut it out.

Topping left for New York and, according to Lana, she thought the episode was at an end.

Topping certainly wasn't the perfect male animal that automatically attracted Lana, and his campaign probably would have been a failure had it not been for her abrupt split with Power.

While Lana was in New York in November, she again encountered Topping. She has said that she finally met him as a favor to her friend, ex-Howard Hughes aide and MGM publicist Johnny Meyer. Lana was lunching with Meyer one day at the Stork Club and he said, "A good friend of mine wants to meet you, Lana. Listen, you've got to get me off the hook. I promised the guy. I bragged. I said I would arrange it. All you have to do is meet the fellow." Meyer also confided to Lana that Topping was "a Cartier man," which he described as a guy who gives girls baubles from the famous jewelry store.

She had her own jewels, and told Meyer so. But, according to Lana, she agreed to meet Topping the next day and, although she was a half hour late, he waited patiently.

In any event, several weeks later, after Power had jilted her and Talbot had been discarded, Lana needed an escort for the New York premiere of *The Bishop's Wife*. The film's star, Loretta Young, was at sea on the *Queen Mary* and wouldn't arrive in time for the premiere. It wasn't an MGM film, but producer Sam Goldwyn telephoned Louis B. Mayer and asked if one of Metro's stars in New York would attend the premiere to add glamour and insure publicity. Who could have obtained more coverage in December, 1947, than the film colony's leading newsmaker?

Lana has said that she telephoned Topping, who was in the midst of a card game with his cronies. He delightedly accepted her invitation to escort her to the premiere and, after he hung up, gleefully bragged about it to his pals, who hadn't until then believed that he was really seeing Lana Turner. "You didn't think I could make it with the little lady did you, you bums?" he said.

Topping and the little lady made all the newspapers when they attended the premiere of *The Bishop's Wife*. It was not an uneventful evening. Lana has said, "On our way, with Topping appropriately in tails and me in all the white glamour and fur that I could wear, I was fumbling in my purse for the little card bearing the impromptu words I was to say into the foyer microphone." Supposedly Topping then reached over, took her purse and dropped a little paper-wrapped package into it.

Lana has recalled their ensuing conversation.

"Now what's that?" Lana asked.

"Nothing much," he replied. "Little things I picked up. Open it if you like."

When she snapped open the little box, she saw two diamond earrings "so large and so glittering they could have been used for headlights." Cartier's.

Lana says she turned stuffy again. How fast did a guy think he could work? she thought.

"I can't accept these," Lana said coldly.

"Why these are just little things," said Topping. "I kind of thought they looked like you."

To Lana, Topping seemed hurt and baffled.

"Well, I could just try them on," Lana conceded.

At the premiere they were besieged by photographers and Lana's fans. Lana and Bob didn't like the film, and while Cary Grant and Loretta Young cavorted on screen Topping motioned to a convenient exit. He and Lana sneaked out and went to a nearby bar. Lana has remembered, "I began to admire this fellow. He seemed competent."

Later in the evening Topping escorted Lana to the posh post-premiere society party. They arrived hours late, and society columnist Elsa Maxwell was going out the door just as Bob and Lana were arriving.

"Hello," Lana said to Elsa and they shook hands.

"Hello," Elsa replied.

"Meet Mr. Topping," said Lana, waving casually to her escort.

"I've already met Mr. Topping," said Elsa cheerfully.

"Where are you going?" Lana asked Elsa. It was a quarter to one.

"I'm going home," answered Miss Maxwell. "But come on in now and meet the crowd. They've been waiting for you for hours."

Lana flipped off her fur coat. "Where's the hatcheck girl?" she asked.

The butler waiting to take her coat stiffened perceptibly.

"This isn't a night club," whispered Elsa to Lana. "This is a private house. They don't have hatcheck girls."

At that moment Lynn Farnol, Goldwyn's publicity agent, rushed to the rescue and Elsa and Farnol both escorted Lana into Mrs. Evander Schley's large drawing room on Park Avenue, which was crammed to its rafters with a supper party given for members of the cast of the film.

Elsa later wrote in her syndicated column, "Now the one fault Miss Turner shares with most Hollywood stars is the art of not being smartly dressed so I watched Lana's innocent blue eyes as she was presented to the Duchess of Windsor, Mrs. Harrison Williams, Mrs. Harry Payne Bingham, Mrs. Carol Carstairs and others in Christian Dior and Hattie Carnegie dresses which were very becoming, I thought, but Lana didn't. She said to a friend, 'If they're the best-dressed, then somebody's looney!"

As was characteristic of Lana's private life, her relationship with Topping snowballed at breakneck speed.

"Ever spend a white Christmas?" asked Topping. Indeed he was competent, and quick.

Lana never had spent a white Christmas.

"How about it with my family at Round Hill, Connecticut? We'll just have your baby and a governess and your mother fly in, and we'll all go up there in the snow and quiet and have a real Christmas. Away from all this. Just my family and yours."

Lana was probably relieved to leave New York and the avalanche of publicity, much of it mocking, that she had been receiving over the past two months. And perhaps it would help her forget the Ty Power bust-up, which hovered like a dark cloud over her life.

The Topping family was a different breed from others Lana had known. Although they had been involved with show-business people, their "landed gentry" status, and wealth that spanned three generations, gave them a sense of quiet security which was conveyed to Lana.

The newspapers immediately picked up on the Topping-Turner affair. MGM was at their wit's end with Lana. She was succeeding in stripping away the carefully built-up image the studio had developed. First Ty Power, then Talbot, now Topping—all, after all, married men. Topping, in fact, was newly married, though separated. Arline Judge was giving out statements that she still loved Topping and, to prove it, she was going to make it very tough for him. It might take her a long time, she said, but she would ruin him.

Arline wasn't the only one to be surprised by the quick events of the Turner-Topping relationship. On the heels of the Ty Power and John Alden Talbot affairs, with the newspapers saying Lana was being named corespondent in the Talbot separation and subsequent divorce action, MGM was angry with "Miss Public Nuisance" and suspended her when she refused to play Dumas's female menace, Lady De Wynter, in *The Three Musketeers*.

Right after the new year, before Lana's suspension, it was announced that Topping was going to throw a $25,000 gala engagement party for Lana at the Mocambo. Somewhere between four hundred and seven hundred telegraphed invitations went out, signed Lana and Bob Topping. But the party was canceled and Topping gave out a statement that he had never planned it in the first place. However, Lana now had a fifteen-carat marquise diamond engagement ring, and she wasn't shy about wearing it.

On January 10, Lana and Bob arrived in Hollywood. Mildred, Cheryl and the child's governess had preceded them, and Mildred met Lana at the terminal. The press was there in force, and Lana quipped, "I hope I still have a job at MGM." Topping was grumpy, refused to talk to the press and growled, "There's been too much publicity already."

Associated Press announced Lana's suspension on January 14, and MGM said the suspension was because of her refusal to play a role and denied the action had "anything to do with her recent cross-country romancing with Tyrone Power and Bob Topping."

According to Hedda Hopper, when Hedda found out that an angry Metro was planning to make an example of Lana and "teach her a lesson"—one that would also keep the rest of the MGM roster in line—she telephoned Lana and filled her in, telling her to "get the hell out here and do the picture if you care anything at all about your career."

Lana apparently still cared.

A studio spokesman said, "Miss Turner had agreed ten weeks ago to start the picture on January 5th and had requested and received a $25,000 advance against her salary to spend on a New York vacation." He estimated that Lana's refusal to do the picture would cost MGM between three and four hundred thousand dollars.

The next day, January 15, the *Hollywood Reporter* speculated that "Lana is taking outside advice—and none too good. She has never been a headache to the studio along these lines before."

A day later even Louella was in the act. She reported, "Yesterday afternoon at the home of Bert Friedlob, a mutual friend, Eddie Mannix and Bob Topping met to discuss Lana's refusal to make the picture.

"Later I talked with Topping, who said: 'It's true Mr. Mannix and I had a little social get-together, but I had nothing to do with Lana's refusing to make 'Three Musketeers.' I don't feel I should interfere in any way. Our meeting was very amicable, but Lana must do what she feels is best for her own future.'

"It was pointed out to Mr. Topping that it would be far better to have Lana have the studio in back of her now and that she has had three tremendous parts in 'Green Dolphin Street,' 'Cass Timberlaine' and 'Homecoming,' and since she had agreed to play in 'Three Musketeers' the general consensus is that she should not leave the studio in a spot.

"I personally don't think Lana would be happy quarreling with MGM. She told me not very long ago she couldn't understand why stars walked out and refused to do parts.

" 'I couldn't see myself ever disappointing Louis B. Mayer. He's been too good to me,' Lana said.

"So with the memory of what she said to me on the set of 'Homecoming,' I firmly believe before 24 hours is over that Lana will be back at the studio.

"It will take only a month to make the picture, and she would be through in time to marry Topping when he is free to marry her."

For almost a week the trade newspapers and the columnists guessed at the behind-the-scenes negotiations. On January 19, Edith Gwynn, the gossip columnist for the *Hollywood Reporter*, noted that "the latest on the MGM-Lana Turner affair is that Miss Turner offers to do 'The Three Musketeers' (which will require 21 days of her time) if MGM will at the end of the picture give her a year's vacation with pay. MGM turned it down."

Later, when the suspension was settled, Eddie Mannix denied that Lana had ever made such demands. The star told her favorite columnist, Louella, "I have always been cooperative and certainly there never has been a time when cooperation is more needed in our industry." Miss Parsons went on to report that *Musketeers* producer Pandro Berman had assured Lana that her role would be completed in twenty-one days so she could make marriage plans.

Hedda Hopper had something to say, too: "I never for one moment doubted that Lana would make the picture. Her career means too much to her and she is much too good an actress and too sensible to throw it away."

Hedda was right. The suspension was short-lived. Less than a week after it was announced, Lana was back at MGM for pre-production work on *The Three Musketeers*. Although Angela Lansbury had begged L. B. Mayer for the Lady De Wynter role, he insisted on Lana, knowing she was needed for box-office insurance. Lana was a very valuable property in 1948. Her last three films had been tremendous grossers. Her offscreen publicity was staggering. There could be very few people in the world who weren't aware of Lana Turner. Despite the problems she gave the studio, they had no intention of dropping her or letting her buy up her contract. They knew the other studios would fight to sign her and reap profits with the glamour girl that MGM had created.

An observer remarked, "No matter what Lana does she's safe. She's so into Metro now that MGM can't fire her. It has to protect its investment."

So at $5,000 a week, Lana began *The Three Musketeers* under the direction of her friend George Sidney. And MGM prepared *Homecoming*, her film with Clark Gable, for an Easter release.

In the midst of all the ballyhoo about the suspension, Lana and Topping made a glittering appearance at the Hollywood premiere of *Cass Timberlaine*. Mildred accompanied them to the event, which was a benefit for the John Tracy Clinic. Spencer Tracy and his wife Louise (who had founded the Clinic for the Deaf) were the hosts.

Lana's entrance, because of all the suspension publicity and also because of her spectacular fifteen-carat engagement ring, made news and heralded the fact that 1948 would be an even bigger year for her, publicitywise, than 1947 had been.

To set the pace, Bob Topping was suing Arline Judge for divorce, and she was contesting it. Topping rented Carole Landis's house in Beverly Hills and planned to spend the winter there.

Obviously MGM was unhappy and had a serious talk with Lana. The next few months were relatively quiet and, although gossip columnists made much of the Topping-Turner affair, Lana gave out no statements.

Finally on March 3 she broke the silence and said that she and Topping had no plans for marriage. A United Press International story reported that Lana said she had shut up about the Topping "romance" because the studio had told her to.

"I'm their property," she said. "If they tell me not to talk, I don't talk. I feel maybe I've been quiet too long. Everybody else has been quoted on this but nobody ever talked to me."

Lana went on to say she was never involved, either, with John Alden Talbot. "I have dinner with a fellow a couple of times and I'm a homebreaker. Great big lecherous Lana, that's me."

The following month, however, Topping announced he would marry Lana. His lawyers obviously had reached a settlement with Arline Judge, and on April 23, in Bridgeport, Connecticut, Arline won an uncontested divorce and cleared the way for Topping to marry Lana.

Miss Judge received a lump sum of $100,000 and was awarded $15,000 more for counsel fees. The money wasn't the newsmaking aspect of the divorce, however. The actress was awarded the divorce when she testified that Topping was insanely jealous and that he beat her. She also testified that he had twice threatened to shoot her.

The trouble began, according to Arline, about a month after she and the tin-plate heir were married in Miami Beach. She declared that he threw her down a flight of stairs when they were cruising the Bahamas on his yacht. She then told the judge that she couldn't walk for two months. She testified that Topping's acts of violence continued almost uninterruptedly despite her efforts to patch things up. On one occasion, she said, after she had had an appendix operation, Topping flew into a rage and kicked her on the incision. After that she needed a day and night nurse for three weeks. She wound up her testimony by saying that she would have been killed eventually if she had stayed with him.

Obviously Lana wasn't intimidated. Literally moments after the divorce was final on a Friday, Lana blissfully confirmed that she and Topping would wed the following Monday. She and Bob were vacationing in Palm Springs when they heard the news of the divorce and they rushed to Hollywood, where Lana had a last fitting on her "cocoa lace over nude satin" wedding dress, as United Press International described it. Lana later remembered it as "champagne Alençon lace from France over champagne satin." She also recalled a trousseau of "dozens of nightgowns in flowered chiffon." In 1948 the press delighted in reporting extravagance. Twenty-five thousand dollars for a wedding trousseau! And Lana has said, "I arranged for a handsome suit for my mother and for a little 1820-period dress for Cheryl."

Cheryl was to be a flower girl at this, what Lana considered "my first wedding." And the setting for the wedding couldn't have been more appropriate: Billy Wilkerson's Bel-Air mansion.

Wilkerson had suggested they use his mansion for the gala wedding when Topping had asked Wilkerson to be best man. The publisher was delighted. It was to be a small affair, only twelve at the ceremony and seventy-five at the reception.

Lana wanted the impossible. She wanted the wedding to be dignified and quiet, but she made the major blunder of trying to exclude the press. Police stood by to keep the service private and quiet. But the event was too newsworthy for the press and public to ignore.

Special police from MGM and a dozen studio press agents were on hand to strong-arm the press, who were kept waiting on the lawns of the estate to record the details for Lana's public.

Lana has said that she knew her wedding would cause publicity. She knew that no actor escapes publicity and that actors who accept it when they want it and then complain about it when they don't are unrealistic. But in recalling her wedding to Topping, she remembered: "But I hoped to be married to Bob decently and reverently and with as little fanfare as possible." Years after the marriage, she remembered that the press "were wretched and noisy and they made a mockery of my wedding."

Almost every news account of the wedding contained two points of information which would be rewritten in every account of every subsequent Lana Turner wedding and in every rehashing of her love life—one, that Lana, although twice married, went through the ceremony like a breathless teen-age novice; two, that after the ceremony, Topping whispered to her, "This is forever," and Lana concurred, "Yes, darling."

The United Press International account also quoted Lana as being so ecstatic when she managed to complete the ceremony that she "squealed to a feminine friend, 'I did it! I did it!' "

The wedding lived up to every shopgirl's dream of what a Movie Star's wedding to A Millionaire should be. Lana not only wore her fifteen-carat engagement ring, but a glittering two-inch-wide diamond bracelet, Topping's wedding gift.

The altar at the ceremony was covered with gardenias. Lana later remembered, "I asked for three hundred dozen flowers—delphiniums, roses, gladiola, daisies and gardenias, to fill Billy's house. Bob approved of my somewhat elaborate ideas about clothes and decorations."

The sedate ceremony was performed by the Reverend Stewart P. MacLennan, retired pastor of the Hollywood First Presbyterian

Church. "Lana is such a sweet girl," the Reverend beamed after it was all over. "She has such a fine, earthy quality in her face. There is spiritual quality in that woman."

After the ceremony, more guests began to arrive (the number was closer to 150 than 75) and three hours later the reception began. Guests, including Joan Crawford, George Jessel, Beverly Tyler, Anita Louise, Errol Flynn, Greg Bautzer, dined on caviar, roast pheasant, smoked salmon and six-pound lobsters especially flown in from Boston. "She Loves Me" was inscribed in glazing on a huge ham. "I Love You" was written in glazing on a roast beef.

It was one of the biggest news stories of the year, and even the overseas Voice of America radio network allotted a full fifteen minutes to cover it. The national magazines covered as well, and a *Life*-magazine staffer sent the following confidential memo back to the home office:

"The bride and groom posed while innumerable flashbulbs went off in their faces. Lana was pancaked up to the hairline. The colors she wore, including that of her hair, were not becoming and neither was the fact that she was exceedingly nervous. The big bouquet of white orchids she carried trembled as though they were back in the jungle in a storm. In a way they were.

"The bride and groom stood before a lavish flower screen made up of gardenias, greenery and lined along the floor was a row of white gladiolas. There were more of these complicated little floral effects scattered about everywhere.

"Cheryl comes in for her share of attention. She was vastly confused and a little unhappy about it all with her nurse, an aged lady who showed up bedecked in foxes and mauve silver satin and who would only identify herself as Nanny.

"Cheryl was photographed with the wedding cake, which was just sitting around on the terrace. She was seen with Mrs. Turner who was not at all pleased to discover her [Cheryl] being photographed and yanked her away but quick.

"That's all, I guess," concluded the correspondent, "unless you

116

consider how dumb the MGM publicity department was to say, with great emphasis and reiteration, that the wedding was to be completely simple and dignified in the face of the obvious facts.

"Or unless you're interested in the curious selection of musical numbers the string orchestra kept playing—'If I Loved You,' 'People Will Say We're in Love,' 'Make Believe,' 'You're a Lucky Boy and I'm a Lucky Girl.' "

Covering the wedding, *Life* ran an unflattering picture of Lana. For years after, she refused to pose for them.

Lana informed MGM officials that she and Bob planned to go to New York, where on May 5 they would sail to London on the *Mauretania*. The day of the wedding they sped off in a Cadillac painted "Lana Loves Bob," "Bob Loves Lana," to spend their wedding night at the Beverly Hills Hotel.

The publicity, of course, was overwhelming. It was impossible for Lana to escape the press. Reporters and photographers followed the Toppings everywhere. Lana has remembered that at 10:30 a.m. the morning after the wedding, when she and Topping walked out of their cottage at the Beverly Hills Hotel, they found columnist Hedda Hopper sitting at the breakfast table of their front porch.

"Bob, why do you love Lana?" shot Hedda. "Do you think this marriage is going to last?" she asked him. "What about you, Lana? Is this just a rebound from Ty Power?"

Flinty Hedda had come close to the truth. Years later Lana said, referring to her marriage to Topping, "This was the one and only time in my life that I married for security."

But at the time Lana swore she was head over heels in love with Bob. And she undoubtedly, even if fleetingly, was.

Interest in the Toppings was intense. The publicity circus continued. When they arrived in New York to sail on the *Mauretania*, the mass hysteria started again.

Lana's relations with the studio were strained. But they capitalized on the publicity once again, and released *Homecoming*. Movie critic Alton Cook wrote in the *World-Telegram*, "In the wake of all the headlines of Lana Turner's wedding along came her new picture *Homecoming* to the Capitol. The combination of the wedding uproar and the reunion with Gable should assure large crowds at the Capitol. That is the only guarantee that can be offered for the picture there. As entertainment it sticks close to a nice, slick soap opera level." And the MGM ad boys were at it again, tagging Gable and Turner as "The *TEAM* that generates *STEAM!*"

Topping supposedly encouraged Lana to give up her career long before her suspension and was still urging her to do so.

"Lana considered giving up her career," says Adela Rogers St. Johns. "They all do. But considering and doing are different things. They get worn with fatigue—the hazards—the gold fish bowl—and want out. Who doesn't? But I think they all *love* their *work* really —and Lana would not have retired."

MGM was not happy with the situation. Lana had always been independent and unpredictable. Now, married to a millionaire, she no longer urgently required her $5,000 weekly paycheck, which undoubtedly induced her, during previous crises—along with personal loans from L. B. Mayer—to go along with the studio's wishes.

As was the practice, when a star became too independent, the studio waged a subtle campaign to scare her back into the fold.

It seems incredible that MGM would allow a star of Lana's stature to cope with the press without benefit of press agents. Perhaps Topping was fed up with the studio's interference and specifically requested "no help" from them. In any case, there were no public relations people to handle the news hawks when Lana and Topping sailed on the *Mauretania*.

It was bedlam. Lana has said, "With no one on hand to handle the press, which can be a very good press indeed if you supply the information they want but can bare its teeth and eat you if you don't, the press went wild.

" 'How much luggage, Lana?' they asked. I hadn't counted at that time. I didn't know, and failure to specify was held against me.

Photographers dashed up and down gangplanks and slammed at stateroom doors. Some of them failed to get their pictures in the confusion. Naturally all of this was considered my fault. The stories the reporters wrote about us, about the fabulous honeymoon of the movie queen and the millionaire, were jeering and sarcastic. We sailed away, sad and upset, and were met by the same kind of thing in London."

Helen Young went to Europe on the Topping-Turner honeymoon. "Since Bob was writing off their honeymoon as a business trip, Lana was able to take me along. We traveled with Bert Friedlob and his wife Eleanor Parker. It was a dreadful trip and I was probably the only one who had a good time."

Even for Helen it wasn't altogether a good time though. "I'm not a good sailor," she relates. "At least eighty percent of the people on that crossing were sick. The first three days out I was really seasick. Lana kept coming down to my cabin. Bringing me soup. I wasn't able to walk. She was really that concerned about me. She is a good sailor, though, on anything—planes, trains, ships.

"She and Topping used to go fishing and yachting and she never got seasick."

The month of May, 1948, was a dark one publicitywise for Lana Turner. The London press was harsh. While the Hollywood press corps might wait an hour or more for the start of a press conference, without being nasty in their reportage, the British wouldn't.

Shortly after arrival, Lana and Bob held two press conferences, one at the Savoy Hotel and one at the Empire Theatre. They kept the press waiting at both. Asked about her marriage, she said, "This is the last of them, this really does it." Thirteen trunkloads of her clothes were photographed piled high in front of the hotel, with accompanying copy about the "wastefulness" of the Hollywood movie star.

This was postwar England, and austere conditions prevailed throughout the country. The British press leaped at the chance to contrast the free-wheeling Hollywood-therefore-American life style with England's, pointing to Lana as an example of vulgarity and bad taste.

While the London press blasted her, back in the States Lana received fresh bad publicity on the home front. And it was bad publicity with a new twist.

Headlines screamed: MINISTER IN LANA TURNER WEDDING FACES PRESBYTERIAN CHARGES. It seems that under the laws of the Presbyterian Church in 1948, it was forbidden for ministers to officiate at marriages of divorced people until a year had passed from the time of divorce. Lana, of course, had been divorced from Crane for several years, but Topping had been divorced from Arline Judge for less than a week. Although the cause of the problem was Topping's divorce, it was Lana who received the adverse publicity.

The Reverend MacLennan was being tried under the laws of the Presbyterian Church. The elaborate Turner-Topping ceremony he performed had drawn immediate protests from Presbyterian groups. Reverend MacLennan admitted ignorance of the Church law but stated that he had thoroughly investigated the basis of the Turner-Topping marriage as well as "whether or not they had honestly determined to break completely with 'their old past.' If that were not the case," said the Reverend, "I could not perform the ceremony. I felt that I sensed an earnestness that their life together should be started on an entirely new basis."

In commenting on the future of Lana's four-and-a-half-year-old daughter, the Reverend said that the child's nurse and companion was a "very fine, godly Scotswoman who is doing everything in her power to bring the child up in the fear of God.

"As an evidence of the kind of training the daughter is receiving," Reverend MacLennan added, "the little girl told me it was her ambition to be a missionary when she grows up." The Reverend said all this in a letter to a Washington attorney in defending his role in the ceremony.

120

Reverend MacLennan was already retired, and in church circles the story would soon die. But not before every newspaper, wire service and news magazine in the country ran the item. This was a period when morally outraged women's organizations ganged up on public personalities, whom they expected to be on pedestals off-screen as well as on. These "super-puritanical pressure groups" were easily capable of calling a halt to someone's career. And late in May, reports were carried that MGM was grooming Ava Gardner for Lana Turner roles, "in case Lana's recent unfavorable publicity reacts strongly against her."

To top off the Topping honeymoon, in England Bob suffered a $400,000 loss in a midget auto-racing venture. Lana had been advertised to appear at the opening of the track. She has said, "I didn't go on my honeymoon to open a midget auto track nor did my husband want me to." Nevertheless, Lana did appear, riding around the oval in a sports car, waving to the crowd. The auto-racing venture was a disaster.

"Topping's business partners had yessed him to death, but then he discovered that the import taxes on the special gas needed for the midget cars made the whole venture impossible," says Helen Young.

Word was getting back to America that, although a millionaire married to a glamorous movie star should have been delightfully happy, he seemed more than slightly miserable.

In June, a London crowd showed their disdain by tossing a few casual but well-aimed rocks at the car that Lana and Bob were riding in, leaving the BBC.

Lana later said, "Our honeymoon was one big fat fiasco."

With the security blanket of the Topping millions, Lana was not as concerned as she had been with maintaining her physical beauty. She was gaining weight, and often candid shots of her appeared showing her without her penciled-in eyebrows. "She became very casual while married to Bob," remembers Helen Young. "To me,

121

that's when she's prettiest—just her natural self. She'd portrayed the glamour girl so long, few people have seen her in this natural little girl look that is so lovely."

That summer, Bob and Lana went to Germany to visit the GI Summer Theatre circuit. Helen Young remembers, "One nice part of the trip was that we toured Germany—the bases and the army hospitals. It was very gratifying. And it was interesting to see Germany at that time, being rebuilt after the war. But Lana got strep throat and we had to go back to London."

Helen returned home from London, and the Toppings continued to the Riviera and on to Italy. Lana became indignant at all the publicity about her gaining weight. Under a headline "Meow," *Newsweek* said, "Lana Turner wrote from Europe to a friend, 'Why do they concentrate on me? I just saw Rita Hayworth and she's fatter than I am.' "

In September, the Toppings returned to live in New York and with the announcement late in the month that Lana was expecting a baby in April or May, it was reported that Lana would retire from motion pictures. In October, MGM released *The Three Musketeers*, Lana's first major role in Technicolor.

Filmed during her courtship and romance with Topping, *The Three Musketeers* presented an incredibly photogenic Lana Turner. Her performance was excellent and her role as the villainess gave the film its few believable moments. With a cast headed by Lana, Gene Kelly, June Allyson, Van Heflin and Angela Lansbury, the film was one of the commercial hits of the year, though not a critical success. The ads focused on the fact that it was Lana's first picture in Technicolor, although she had made a brief, unbilled "cameo" appearance in *DuBarry Was a Lady* in 1944.

Musketeers had been produced at relatively low cost (the stars were all under long-term contract) and grossed over $4.5 million in film rentals in the United States alone. Lana was bigger at the box office than ever, and MGM was eager to have their "retired" star return to work.

There seems no doubt that Lana really wanted a child with Bob
Topping. The RH factor was again working against her, and reports
were that she was suffering from anemia. Close to her sixth month
of pregnancy, she suffered a miscarriage in New York's Doctors
Hospital after being admitted for what officials termed "a routine
checkup." This was a physical and emotional ordeal. Lana has said
that, had she not had that miscarriage, she might really have retired
from films.

Looking back on this marriage, Lana has admitted that she
didn't truly love Topping. "Bob felt that I would learn to care
more deeply for him," she has said, "and I must say that when
things were right he was a joy to be with. But things went wrong
pretty fast."

She had told a friend at the time of the wedding to Topping, "I want dignity and peace, and a home where I can bring up Cheryl right."

Topping had married Hollywood's Number One Party Girl, but Lana appeared to want to settle down, while Topping seemed to want to continue his night club-playboy antics. Or was it the other way around? cynics asked.

After her miscarriage, it was reported that Lana and Bob had become "homebodies." They had five television sets. "We're very folksy," Lana said in late 1949. "I'm strictly a home girl now. Maybe it's hard to believe but I like it. This is the good life."

Lana spent most of 1949 living the café-society life—yachting, tennis, dinner parties, entertaining, traveling. She seemed determined to have a child. After her thirtieth birthday in February, 1950, she said, "No more birthdays. I'm not telling how old I am any more."

Reaching the age of thirty can be traumatic for many people. For Lana it must have caused disbelief. People close to Lana said, "It must have been hard for her to accept the fact that her twenties were behind her." And disenchantment with her marriage to Topping was setting in.

Psychologically it was obviously the right time to convince her to return to work. MGM needed her, and it was a good feeling to be needed. Lana had been voted Number One Box Office in a national poll by the respected fan magazine, *Modern Screen*. She had received a special award from all of the fan magazines in 1949, since they deemed her (because of the stories about her) responsible for selling more fan books than any other star.

The studio had planted a lot of publicity about Lana's competition at MGM. Her absence from the screen was causing them to build up Elizabeth Taylor and Ava Gardner, with long-range plans for the two girls who were "younger than Lana"—Liz was eighteen, but Ava was twenty-seven. But the fact was, with the new "gimmick" of television keeping people away from theatres, MGM still needed Lana. She was dependable box office. Her last four pictures had grossed over $20 million—a record untouched by any other glamour girl.

While she never considered herself a great thespian, Lana always had an instinct for a good script and what would be a right role for her. But A *Life of Her Own*, co-starring Ray Milland, was the first in a series of bad films that MGM would cast her in for the next few years. Lana had to carry the pictures with her name value.

That July, on Cheryl's sixth birthday, Lana and Bob gave the girl a black pony and held a western rodeo party for her and her young friends.

The young girl's upbringing was difficult. Lana gave her lavish gifts, expensive clothes, and nannies, and would later send her to private schools. But authority was divided five ways—among Lana, Mildred, Steve Crane, a governess and now stepfather Topping. Cheryl, like any child, learned to play one against the other to get what she wanted.

If Lana's private life wasn't on a solid footing, neither, for the first time, was her professional life. Even noted director George Cukor couldn't salvage A *Life of Her Own*. Lana played a young fashion model and wore a lavish wardrobe. In the initial ending her character committed suicide. But at a sneak preview the reaction to this was so adverse that a new ending had to be shot.

Although this was her first picture to be released in two years, Lana was still a Star. Her "comeback" build-up began. In the next two months photographs of her ran on the covers of all thirteen movie fan magazines.

Already Lana's endurance in films was being evidenced. Other glamour stars of the forties were fading—Dorothy Lamour, Betty Grable, Veronica Lake, Paulette Goddard, Ann Sheridan.

A sexy new blonde, six years younger than Lana, a girl named Marilyn Monroe, was beginning to be noticed by the movie studios. She had been offered to MGM for a long-term contract on the basis of her brief role in *The Asphalt Jungle*, filmed at Metro. But MGM turned her down. They already had their box-office blonde.

In May, 1950, Lana made news when she officially changed her name from Julia Jean Mildred Frances Turner to Lana Turner, explaining that it was "pronounced Lana as in lah-de-da, not lady."

That June, Lana was involved in one of the most momentous occasions of a movie star's career. She was invited to put her hand and footprints in the concrete in front of Grauman's Chinese Theatre in Hollywood. Jittery with excitement, Lana stuck her hand and footprints in the wet pink concrete. Disappointed fans on the sidelines cried out, "Come on, sweater girl!" and similar exhortations, implying that Lana should imprint the part of her anatomy that made her famous. After all, Monty Woolley had imprinted his beard, Bob Hope had imprinted his nose, Betty Grable had imprinted her legs.

Lana giggled, and said she would imprint her hands and feet and nothing else, to keep the ceremony "in good taste." She added, "Gee, this is an honor," and sighed as she wrote her name for posterity in the concrete.

Later that month, Lana and Bob announced they were expecting again. "Bob and I couldn't be happier," she said. "Both of us have wanted and planned for a family." The announcement had come after her physician gave her the go-ahead to continue working, and she said she was "anxious to keep on working," which would seem to indicate all was not well at home.

MGM cast her in *Mr. Imperium*, co-starring her with the singing idol of the day, fifty-eight-year-old Ezio Pinza. The Italian star, who made a hit at the Metropolitan Opera, had turned to musical comedy, and he came to Hollywood fresh from the success of his role in the Broadway hit, *South Pacific*.

Mr. Imperium was another poor script—so bad that Greer Garson had refused to do the role that went to Lana. At this point, Lana was obviously more concerned with her personal life than her career. She undoubtedly knew the script was bad, but—all things considered—MGM had been good to her. And she wanted to keep busy.

A publicity girl working on *Mr. Imperium* remembers: "Pinza considered himself the Great Lover. He had 'heard stories' about Lana, thought she was 'easy' and therefore treated her rather trampy. She froze, became 'Miss Turner' for the rest of the picture and no matter how Pinza tried he couldn't make it up to her. And he tried. He sent flowers, candy, invited her to lunch, the whole continental approach. But it was no use."

A Life of Her Own was released in August. The reviews were bad. Worse yet, the picture didn't do much business. For the first time Lana Turner was in a flop film.

But her star image was maintained. Adela Rogers St. Johns observed that year: "Lana is an exaggerated, unconventional, slightly mad, utterly enchanting creature unlike anybody else in the world, with plenty of brains and practically no sense at all. She drinks martinis and assorted beverages from 86 to 100 proof . . . collects elaborate negligees and embroidered nighties . . . loves Clark Gable pictures . . . Palm Springs . . . sun-bathing . . . owns 250 pairs of shoes but roams the house barefoot . . . drives a robin's-egg blue Cadillac convertible with red leather cushions and lives in a 12-room $100,000 mansion on three rolling acres above Sunset Boulevard with daughter Cheryl, husband Topping (whom she calls Poppa) and six TV sets."

Adela's opinion was that "Lana is a success story in search of an explanation, a love story in search of a happy ending and an endless list of contradictory quotes."

Tragedy again befell Lana when, in October, she reportedly slipped on a polished floor in her Hollywood home and suffered a second miscarriage. From that point on the Topping-Turner marriage disintegrated fast. After this second miscarriage and *Mr. Imperium*, Lana took it easy for a while.

Her old affair with Charles Jaeger popped into the news when,

127

during a three-day child custody battle concerning Jaeger's son, clippings from gossip columnists and testimony representing Jaeger's association with Lana and others were placed in evidence. The judge ruled, however, that Jaeger's reported activities did not make him an unfit father.

Topping by now had become involved in a new business venture —a project concerning plastic boats for the navy. Lana was between pictures and bored, although she had time to be with Cheryl and Bob. But in 1951 the question being asked was: Did Bob want to be with Lana? Her relationship with him had deteriorated to the point where they were arguing in public.

She tried to share Topping's interests—even went fishing with him on their yacht. But it wasn't working. She claimed that she was displeased because he did not even show affection for Cheryl.

Then Topping left without Lana for a fishing trip in Oregon. Lana picked up the cue. She retained a new lawyer, Arnold Grant, who was handling Nancy Sinatra's divorce. Lana and Grant decided on a legal separation from Topping, and Grant filed a suit for separate maintenance. Topping was undoubtedly in agreement, and preparations were made for Lana's lawyers to meet with Topping's lawyers in Chicago to work out a property settlement.

On September 11, 1951, the separation was officially announced. The reason given was that they had a misunderstanding because Topping did not want Lana to return to the screen.

Lana didn't divorce Topping until over a year later. There were several schools of thought on this matter: One was that she sincerely thought the marriage could be saved; second, she was holding out for a big settlement; third, she wanted to find a suitable replacement for Topping before letting him go.

There would, in fact, be two important men in her life before the Topping divorce became final.

Several days after the Topping separation was announced, sensational headlines implied Lana had attempted to commit suicide by slashing her wrists. The stories were so widespread that Lana telephoned columnist Louella Parsons to deny the reports. "It's ridiculous for anyone to think I'd attempt suicide. I'm not the type," Lana, arm bandaged, told Louella. "I became dizzy in the shower and my hand went through the glass and I cut myself. It's as simple as that."

While slashed wrists are not unusual occurrences in Hollywood circles, many in the film colony concurred that Lana was definitely not the suicidal type—"She's been through a lot worse than this, and she's always managed to bounce back." Others thought impulsive Lana capable of suicide.

At the time, the most accepted version of the story was that Lana was despondent and alone and, when Topping returned from Oregon and didn't phone her because his interests were elsewhere, she had one too many to drink. One report then continued that she decided to take a shower to clear her head. The shock of the hot water caused her to stumble and fall through the door. Mildred was on the premises and quickly called Dr. John McDonald (the same doctor Mildred and Lana would frantically call years later when Johnny Stompanato was stabbed).

By the time Dr. McDonald arrived, Lana's associate Ben Cole was on the scene, and they took Lana to Hollywood Presbyterian Hospital, where her wound was attended to and she was given a sedative. She stayed at the hospital only fifteen hours, but there were enough ingredients for a sensational story to fill the press for days.

Her fall-through-the-shower-door story seemed questionable after certain other facts came to light. The *L.A. Times* said that Dr. McDonald was called to Lana's home at about 2:00 a.m. The doctor said he found Mrs. Turner, white-faced and excited, trying to staunch the flow of blood from a forearm wound while Cole was applying a tourniquet. "There was blood all over," the doctor said.

McDonald described her wound as a "jagged laceration across the lower quarter of the left forearm. Two tendons had been cut," he said, "but only about halfway through, fortunately."

Cole said he was called to the Turner house "about fifteen or thirty minutes after 1:00 a.m." He did not explain why the physician was not called until later.

He said he had seen the broken shower door but quickly added, "It's been fixed now."

According to studio officials, Mrs. Turner had been staying with her daughter since Lana separated from Topping.

It was said that Lana was annoyed with Topping and jealous over his new love interest, so she hired a private detective to shadow him. Chances are, however, that a private detective was hired by Lana's lawyers during this period, since this was standard procedure in pre-divorce cases.

In periods of crisis Lana prefers to return to work. But *Mr. Imperium* had been a flop. Radio City Music Hall originally scheduled the film but turned it down when they saw the final cut. It was Lana's second flop in a row, something to which she was not accustomed. It seemed that her career was turning sour. The reviewers of the day noted that she was "plump" in the film. MGM obviously realized *Imperium* was a bomb. They had held up its release so that Pinza's second film, Preston Sturges's *Strictly Dishonorable*, was released first.

"I think Lana was very conscious and aware that her personal life affected her screen image," says a close friend, "although it may not seem so since her life has been so full—different marriages and lovers and all the other excitement and tragedy in her life.

"I know in a couple of cases she kept a marriage going longer than it should have," the friend recalls. "Despite what people think, she was, and is, concerned about the scandals and divorces.

"She tried and worked desperately to keep the marriages going because she didn't want another divorce, with all the publicity and what it does to an image."

Lana's marriage was over, but work continued. It is generally acknowledged by Hollywood savants that three flop pictures in a row spell disaster for any movie star's future. Lana needed a hit. Al-

130

though she hated costume pictures (she loved the costumes but thought the scripts unsuitable, since she thought of herself as a "modern" woman) Metro convinced her she'd have a hit in a lavish Technicolor remake of *The Merry Widow* (a title that wouldn't be overlooked by the columnists.) Her co-star would be the dashing, sexy new South American heartthrob Fernando Lamas. Lana was ready for a new co-star in her private life as well. The beginning of their relationship was described as "spontaneous combustion."

In almost no time, Lana and Lamas were inseparable, and the word on the MGM lot was "Lana's in love again." Helen Young remembers, "In *Merry Widow* I think the reason Lana looked so great was because she felt so great. She had a new romance with Fernando, and it was a beautiful time of life for her. Her personal life was more beautiful so she looked more beautiful.

"It was one of her peaks in beauty, I think. When Lana found out she was going to do the picture, she perked up and began taking care of herself. And dieting. When she was married to Topping there was a long time when she didn't work, and it's easy to let yourself go when you're not acting for the cameras."

The studio was pleased, since Lana was again career-oriented. And her newest lover was equally career-oriented.

Like Lana, Lamas enjoyed the recognition that goes with success. He was an ambitious man. He had been moderately successful in his native Argentina and had a short-lived marriage to another Argentine star, Pearla Mux. But he was irked when her career took off before his. After divorcing Pearla, he married Lydia Babachi, daughter of a socially prominent and wealthy Uruguayan. The marriage was considered beneath her, since her father was a large property owner. Although she and Fernando had a child, Alexandria, the marriage broke up when Lamas came to Hollywood in 1949. Lydia joined him a year later and tried for a reconciliation, but the marriage was over.

Lamas's contract at MGM occurred after Republic Pictures made *The Avengers* in Argentina in 1949. The stars were John Carroll and Vera Hruba Ralston. The film was done in English and Spanish, and Lamas was hired to dub the Spanish for Carroll. Carroll's wife was Lucille Ryman, dramatic coach and talent scout for MGM. She arranged for Lamas to test for the studio.

Lamas went to Hollywood and started a concentrated campaign to learn English. (He also speaks Portuguese, Italian and French.)

The Merry Widow was his third film. He had already completed *Rich, Young and Pretty* with Jane Powell and *The Law and the Lady* with Greer Garson. MGM was giving him the big push, and the new film with Lana was his most important opportunity.

In the early days of their affair, Lamas preferred not to discuss his romance with Lana, except to mention that, like many Latins, he preferred blondes. The studio exploited their relationship in magazine and newspaper publicity, and announced that Turner and Lamas would co-star in a second film, *Latin Lovers*, to be directed by Mervyn LeRoy.

In December, United Press International reported that the U.S. Marines had adopted a new word and a movie queen to go with it: "Orality is the word. It means, 'A desire to be kissed frequently and thoroughly.' Lana Turner is the movie star. No further explanation is required." (Jane Russell was second in the Marines' Servicemen Poll, Faye Emerson third, Ava Gardner fourth, and "fifth . . . stripper Lili St. Cyr, who else?")

Meanwhile, Lana's career was about to be revitalized. After *The Merry Widow* she signed a new seven-year contract with Metro, with options at the end of the third and fifth years. And then the studio gave her career a needed shot of adrenalin when they cast her as the Diana Barrymore-like character in director Vincente Minnelli's film, *The Bad and the Beautiful.* It was a hard-hitting contemporary account of a Selznick-like independent film mogul's rise and fall. Although Lana was only on screen during half the picture, she delivered a memorable performance and received top billing. The film would garner a lot of favorable attention for her and fresh and needed recognition as an actress.

Vincente Minnelli recalls, "The studio wanted me to do *Lili* but I didn't want to follow *An American in Paris* with another ballet movie. Producer John Houseman had a script called *A Tribute to a Bad Man* [retitled *The Bad and the Beautiful*], which I wanted to direct. The studio said OK.

"Lana liked the script too. Everyone at MGM always wanted to work with Lana. I had been told she wasn't a good actress but I discovered it wasn't true. I found she had great imagination. She could do things I had no idea she could. She had great depth and color and rose to the part. That famous hysterical scene in the car was shot in one take. I had a special apparatus so the car revolved and the cameras moved in and out. I explained the whole routine to her, and she went in and did it in one take.

"She was a marvelous person as well as actress because if you were appreciative and responded to her doing a good job, she responded as well." Minnelli regrets never having worked with her again, but at MGM she was stuck with her kind of picture and he was stuck with his.

Despite rumors to the contrary, the hysterical car scene was always in the script. It wasn't written after shooting on the rest of the picture was completed, as has been reported.

"Lana loved working with Minnelli," recalls Helen Young. "The first time with new directors, they are absolutely floored with the way Lana responds to direction—to mood, feeling, everything. Lana was well liked at MGM. Everybody loved to do a film with her. All the departments—make-up, grips, all of them. She always had music on the set playing from a phonograph outside her dressing room. Crews heard music all day. One of the little messenger girls was assigned to her phonograph.

"Lana always liked to do things that would keep work interesting. On *The Bad and the Beautiful* it called for a scene with a make-up man and hairdresser. Lana went to Vincente and asked if Del and I could play the parts. After Del made me up during my lunch hour, I went on the set and Lana followed me on, playing as if she were *my* make-up girl. With *my* make-up case.

"She's just so cute about things like that. In the scene, Minnelli told us what to do: 'Do what you'd ordinarily do,' he said. When he called 'Action,' I started twirling around this curling iron. Minnelli yelled 'Cut!'

" 'Jesus Christ, Helen, what are you doing??' he cried. I was too busy. Who was gonna watch the scene with all this twirling? So Lana said, 'Helen, we're going to have to re-cast if you don't straighten up.'

"In rehearsal they had set up her key light and, when we were shooting, she was right in it. She can tell by the feeling of the heat on her face, I think. I pretended I was curling her hair and I tried moving over into her light and Lana kidded, 'No, that won't work.' She's great fun."

Lana's co-star in the film was Kirk Douglas. Douglas certainly possessed the physical qualities Lana was attracted to. But she denied their relationship was anything but professional. Louella Parsons wrote at the time, "Lana wondered who started the tall tale that she is carrying on secretly with Kirk Douglas. 'You've got to straighten this out, Louella,' she told me. 'It does no good for me to get myself in a temper. I don't know who is starting these things, which are a pack of lies.

" 'I've denied again and again that I have ever seen Kirk away from the set, but items have appeared twice. I'm in love with Fernando Lamas, and no other man means a thing to me."

Lana's professional relationship with Louella, right up to Louella's retirement, was ideal. Lana often called upon the columnist to help her squelch unfavorable publicity, such as the Sinatra home-wrecking rumor and this Kirk Douglas story. Louella always loved Lana especially because the golden girl represented the Hollywood of bygone days when stars were flashy, colorful people. Louella loved to report incidents such as, "I had heard about Lana driving into the MGM lot in her low-slung white Jaguar, upholstered in white leather with a silver monogram on the door—and just to make it more effective she was dressed all in white, a dazzling sight for both MGMers and visiting tourists."

Bob Topping wasn't exactly idle during this period. He had lost interest in Hollywood but had discovered Mona Moedl, a one-time ice-skating instructress at Sun Valley. She didn't seem to fit the pattern of Bob's former wives. She wasn't a news-grabbing glamorous sophisticate. She was twenty-five, five feet six, well-stacked but not sensationally so. She was an outdoor girl who had led an uneventful early life until her meeting with the wealthy playboy. Mona had been married and divorced before meeting Topping, but had no children. Topping was in love with her and wanted to marry her, but there was a minor detail: Lana had not yet agreed to the property settlement and had not yet divorced him.

Topping was staying about a mile from Sun Valley, not far from Mona. He wanted to keep his affair with her as quiet as possible, afraid that the publicity might work against him and enable Lana's lawyers to hold him up for a huge settlement. Also during this period Topping vehemently denied reports that he and Mona had flown to Mexico, where he supposedly got a quickie divorce to marry her.

The summer of 1952 found Lana vacationing in Nevada. She left for Reno on June 27, and her friends in Hollywood were saying that she planned to divorce Topping and marry Lamas as soon as possible.

In July she and Cheryl, now nine, vacationed at Lake Tahoe. Lana confirmed that she *might* file for divorce in mid-August on the mildest grounds, mental cruelty, if her attorneys could wangle a suitable settlement from Topping's lawyers. "My attorney," she then said, "is handling it well and what I'm asking is not out of line. I will not get a divorce until the settlement is made." Asked about Miss Moedl, Lana said, "She must have taught him how to skate. He never skated with me."

That summer *The Merry Widow* was ready for release. It was

135

not a particularly good film, but Lana carried it and it was commercial. Lana did not divorce Topping that summer. She returned to California, but her romance with Lamas was taking a new turn.

Lamas had initially skirted the "When will you marry Lana?" questions by saying, "I have no intention of starting divorce proceedings against my wife. It is not up to a man to ask for a divorce anyway." But when Lamas's wife had obtained a divorce, the suave actor changed his tactics and was giving out statements to the press that he was not interested in marriage to anyone. This was not exactly flattering to Lana, and her friends felt that she was justifiably furious and hurt at his ungentlemanliness, considering how she had helped further his career at MGM.

Their relationship ended spectacularly. The setting for the blow-up was appropriate—the most prestigious Hollywood social function of the year, Marion Davies's gala party for singer Johnny Ray.

At the lavish party Lana, who had come with Lamas, met screen Tarzan Lex Barker, who was then married to, but separated from, Arlene Dahl. One report said it was Lana who impulsively asked Lex for a dance, although he was with a date.

Lamas was reportedly furious at Lana's drinking and dancing with Barker at this party, and supposedly made a scene by accusing her of never being any good at lovemaking anyway and chastising her with words to the effect, "If you must be intimate with this man, don't do it in public."

The episode was followed by some ungallant remarks emanating from Fernando about how he wasn't interested in marriage.

Lana and Lamas were through. Louella came to Lana's defense and reported, "I assume Lana was as shocked as all of us at some of the things Lamas is reported to have said."

It is important to keep in mind that this was all taking place in 1952, when accepted public behavior was considerably different from the 1970s. The implication of the breakup didn't place America's Dream Girl in a very flattering light. She had been jilted by a

136

Latin American Romeo who had apparently been sleeping with her but now seemed to consider her beneath the status of marriage.

A good many people had been horrified by Lana's string of affairs and her seemingly endless emotional improvisations. Some offered the explanation that little bits of all the various parts she played had rubbed off on her and that she was continually acting out those bits in real life. And she couldn't make up her mind which of the various characters she wanted to be.

In early October, Lana gave out a statement that she and Lamas were finished. It was a typical studio whitewash of Lana's latest fling: "It's just one of those things," she said. "We're still friends but, as far as romance is concerned, that's out. We are making *Latin Lovers* together within a month, but from now on I'm interested in one person—and that's Lana Turner."

A week before shooting of *Latin Lovers* was supposed to start, however, MGM announced that Lamas had been replaced by Ricardo Montalban. It was obviously made clear to the brass at the studio (Louis B. Mayer had been ousted by this time and Dore Schary was now studio chief) that there would be "less friction" on the set if another actor were playing the love scenes with Lana. Not long after, Lamas was out of MGM completely.

Lana continued to make sensational news when later that October she spent what would become a famous Palm Springs weekend at the home of Ava Gardner and Frank Sinatra, who by this time had married. Correspondent Florabel Muir reported the event as best she could, and insiders liked to think they could read between the lines. Scandal and fan magazines of the day would give more colorful accounts.

Florabel reported, "Ava Gardner and Frankie Sinatra were not talking to anybody today—including each other—about the spectacular row they had Saturday night which brought out the Palm Springs cops.

"News of the battle first hit the Hollywood scandal circuit

today," Miss Muir continued. "The story, as we get it, began when Ava offered the hospitality of the Palm Springs home to Lana Turner and her friend, Benton Cole, who also is Ava's agent. Ava herself said she could not be with them because of a TV show in Hollywood Saturday night.

"Lana and Cole did the town a bit and were back in the Gardner-Sinatra living room, having a nightcap or so, when Frankie walked in. He seemed surprised and even put out to find them there.

" 'Why, Frank, you know that Ava asked us here,' Lana said.

" 'I don't know anything of the sort,' Sinatra answered.

" 'If that's the way you feel, I have other friends in Palm Springs who'll be glad to have me,' Lana huffed.

"About that point Ava arrived unexpectedly, and the battle began."

Other accounts claimed that Ava was already there when Frank arrived unexpectedly and supposedly heard himself being discussed. Only the principals know the actual story. Florabel concluded, "Nobody got hurt and nobody was arrested, as far as can be learned. But everybody was madder than hops. Ava came back to Hollywood. Sinatra went to stay with composer Jimmy Van Heusen."

Associated Press reported the event a bit differently: "Movieland gossiped today about a new tiff between Frankie Sinatra and Ava Gardner, but the spindly crooner and his curvacious bride remained silent. Those who professed to know," AP continued, "said that the incident occurred at Sinatra's home in Palm Springs. Rumors said the affair was so heated that police were called. Police denied it.

"One version said Sinatra became angry when he went to the house to meet Ava and found film actress Lana Turner there. He was said to have ordered them out of the house and Miss Turner and Miss Gardner left together.

138

"Palm Springs police said, 'Nothing on the record' indicated a disturbance at the home."

This particular episode of Lana's life would crop up again over the years in various gossip columns and scandal magazines. The episode was recounted in at least two stories bylined by Barbara Payton. An extraordinarily beautiful blonde, Miss Payton achieved brief celebrity in the late forties and early fifties, made several films for Universal, married Franchot Tone and traveled in the Hollywood social set. Her fall was as quick as her rise, however, and a few years later she was arrested on suspicion of prostitution. (The charges were later dropped.)

Whether Barbara Payton actually participated in the Palm Springs weekend or not, she revived the incident—much to the horror of both Ava Gardner and Lana Turner. Miss Payton claimed, "I became good friends with Ava Gardner and Lana Turner. We three were in Palm Springs together. We were drinking and lying around with not many clothes on and talking about things. Ava was married to Frank Sinatra in those days. He was screaming crazy about her. Well, he didn't approve of the way we were carrying on like that, and one night he came in and caught us all together. Well, I jumped out the window and into the bushes but he caught Lana and Ava together and he was mad as hell. It got into the gossip columns and contributed to the end of their marriage."

By this time, Lex Barker was getting divorced from Arlene Dahl, who was now dating Fernando Lamas. Although, while dating Lana, Fernando claimed he wasn't interested in marriage, he subsequently married Miss Dahl. But not before Lana married Lex.

Despite the adverse Palm Springs publicity, back in Hollywood the word was circulating that *The Bad and the Beautiful* was a terrific film, one of the best MGM had produced in recent years. And there was talk of an Oscar nomination for Lana's performance.

After fifteen years in films it was recognized by many that Lana Turner had accomplished the impossible. She had become an actress while she continued to play the role of the complete movie star.

Although key critics praised Lana's acting, the advertising campaign as usual exploited Lana's sex image and slightly misrepresented the plot with lines like: NO HOLDS BARRED IN THIS STORY OF A BLONDE WHO WANTED TO GO PLACES . . . AND A BIG-SHOT WHO GOT HER THERE THE HARD WAY!

Lana at thirty-two was slimmed down and looking beautiful. She was back in the Hollywood social whirl, and in addition to Lex Barker she was dating department store heir Jerry Ohrbach and found a few evenings' diversion with Mexican bullfighter Luis Sallano.

At about this time Metro executives reprimanded their leading raven-haired glamour girl for picking up a gas station attendant and sharing him with her equally famous blonde girl friend. The soft-spoken love goddess shrugged nonchalantly and said, unconcernedly, "Look, honey, don't worry. Who's gonna believe it?"

On December 15, 1952, in Carson City, Nevada, Lana Turner divorced Bob Topping after four years and seven months of marriage. Newspapers were caught off guard by what they described as "a sudden and surprise move considering the lengthy separation." She was in Hollywood filming *Latin Lovers* but, unknown to the press, she had set up residency in Douglas County, Nevada, to obtain the divorce. The lawyers had come to an agreement on the property settlement, and Topping was anxious to marry Mona.

When asked if she had wedding plans, Lana replied, "I certainly do not. As for Topping, you'll have to call him because I'm no longer keeping track of his heart interests."

Although the details of the financial settlement were never made public, they were undoubtedly satisfactory. A British paper reported the settlement as being in the neighborhood of 45,000 pounds—about $216,000. And it was said that Lana kept the fabulous jewels Topping had given her.

At the time Lana commented, "All I can say is that it's taken the lawyers more than a year to work it out. If it wasn't satisfactory, I wouldn't be laughing."

Topping married Mona Moedl, and remained married to her until his death fifteen years later in April, 1968.

Referring to what was said at the Turner-Topping wedding—"This is forever"—newspapers said: "A new definition of infinity —four years, seven months, eighteen days, nineteen hours, twenty-six minutes."

Judge J. Guild granted the divorce on the charge of extreme mental cruelty. Lana appeared in court in a black fur coat, form-fitting black sheath and a blonde upswept hairdo. Even the judge was reported to remark that the plaintiff's getup was "very becoming, to say the least."

Lana met reporters while celebrating her freedom with a bottle of champagne. "I'm finished with Fernando," she was quoted as saying, "and you can say I'll never, never marry again."

By this time, more and more of Hollywood's film stars were taking the high road to Europe. Lana was disillusioned and unhappy with recent events in her life, and the idea of a change of scenery must have appealed to her. Clark Gable, Gene Tierney, Errol Flynn and Gene Kelly had already made the move.

There was an eighteen-month tax holiday available to stars who stayed out of the United States for that period, and at least three of Hollywood's major stars already qualified—Gable, Flynn and Kelly. (The tax cut was originally designed to aid big business in securing top workers to develop American interests abroad.)

Hollywood observers noted that Lex Barker was determined to develop Lana's interest in him beyond the stage of "good friends." In addition to her obvious attributes, and the genuine feeling he had for her, it was noted that Lex was not unaware of Lana's stature in the film community, in which he aspired to do great things. She knew everyone of importance in town, was respected by them and socialized with them.

Lana certainly couldn't have been in a marrying mood as 1953 rolled around. If she had appeared carefree and unconcerned at the time of her divorce from Topping, it was in part a façade and not totally representative of her true feelings.

"She was disillusioned, believe me," says a close friend. "She had lost Ty, Topping and Lamas and, by this point, the memories couldn't be wiped away quite so easily. Lana wasn't a teen-ager anymore but she was living the same emotional existence as when she was and it was like a treadmill by now. She was getting older but not wiser."

"There she was, a woman who typified American sex appeal, and she couldn't hold on to a man for very long. She was—still is, I think—emotionally uneducated," conjectured a friend. "Even though she hadn't loved Topping, it was a terrible slap at her ego when *he* lost interest in *her!*"

Two weeks after she appeared in court for her divorce, Lana collapsed on the set of *Latin Lovers*. Dr. McDonald was called and diagnosed her illness as "a bad virus flu plus nerves." Friends thought the statement the usual public-relations masterpiece of understatement.

"She was the most depressed girl I've ever seen when she was forced to end her marriage to Topping," said one friend.

Lex Barker was a shrewd man, and it was no secret that he had every intention of marrying Lana Turner. He was exactly the type of physical specimen that Lana was attracted to, and he had brains as well.

Born Alexander C. Barker in Rye, New York, Lex was the first screen Tarzan who could boast a social background. Prior to his marriage to Arlene Dahl, he had been married to Constance Thurlow, and they had two children, Lynne and Alexander Barker III.

Lamas had been described as Lana's Argentine Clark Gable, and

143

now Barker was her Tarzan in the flesh. He was no newcomer to Hollywood. He had been appearing in numerous small roles since the late forties. He had a bit role as a construction worker in *Mr. Blandings Builds His Dream House* in 1947 and appeared in a couple of other pictures. In the late forties, Lex was picked to play Tarzan. Sol Lesser, the series' producer, had reportedly scrutinized over two thousand photographs of applicants, sent scouts to college campuses, model agencies and gyms full of musclemen to "discover" the new screen Tarzan. "Because," Lesser had explained, "we find women are coming to see Tarzan along with the kids."

But after a few years, Barker was anxious to rid himself of the Tarzan image. No important offers to do anything different came in Hollywood. Able to speak French and other languages, Lex thought he'd try films overseas and at about the same time Lana decided to switch her base of operations to Europe. Lana claimed that tax benefits had absolutely nothing to do with her going to Europe. She said she went there to be with Lex.

Lana's remarkable ability to turn her back on the past and make the most of a hopefully bright and shiny future again asserted itself. Lamas, Topping *et al.* were not to be brooded about. Perhaps she realized it was not the individuals as much as the pattern of her life that depressed her. Getting away from Hollywood would be good for her. Of course, it wouldn't change the fact that she seemed incapable of maintaining a meaningful relationship. But, " 'Never look back' is my philosophy," she has said.

Friends have said that if Lex had disappeared from Lana's life at this early point, she wouldn't have been too distraught. But Lana had to have a man in her life, and Lex saw to it that he filled the bill.

MGM arranged to shoot Lana's next picture, *The Flame and the Flesh*, in Rome. It was her first picture outside the Culver City lot. She had been offered the lead opposite Gable in *Mogambo*, which would have been an excellent follow-up success to *The Bad and the Beautiful*. But she turned it down. It would be shot in Africa, and Lana's doctor advised her against long-term location shooting on the dark continent because of her rare blood type.

"But the *Mogambo* script I read wasn't the script they shot," Lana later said. "The picture was perfect for Ava Gardner. I couldn't have done as well as she. I didn't know, until Clark Gable told me, that the safari was the living end. They had all the comforts of home."

Lana and Lex departed for Europe. Separately, of course, but that didn't stop the gossip.

A friend of Hedda Hopper's dined with Lana and Lex in Europe and wrote back to Hedda that she could safely predict an early breakup of that romance. According to the friend, at that dinner Lex just sat and pouted, while Lana was just plain bored. "Lana later told the girls present," wrote the friend, " 'this guy has got to go.' " But Lex was not the going type, concluded Hedda's friend, and he was lining up all pictures possible in Europe.

Before leaving the states, Lana had told a reporter, "I have reached the point where I am filled with skepticism about any marriage. There is no possibility of a marriage for Lex and myself, though we are wonderful friends, and will continue to be that. I want to concentrate only on the future," she said. "I have found work, and work alone, the only sure panacea. I am glad that I have learned that."

What were her European plans? "I'm going on a motor trip through Italy from Paris because I want to learn about the Italian people for this picture," she said. She was to play a blonde girl (so it was announced) from northern Italy in the Joe Pasternak production, *The Flame and the Flesh.*

But Lana turned brunette, supposedly because Barker preferred her that way. However, considering Lana's long history of hair-color changes, Barker's preferences may not have had much to do with it.

"I let my hair go brown for a very simple reason," said Lana. "I had to do two pictures that called for it. In *Flame and the Flesh* I played a real earthy Italian girl. Unlike anything I'd ever done before. Now I couldn't very well play a role like that as a blonde. In *Betrayed*, I'm a Dutch spy who dyes her hair."

In *Flesh*, directed by Richard Brooks, Lana played a tough, convincing tramp—at least in the early portion of the film. Then the old-fashioned MGM "keep Lana's character sympathetic" soap-opera thinking took over in the script, and the picture deteriorated into melodramatic slush. The trailers for the film described "That *Bad and the Beautiful* Girl" as "even more dangerous as a brunette."

Lana was delighted with the amazing amount of worldwide publicity about her hair-color change. "You couldn't buy that much publicity for $1 million," she said. "And the wonderful thing about it, there was no scandal. A controversy without a scandal! That kind of publicity is rare these days." For Lana, it certainly was.

In June, filming stopped for several days on *The Flame and the Flesh* when Lana and Pasternak suffered food poisoning in Naples.

After completing the picture, Lana was sent to Holland and England to film *Betrayed*, her last film with Clark Gable, and Gable's last for MGM. Also in London at the time was Ava Gardner, and Ava and Lana again made headlines when they scored a big hit in an impromptu dance routine at a party hosted by the Duke of Manchester. "It caused the biggest talk in London since the Princess Margaret Rose's famous can-can," wrote Harrison Carroll. "The girls harmonized on 'Take Me Out to the Ball Game,' and then went into their terpsichorean routine that sent the guests, more famous names than you can shake a stick at, into hysterics. Other hosts and hostesses have cajoled like mad but nary a repeat have they been able to get out of Hollywood's two glamour-pusses. And the news photographers over there are gnashing their teeth: not a flashbulb popped during the entire proceedings."

Another London party story demonstrates Lana's kindness, sense of humor and unaffectedness. Director Tay Garnett remembers, "One night at producer Cubby Broccoli's place, Ava, Frank, Gable and other stars were there. A man who owned a chain of movie

At sixteen, a student at Hollywood High School, 1936.

With agent Henry Willson at the Trocadero, 1936.

Julia Jean Mildred Frances "Judy" Turner, age eight.

Mervyn LeRoy named her Lana, cast her in his 1937 film for Warner Bros. *They Won't Forget.*

Lana was a fast study at mastering the art of make-up.

Results: Lana Turner, seventeen-year-old Hollywood starlet.

Louis B. Mayer dances with his twenty-one-year-old star.

1941 Hollywood foursome: Lana, Tony Martin, Judy Garland and her husband David Rose.

Twenty-one-year-old Lana Turner and Clark Gable. She was at the top.

Lana and Victor Mature. Their "romance" was short-lived.

(Left Page)

Transformation into Hollywood Glamour Girl, 1938-style.

Lana and new husband Steve Crane, with Lana's mother, at their 1942 Hollywood wedding reception. A few surprises were in store.

With Cheryl, about eighteen months old.

Lana and Steve with newborn daughter, Cheryl Christine, 1943.

It was "serious"
with Turhan Bey.

With Tommy Dorsey.

By 1943, Lana's on-screen development into sultry
love goddess was complete.

With Cheryl, about three.

Interviewed on radio by Louella Parsons. Lana's uniform was a costume for her current picture.

With Frank Sinatra. Lana was labeled "a homewrecker."

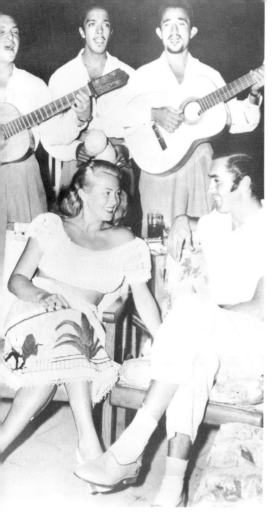

With Tyrone Power in 1947: "the one great love of her life."

"No other man means a thing to me," declared Lana about Fernando Lamas in 1951.

About to embark on her honeymoon with third husband, Henry J. "Bob" Topping, 1948.

Lana, almost thirty-five, still sexy in a
scanty costume.

Cheryl, eight, visits her mother on the set.

Cheryl, five, poses with her mommy at the
Topping wedding.

With Hedda Hopper, 1955.

na Turner and her "intimate friend," Ava Gardner, 1951.

57 prelude to tragedy: Lana and
ve Crane pick up thirteen-year-old
eryl at Los Angeles police station.

Lana and her fourth husband, screen
Tarzan Lex Barker.

Lana Turner rarely allowed herself to [be] photographed with her new boyfrien[d] Johnny Stompanato.

Darling Juanito —

Just a tiny note for now —
It's been so strange these last few days, all hectic, and no letters from you — I keep saying to myself — (good old English phrase)(I'm pshed up.) "never mind love, it'll be allright" — what the hell they mean by that — I don't know — supposed to cover everything including a Heart-ache, I imagine !!!!. So Dear, I'll write again, hope all is going well with you! I do miss you terribly ! —

Cuidado,
Baci,
Ceau,
Lunita my love,

P.S. Typing getting far "" ... between you so much !!

One of many letters Lana wrote Stompanato.

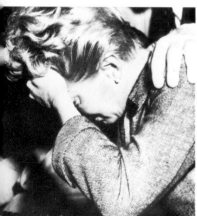

After Stompanato's tragic death, Lana faced the most harrowing ordeal of her life.

Lana and attorney Jerry Geisler, besieged by the press.

Real-life 1958 courtroom drama: Lana Turner on the witness stand.

In court: Steve Crane, Lana Turner, Mildred Turner.

Lana reassures Cheryl as Jerry Geisler looks on.

Cheryl and Lana at the 1959 premiere of
Imitation of Life.

Husband number five: Fred May.

Husband number six: Robert Eaton.

Twenty-three-year-old Cheryl, Mildred Turner and Lana at a preview screening of *Madame X*.

Holding hands with Harold Robbins at the party announcing their joint TV venture, *The Survivors*.

With husband number seven,
Ronald Dante.

theatres in the south was there with his little southern wife, a typical southern belle—one of those girls who worked at it, you know.

"Lana landed beside this ole gal, who kept asking her, 'Who's that? Who's that?' And Lana was telling her. Ava Gardner walked by, and the woman asked, 'Who's that?'

" 'Ava. Ava Gardner,' Lana told her. 'You must have played *Mogambo.*'

" 'No, I don't think we've played that in Knoxville yet. We play a lot of canasta though.'

"After a while, Lana said, 'Well, I think I'd better circulate.'

"The woman asked, 'Honey, what was your name?'

"Lana sweetly said, 'Mrs. Barker, dear.' The woman didn't know who Lana was till the next day when her husband told her."

Back at home, *Latin Lovers* was released. Whereas *The Bad and the Beautiful* had been excellent contemporary filmmaking, *Lovers* was at the opposite end of the scale—a ponderous and dull romantic pastiche totally irrelevant even to filmgoers of 1953. LeRoy and Lana had done the best they could with a turkey of a script. Lana's beauty was the film's solitary saving grace, and Metro knew it—ads for the film read: SHE'S GORGEOUS IN TECHNICOLOR. And she was. But the public was starting to demand good stories in addition to pretty faces.

A new generation of stars were making their impact—Marilyn Monroe, Montgomery Clift, Marlon Brando. All the major studios were hard-hit by the tremendous slump in film revenues attributed to television. High-priced contract stars were being let go, and even Gable's days at Metro were numbered. But Lana was safe, for the time being.

Gable was at the end of his MGM contract, and the studio wanted to squeeze the last bit from him. And so Gable and Lana, the two heartthrobs of 1941 who had created cinema electricity together in *Honky-Tonk* and succeeding films, were together for the last time. Only this time she was brunette and thirty-three, and he was tired and old-looking at fifty-three. The team who were sup-

147

posed to have created screen history with their kisses now prompted one critic to note, "Clark Gable kisses Lana Turner like a husband with a hangover."

The Gable-Turner electricity fizzled under the labored direction of Gottfried Reinhardt, and *Betrayed*, an old-fashioned war melodrama filmed in Holland and London, had no pace. Also starred in the film was Lana's old flame, Victor Mature. But the public had long since forgotten that romance, and *Betrayed* stirred remarkly little interest. It was, in short, a dud.

Lana and Lex attended the Cannes Film Festival together, generating more outraged gossip on the home front about their "flaunting of morality" by traveling around the world together "without benefit of clergy."

Finally, on September 8, 1953, she gave in. Lana Turner became Mrs. Lex Barker in what she had hoped would be a secret wedding ceremony in the sixteenth-century city hall in Turin, Italy.

Not surprisingly, there would be legal problems ahead, since Barker's divorce from Arlene Dahl wouldn't become final until October.

At the ancient church Lana was mobbed by reporters and women bystanders. She was visibly upset and distraught by the crowds. Cheryl and Lex's two children were present. Half an hour before Lana and Lex departed, the couple's gardener took Lex's two youngsters and Lana's daughter to the station, where the children were placed on a train for Paris. Associated Press reported that Lana looked "very happy."

The next day Lana and Lex left their luxury villa by car for a honeymoon on the isle of Capri after spending the first night of their marriage in Barker's villa in the hills overlooking Turin.

Members of the household said that the newlyweds planned to spend two weeks in Capri and after that they would go to Paris to join their children. The Barkers would then tour Europe with their familial entourage.

148

Legally the marriage was complicated in more ways than one. Not only was Barker's divorce from Arlene Dahl not final, but there was an Italian law that three hundred days must elapse after the dissolution of a previous marriage before a man or woman may remarry. Lana was divorced from Topping in December, 1952, which meant that the Italian legal period hadn't elapsed for her either.

Italian laws also required a public posting of intentions to wed two weeks before marriage. To get around these technicalities Lana and Lex asked the state attorney's office to exempt them from both rulings. Italian sources said that, since they were both foreigners temporarily visiting Italy, they might win such an exemption.

In spite of these legal complications, which were certainly nothing new in Lana's complex private life, Lana and her new consort were man and wife.

At an interview, Lana got up from a chair, walked across the room and took away a large vase of flowers that was blocking her view of Lex Barker. "He's brand new, and I want to look at him," she said.

Columnist Hedda Hopper, always one for direct questions, later asked the Barkers, "Why did it take you so long to get married?" They parried, "It took that much time for me to convince her she loved me," explained Lex.

"I chased him until he caught me," added Lana. Hedda wasn't laughing. "No, seriously, we weren't playing a game," said Lana. "We couldn't make up our minds, and we didn't feel obligated to check with anyone. We were apart for six weeks, and that really did it. Being apart was no good, so we got married. And what a honeymoon! We had my mother and daughter, Lex's two children, a nurse and a governess."

The *Herald Tribune*'s Paris-based wit-in-residence, Art Buchwald, interviewed Lana and Lex. The last time Buchwald saw Lex in Paris, he said, was when Lex was playing Tarzan and was on his honeymoon with movie actress Arlene Dahl. This time Barker informed him that he was no longer playing Tarzan but he was still on his honeymoon, this time with Lana Turner.

"I've given up playing Tarzan. You can't play Tarzan forever or you'll get typed," Barker told Buchwald. As a start in the right direction, he said, he had just completed two pictures in Italy—*The Tiger of Malaya* and *The Temple of Kali.*

Lana told Buchwald that she didn't come over to Europe for the eighteen-months tax holiday. "I came here to be near Lex," she said.

The Barkers explained that the wedding was a simple affair in Turin, and that they had tried to avoid publicity, but it was to no avail. They got too much publicity, they complained.

"Let's get a few things straight about that wedding," said Lana. "They wrote some terrible lies. I did not faint, as reported in the press."

"Yes," said Barker to Buchwald, "and I did not slug a photographer—I would have liked to have slugged him, but I didn't."

"One of the papers," continued Lana, "reported that, when a guy pulled out a document proving he could take a photo, Lex grabbed the paper, threw it on the floor and stamped on it."

"I stamped on no documents," said Mr. Barker.

Miss Turner added: "They also quoted me as saying peevishly that if the newspapermen did not leave I would not get married. Now isn't that ridiculous?

"Back home they were even worse. The columnists wrote before we were married that we had shocked Europe. Is this possible?"

Lex said: "If two people want to travel together and see Europe, what's wrong with that?"

Lana said: "We always used discretion before we were married, but they still kept sniping at us."

Mr. Barker agreed: "As soon as we were married they started on Rita Hayworth and Dick Haymes. Now that they're married they'll have to find somebody else. Besides, I don't see why anything we do should be anybody's business."

"What is your advice to young people wanting to get married?" Buchwald asked them.

"That," said Mr. Barker, "is none of your business either."

Dorothy Kilgallen wrote shortly afterward, "It's hard to tell but that Lana Turner would burn or just laugh disdainfully if she knew it, but several of her most cynical friends have organized a pool, to which they each contributed $100, on the duration of her marriage to Lex Barker."

That fall of 1953, Florabel Muir interviewed Arlene Dahl, who had no plans for marriage with Fernando Lamas (yet) but had no objection to discussing Lex and Lana. "I wish them happiness," Arlene said. Then, according to Florabel, Arlene added rather cryptically, "I think they have a lot in common."

The New York *Daily News*, which carried Florabel's column, also ran a picture of Lana and Lex with a caption: "Lex Barker, Arlene Dahl's ex, and Lana Turner, Fernando's ex (in a way) didn't hesitate. They tied the knot."

Christmas, 1953, found Lana and Lex on a second honeymoon, literally. Their second surprise wedding ceremony was for benefit of friends, family and the law, and took place an hour after the stars, unrecognized, took out a wedding license in Santa Monica, California. It would clear up once and for all the legal complications raised at the time of their September wedding.

The bride's attendants were her mother, daughter (now ten but always referred to as "the baby" by Lana), and Nat Willis, described as "an old family friend."

On their license, Barker gave his age as thirty-four and Lana said she was thirty-two.

Lana hoped Lex would sign with MGM, but, to her surprise and to the surprise of many Hollywood insiders, he decided against it. "Had I accepted MGM's offer," Barker has said, "any success I might have achieved would have been credited to Lana's standing at her studio, not to my own ability."

Others noted that perhaps Lex had enough foresight to realize that marital paradise with Lana might not last forever, and he didn't want to be kicked out of MGM, à la Lamas, if and when Lana decided to call it quits.

Universal-International offered Barker a contract and he was enthusiastic. Lana was against it. He had remembered her advice: "If you don't want to go to MGM, why not free-lance? You can do much better that way." Lana was, of course, looking at it from the point of view of an established top star, in demand by almost every major studio. "My situation was hardly the same," Barker has said. "I explained it to Lana and accepted U-I's offer."

In early December, Metro raised a lot of eyebrows when they announced plans to star Lana and Ava Gardner in a property entitled *My Most Intimate Friend.* The title was another in a series of film titles that Metro had on occasion used for Lana's films that bore a definite connection to her private life (*Marriage Is a Private Affair, Slightly Dangerous, The Merry Widow*). *Intimate,* supposedly intended originally for Eleanor Parker, was a story about two fashion models who are great friends until they fall in love with the same man. At the end of the movie they both lose him and return to being great friends.

Lana was eager to do the film. "Ava and I have to get together on *My Most Intimate Friend,*" she told Hedda Hopper. "I've nothing against Eleanor Parker, but the script was written for Ava and me. We'll have a ball making that one, since in real life we are intimate friends."

During their marriage, the Barkers spent much time in Acapulco. While in Hollywood they lived in the grand style to which Lana had long since been accustomed. She drove a Jaguar, he a Cadillac convertible (he also had a Volkswagen). They belonged to the Bel-Air Country Club, had a cook and a maid, Cheryl had a governess, and they had a full-time gardener. They lived in a modified colonial estate with eleven rooms—four bedrooms, four bathrooms in the main house and servants' quarters above the three-car garage.

An adolescent now, Cheryl was growing up without a feeling of being rooted anywhere. She had been sensitive to her mother's shifting romantic attachments, was aware of all the publicity her mother received, and must have been intimidated by Lana's beauty, since Cheryl went through the usual tall, awkward pre-teenage years.

For a while the girl had been interested in horses and even talked of studying animal husbandry. Like most mothers and daughters, Lana and Cheryl found communication difficult during this adolescent period.

Lana confided in friends and columnists that she and Lex were "dying to have a baby. Lex's blood type cancels out fifty percent of the dangers in having a baby with my RH factor," said Lana.

"That's why she married me," Lex kidded.

Hedda Hopper observed, "Either marriage or the brunette personality had changed Lana. She was keenly interested in her career again."

"If Metro hasn't a picture for us, we should be loaned out," Lana said. "The money makes no difference. I get paid fifty-two weeks a year anyway. But Mama's not going to sit around getting rusty."

Lex and Lana had purchased a script, *The Great Fall*, which they wanted to film together. As for more Tarzan flicks, Lex said, "I would for money, but not for love. If Sol Lesser wants to give me a percentage of the profits, I'm his boy."

Discussing their European sojourn, Lex said, "I was in the army five and a half years. Got wounded three times. Then when I went to Europe for ten months to work, people began to say: 'There goes Barker, ducking income tax.' How dare they question my patriotism? Hollywood was in such a confused, unproductive state we had to go abroad to work."

All things considered, Lana's marriage to Barker was probably her most tranquil to date. Universal was behind Barker and wanted to establish him as a star out of Tarzan roles. And, despite diminishing box-office returns from Lana's pictures (thanks mainly to the lousy scripts they gave her), Lana was still queen of the MGM lot, although she shared the throne with Elizabeth Taylor and Ava Gardner.

In 1954, Lana's picture appeared on the cover of *Look* magazine, along with pictures of Jean Harlow, Jane Russell, Ginger Rogers and Ava Gardner. It was a story about Howard Hughes, "The Fabulous Lone Wolf," and Lana's relationship with Hughes was again dredged up.

Lana made her television debut that year. The Ed Sullivan Show, then called "Toast of the Town," devoted an entire program to saluting MGM and the studio's thirtieth anniversary. In addition to Lana, the star roster still included people such as Ann Blyth, Cyd Charisse, Van Johnson, Howard Keel, Gene Kelly, Ann Miller, Walter Pidgeon, Debbie Reynolds, Jane Powell, Edmund Purdom, Esther Williams, Fred Astaire, Lionel Barrymore, Lucille Ball and Desi Arnaz (at MGM on a multiple-picture commitment). Studio head Dore Schary narrated the show.

Lana had the distinction of being the only star whose number was on film, not performed "live." She performed the "Madame Crematon" routine, complete with chorus boys, which had been introduced by Judy Garland in MGM's *Ziegfeld Follies* in 1946.

She carried it off excitingly, to the surprise of many critics who didn't realize she had a flair for comedy and satire that had never been exploited by the studio (and wouldn't be again). She wore a sexy slit-up-the-side and down-the-front black sheath evening gown, her brunette hair cropped short.

In May, *The Flame and the Flesh* was released and did only average business. Lana was in New York and, unrecognized and with her sister-in-law, she paid to see the film at Loew's State. She later told an interviewer that she sat behind a lady who kept making periodic comments on the movie.

"She kept muttering, 'Tramp! Tramp! Trash!' everytime I came on the screen," said Lana, "and when I got slapped in the picture, the woman shouted, 'Good!' I was rather hurt. I didn't think the character I played was that bad."

Although the lady was watching Lana play a role, Lana pointed out that the lady obviously felt the character was Lana herself.

That fall, on the Barkers' first wedding anniversary (using the Italy date) Lana told Sidney Skolsky, "I know the gag, 'they said it wouldn't last.'"

Skolsky described Lana as a person who didn't evade reality and one who admitted she quarreled with her husband. "Who doesn't?" said Lana. "But we've deleted one word from our vocabulary—divorce."

According to Skolsky, the Lana Turner of 1954 didn't keep old letters and souvenirs. Nor was she interested in yesterday, only tomorrow: "Guess you could say that my philosophy is 'Never look behind.'"

Looking ahead to her career was not too promising at the time, however. Although many stars were free-lancing by now, and earning a great deal of money for individual pictures, Lana was still a studio-contract star, and Metro took advantage of the demand for her services by other studios who no longer had big-name female stars under contract. While Lana earned her contractual sum of $5,000 per week, Metro could loan her out for six times that amount per week to another studio and pocket the difference.

Joseph Mankiewicz was paying MGM $350,000 for Ava Gardner's services for *The Barefoot Contessa* (Ava was on salary at Metro for about $3,500 a week), and Metro made a tidy bundle by lending Lana out for two films—*The Sea Chase* for Warner Brothers, and *The Rains of Ranchipur* at 20th Century-Fox.

Before the loan-outs, however, the studio put Lana into one of her worst movies ever, *The Prodigal*, a biblical costume drama. It was her first film in Cinemascope and utilized her still striking beauty but completely wasted her talents. She knew the script was a dog, and reportedly pleaded with the front office not to put her

155

in costume pictures. She was most effective in contemporary drama, as she had proved in *The Bad and the Beautiful.* But Hollywood was Hollywood and the studio had invested in the costume project.

Her co-star, Edmond Purdom, had been a chorus boy in Lana's "Madame Crematon" routine. The ambitious actor had achieved star status for a brief while when he had replaced Marlon Brando in *The Egyptian* at Fox and Mario Lanza in MGM's *The Student Prince.* Purdom had quite a reputation as a lover, and reportedly made a big play for Lana. But they really didn't like each other. Purdom was having an affair with none other than Linda Christian, who was still married to Tyrone Power (years later Purdom and Miss Christian married). In any event, *The Prodigal* was completed in relative tranquility.

Lana was on a strict diet at the time in order to look good in the sexiest and briefest costumes of her career, described as "a half-dozen beads and a prayer."

The stills from *The Prodigal* were deemed so provocative that re-touchers had to paint on veils. Lana, in one of her scanty costumes, was supposed to be on the cover of *Cosmopolitan,* but the then staid magazine pulled the photograph at the last minute as being "too sexy."

The Sea Chase teamed Lana with John Wayne. She played a femme fatale spy who is really a "good girl" and who dies at the end with sea captain Wayne. It was effective if not distinguished entertainment, and, as a reviewer said, "Once you get used to All-American John Wayne and Sweater Girl Lana Turner as Germans, the film is fairly acceptable."

There was talk of a feud between Lana and Wayne while they were on location in Hawaii, and Lana was obviously unhappy when she told the *Los Angeles Mirror,* "I was loaned out for more than $300,000, more than enough for MGM to pay my entire last year's salary." She noted the film was over schedule, which meant MGM was making even more money.

At one point in *The Sea Chase*, Lana's character is polishing her magnificent jewelry collection and tells skipper Wayne, "These are my trophies. They mean everything to me. I worked hard for them."

For once no rumors circulated about Lana having a love affair with her leading man. However, as usual, she was friendly with the crew.

On returning to the MGM lot, Lana candidly confided to someone with whom she had only a casual acquaintaince that Ava Gardner wasn't coming back from Europe because nobody in Hollywood wanted to do it all night anymore. The friend remembers Lana bemoaning the passing of the good old days with people like Jimmy, Coop, or Hank, who could keep going until you yelled for help.

Lana's opinion, which she frankly offered, was that Ava was looking for another Frankie but wasn't going to find anyone else with his equipment and ability.

Metro cast Lana in another costume drama, *Diane*. It was the story of Diane de Poitiers, mistress of French King Henry IV, a property bought in the thirties for Greta Garbo.

Diane was Lana's last film for Metro, although she wasn't aware of it during production. A young publicist on the film, Quentin Kelly, recalls: "Lana was still 'Queen of the Lot,' and she knew it. But she wasn't a bitch or a snob and she didn't have a star complex.

"She was often late, though. And don't forget, in those days, Metro was really going through a difficult economic period. Dore Schary was head of the studio, and I'll never forget the one day he came down to the set.

"It was about 11:00 a.m., I think, and shooting was supposed to have started at nine. Word was out all over the lot that Schary was furious at this unnecessary delay in production. He had come down to the set to finally have it out with Lana.

"People converged from all different sound stages, and there was a hush when the huge hangarlike doors of the sound stage opened just a crack. A shaft of light streamed through and Lana squeezed in.

"Schary went marching over to her, raised his hands and everyone gasped in anticipation. Suddenly he embraced her, and cooed, 'Lana, sweetheart, what's the matter? Were you sick this morning?'

" 'Yes,' she whispered, 'I wasn't feeling well.'

" 'Well, you go in to make-up now,' Schary told her, 'because we're all ready for you.'

"What an anticlimax that was!" says Kelly.

But it must be remembered that Schary was a pro in dealing with stars of Lana's temperament. He obviously knew the correct approach the moment called for.

"Lana was always very sweet to me," Kelly remembers. As a matter of fact, Kelly, who is now a producer, recalls that, when he was a young man trying to get into production in those days, Lana was a help.

"There was a script knocking around Metro, *My Most Intimate Friend*. No one could decide on an ending. The script was lying around Lana's dressing room, and I said to her, 'You know, I'm a writer. Would it be all right if I tried writing an ending?'

" 'Sure,' she said, 'give it a try.'

"I wrote an ending and a couple of weeks later showed it to her. She read it through and liked it. She picked up the telephone and called Schary's office. She got through immediately and said, 'Dore, I want you to come down to the set right now.' He said, 'Lana, I'm busy. Can't it wait?'

" 'Dore,' Lana said, 'I want you to come down to the set.'

"He was there a few minutes later. Now remember, I was just a junior publicist and she had told—commanded—the head of the studio to come right over for the sole purpose of reading my ending for the script."

Kelly remembers becoming more than a little apprehensive. Schary came in and Lana gave him the script and introduced him

158

to the young publicist. According to Kelly she then said to Schary, " 'I want you to make an appointment to see this boy.'

" 'All right, I'll see him sometime next week,' said Schary.

" 'No,' said Lana. 'Get on the phone and call your secretary and make the appointment right now.'

"Schary got on the phone and called his secretary and made an appointment to see me the following day at one o'clock. I was overwhelmed. When I saw him the next day, he was extremely kind. He said he read my ending and liked it and that if the picture were ever made we'd enter negotiations about using it. But, as we walked out of his office, he said, 'Confidentially, however, believe me the picture will never be made. Ava's in Europe and she's not coming back.' "

Shortly after *Diane* was finished, Lana was lent to Fox for *The Rains of Ranchipur*, a remake of their 1939 hit, *The Rains Came.*

Lana had the role originally played by Myrna Loy, that of a beautiful Western woman who falls in love with an Indian prince. Tyrone Power had played the prince in the original film. The role now went to Richard Burton.

There was no gossip about Lana and leading man Burton, who had failed miserably in films, despite all the efforts of Fox to make him a Movie Star. The relationship between Burton and Turner appeared to be strictly professional, with the talented Welshman not exactly Lana's physical type and vice versa (although certain Hollywood stories at the time said that anything, as long as it was living, was Burton's type).

Lex and Lana practically became fixtures at premieres and parties during the year. Her hair was back to its blonde shade, and photos of the smiling Barkers out on the town made the newspapers frequently.

Lana's marriage to Lex Barker was her only real "Hollywood" marriage. The marriage to Shaw was too short to count; Crane was not really part of the Hollywood set except as Lana's escort; and neither was Topping, although he was an international playboy and sportsman. Ty Power and Fernando Lamas would have qualified as ideal "Hollywood" mates had they married her.

It was Lana and Lex, Lex and Lana—working together, playing together, photographed together. As far as their fans were concerned, the Barkers had reached the ultimate in happiness—one successful star married to another.

During Lana's marriage to Lex, the couple was written about in feature stories, syndicated columns and fan magazines. However, Lana, during this period, wasn't making the kind of news she had in the previous ten years. The events she participated in were not of Associated Press, United Press International or major news caliber.

In February of 1955 Lana turned thirty-five. If thirty had seemed an improbable age for forever-young Lana, thirty-five must have seemed incredible. "She was scared," said a friend. "Sure, she still looked great, especially considering the life she'd led, but in youth-conscious America she had reached *that* age. And she felt that her appearance was her prime commodity and worried how much longer it would last."

In March, *The Prodigal* was released. Lana looked gorgeous as "the pagan goddess of love who tempts the prodigal son," but the picture was awful. It was a commercial disaster. Lana's sense of humor revealed itself when she was discussing the film years later— "It played two weeks in Pomona. It should have played Disneyland," she laughed. But she wasn't laughing when it was released.

In April, 1955, Dorothy Kilgallen wrote that, "All is not well with Lana and Lex. Friends say they've had it—Lana and Lex deny it."

That month *The Sea Chase* sailed into theatres. John Wayne and Lana were a potent draw. The film was a commercial success, and ad lines such as: " 'This is a tramp steamer' . . . 'Okay Captain, where's my cabin?' " helped sell the picture and reinforce Lana's image. Lana's daughter, now nearing twelve, must have been affected by this kind of exploitation of her mother.

In August, during one of the Barkers' frequent vacations in Acapulco and just before she began *The Rains of Ranchipur*, Lana was hurt in a bathtub fall and suffered a concussion of the brain. The extent of the injury wasn't discovered until she was examined after complaining of pains in her back. She had been scheduled to start filming *Ranchipur*, but shooting had to be postponed for two weeks while Lana recuperated.

By the first week in September, she was back in Hollywood and at work on the film. Rumors that all was not well with her marriage continued to filter into the press.

In November, Lana was admitted to the hospital for "a routine checkup." A few days later, Associated Press reported that she was recuperating at her home from an operation for removal of a small tumor. Doctors said the tumor was not malignant.

Lex and Lana were making financial investments, and that month, which seemed to be a bad-luck month for them that year, they were subpoenaed to testify in court regarding $18,000 they allegedly owed a Texas oil promoter. The matter was settled out of court.

Fox had rushed *Rains of Ranchipur* to be ready for a Christmas release, and in December, only three months after production on the film began, it opened at New York's Roxy Theatre. It was the third Lana Turner picture to be released in less than a year, and the critics weren't enthusiastic about it. The film's massive flood sequence garnered all the publicity. The picture didn't do well at the box office, even though they used a provocative advertising campaign utilizing sexy pictures of Lana and catchy ad lines. One for example, had Burton and other men sneering at her, "I wonder what the word for you is in Hindi . . . in English it's got one syllable."

Just before the new year, Metro previewed *Diane*, and the reaction wasn't good. At the emotionally traumatic age of thirty-five, if Lana needed confidence more than anything else, she received instead a punch in the gut—her protector and guardian, MGM, was going to kick her out. The final decision to drop her was made and by February, 1956, as Lana turned thirty-six, she was out of MGM. Her films had earned over $50 million for them. Now, after eighteen coddled, protected years, Lana Turner was on her own.

She didn't waste any time forming her own production company. She was interviewed at her home by Joe Hyams, who found corporation president Turner dressed in black velvet slacks, a black sweater and gold sandals.

"I'm still walking around in a daze," she announced happily. "I've been sprung. After eighteen years at MGM I'm a free agent. I can work for anyone, do anything. For years I was a fixture like the Thalberg Building. If they had a rotten picture and couldn't get anyone to play in it, they'd say, 'Give it to Lana.'

"Then when I turned it down they'd give it to Ava Gardner. What they didn't know is that Ava and I compared notes. She'd call and say she just got a script and did I think she should read it. I'd tell her it was a turkey and to ditch it.

"I used to go in on bended knee to the front office and say, please give me a decent story. I'll work for nothing, just give me a good story. So what happened? Last time I begged for a good story they gave me *The Prodigal*."

Lana's press agent then interrupted. "Let's not make MGM such a heavy, Lana. It's not as though you were in jail."

"Who says I wasn't in jail?" flashed Lana. "I was. They never bought a story for me. They knew I was there, but no one thought of me. Do you know the big question I ask myself now? Why is it that after so many turkeys I still maintained my position at the box office and people will still pay to see me? What could I be if I had decent pictures?"

Since she was now in the driver's seat, what next? "I'm reading everything I can get my hot little hands on, and there's a good story for you, darling—the terrible shortage of material. Nothing."

Lana turned her hands palms upward. "I want to do a variety of things, a wonderful, sophisticated comedy, a romantic drama, and before I have a long gray beard, a musical with a story, if such a thing exists.

"I'm principally interested in getting two great stories. I must have two to prove the first one isn't a fluke. Seventeen years ago my wish was to be successful; today it is to stay successful."

She named her corporation Lanturn and told Hyams, "You know that Korda gong [she meant the Rank Organization gong] and the greasy hand on Mark VII? Well, I plan to have a traditional, old-fasioned lantern. If it's a love story about spring there will be 'love is first' on it."

When Hyams asked what the corporation's principal asset was, Miss Turner looked at him as though he were hanging by his feet from the ceiling. "Me, of course," she said.

"And what greater asset than Lana Turner can a corporation have?" her press agent added solemnly.

Lana was putting on a good front, claiming she was delighted to be out of MGM bondage. But years later, discussing the MGM days, she admitted, "It was all beauty and it was all power. Once you had it made, they protected you, they gave you stardom . . . we had the *best*."

Once again rumors about the imminent breakup of Lana and Lex flared up. September, 1956, would be their third wedding anniversary.

Lana's flamboyant past was dredged up again, this time by Dorothy Kilgallen in connection with a new story she wrote about Frank Sinatra: NANCY IGNORED HIS MANY ROMANCES—THE REAL FRANK SINATRA STORY. Kilgallen said Sinatra didn't care what Nancy knew or what she thought, and during the period of his fling with Lana "he would come home with lipstick on his shirt and not even bother to hide it from Nancy."

Lex gave a lengthy interview to Bob Thomas of Associated Press, lamenting the trials of maintaining a happy marriage in Hollywood. "Barker is perplexed by rumor mongers," wrote Thomas. "Recently he was absent from Lana for five weeks, mostly on location in the

163

Virgin Islands and partly to visit his stricken father in the east. While he was gone the rumors flew. One columnist reported that Lana was hobnobbing with a bullfighter in Tijuana. Another declared her next would be her ex, Steve Crane, after she divorces Lex.

"Lex set the record straight. 'Lana likes bullfights, I don't,' Lex said. 'So while I was gone it looked like a good time to see them in Tijuana. She went down with some friends of mine and a bullfighter happened to be in the party. As for the other rumors, Steve Crane happens to be the father of my stepdaughter. He is entitled to visit his daughter. I was the one in the Virgin Islands, not Lana.' "

Thomas described Lana's marriage to Lex as the most tranquil of her marriages. "You can't win," Barker told him. "Nearly every columnist said it was shocking that we were in Europe together even though we were both working there. Then after we got married, they seemed eager to split us up. You can't win."

However, while Barker was away on location, publicists who worked with Lana in the last months of her MGM contract recall escorting her to some of the night clubs popular in Hollywood at that time. One publicist, who was then a novice in the business, remembers: "If she saw someone at the bar who looked interesting, it was my job to go over and invite him to our table. I was a little nervous, since I had to make it clear to the guy who she was and what was expected of him.

"I almost had my chance with her too," the young press agent recalls. "I was pretty young in those days, but on a certain afternoon things were getting hot and heavy and I thought, Wow! *My* turn with Lana Turner!

"But just at that point Robert Wagner came on the set. He was under contract to 20th Century-Fox but he used to visit MGM a lot in those days. Lana and Bob started carrying on and they laughed and went into her dressing room, locked the door and that was the end of *my* big chance."

That year, when Lex was away on location and Lana stayed in Hollywood, the rumors became so far-fetched some were laughable. One scandal magazine wrote that Lana had an affair with a French actor, George Sorel, and that Monsieur Sorel had been locked in her bedroom for three weeks. Barely given enough nourishment, they said, he could put up no fight when Barker returned and threw him bodily out of the house.

In her professional life Lana was still "at liberty." Incredibly, the Sweater Girl-Sexpot-Sophisticate-Dreamgirl, durable as a diamond, was signed for no films. She, her agent Paul Kohner and Lex "ran into" Universal Vice President of Production Ed Muhl at the premiere of Lex's Universal picture, *Away All Boats*. The meeting resulted in her first picture deal after leaving MGM.

In a *Variety* ad Universal announced that Lana would star in a re-make of *My Man Godfrey*, but Lana backed out when in the spring she learned she was pregnant. She must have been pleased. She and Barker had been talking of having children for the entire three years of their marriage.

But there were other opinions of how she felt about her new pregnancy. "I don't think she wanted another baby," says one of her ex-husbands. "Becoming pregnant proved to the world that Lana Turner was still a young woman, at least young enough to have a baby. She always wanted to be thought of as the eternal young girl.

"It's like an older woman going out with young guys. It says to the world, 'See, I'm still desirable to a young man because I'm still young myself.'

"In my opinion Lana was happy she was pregnant but she had no desire to actually have the baby."

Reportedly Lana was getting giant-sized doses of vitamins. She said she hoped she and Lex would have a boy. She told Louella they'd name the child Christopher whether it was a boy or girl, but they wanted a boy. Miss Parsons was delighted, and sanctioned their union: "Lex is good for Lana," wrote Louella. "They have a home life that Lana has never had in any of her former marriages.

"When Lex was married to Arlene Dahl, he was never completely happy. Their tastes were different and their ideas varied, but in the case of Lana it's different.

"These two people have been through so much that each has made up his mind to make this marriage work out."

Lana "authored" a by-line article for a major fan magazine titled: THE THINGS I'LL TELL MY DAUGHTER. According to the flowery article, Lana was guiding Cheryl into being a thoughtful, understanding person ready for responsibility later. "Darling, I shall tell her," she said in the article, "you have a lovely body. Be proud of it but don't be too vain and always remember this: your life can be one of great happiness or great pain." Lana went on to advise Cheryl that it would all depend on the consideration and respect she showed herself. "Lex and I try to convey to Cheryl now that we are interested in and concerned about the kind of boys she will go out with," she wrote. "Ten to one when she starts dating Cheryl will want the boy to be someone she will be proud to introduce to us." Cheryl will try to grow up in a rush, Lana continued, and she will think the way to do it will be with lipstick, high heels, formal clothes.

Lana, who had been "the night-club queen" at seventeen, went on to state in the article that "lipstick and high heels go with fifteen, sixteen, and seventeen. If you do all these things now, everything will be old hat and then you'll just be restless and dissatisfied with life."

Lana's next bit of advice to Cheryl was to learn to accept responsibility. She pointed out that Cheryl had always had a few chores like making her own bed, feeding her dog and bird, tidying up her quarters and keeping her shoes cleaned. "Now she is getting older," wrote Lana. "These are not enough. She now sets the table, helps with the dishes and cleaning up and soon she is going to learn how to prepare meals." Next Lana said she would tell Cheryl to "remember that you are a lady. If someone says, 'Aw, c'mon, you're being silly,' you can answer honestly if you don't want to join in, 'You kids go ahead, I don't like it, but don't let me stop you.' " Another thing Lana said she would tell Cheryl is always to feel free to invite her friends to her home. "My last bit of advice to my daughter will be, if you have any questions or any problems please come to me and we'll discuss them together."

Features like these are usually written by public-relations people and approved by the by-lined star. But Lana most likely believed all the views stated. If there were mistakes in the upbringing of her daughter, she made them (as most parents do) unintentionally. Some of her friends suggest that Lana, though in her mid-thirties, wasn't emotionally mature enough to cope with a growing child.

On October 2, Lana checked into St. Johns Hospital for "observation and minor surgery." Doctors said there was no danger to the baby she and Lex were expecting in January. But four days later, Lana and Lex had lost their expected child.

There is no doubt that this difficulty in having another child seriously affected Lana. Years later she said, "During my marriages I lost three children, two boys and a girl. I thought of adopting a child, but everytime I'd be getting around to it my married life would be in turmoil so it never happened."

Lana's career got a shot in the arm in January, 1957, when her pre-1948 films appeared on television for the first time. The old movies were tremendous rating-grabbers. In response to a query as to what she thought when she watched herself in her old movies, Lana said, concerning *Honky-Tonk*, "I liked what I saw very much. I am enjoying my old movies. Most of them were good stories, and I had great co-stars. I always knew Clark was good, but I didn't realize how good until I saw him again.

"Seeing myself on the screen," she reminisced, "is like going through an album, looking at pages of old photographs. It brings back memories, and results in mixed emotions. It's also great fun to watch these movies with Cheryl [then thirteen], who was too young to see them before. These movies give talk Cheryl has heard a 'for

167

real' quality. I may be imagining it, or it may be because Cheryl is growing up, but since my old movies have been on television, our companionship has improved.

"These old movies on television also have helped me professionally," she added. Lana hadn't made a new film in a year. "These movies are keeping me before the public. My fan mail is tremendous, haven't had anything like it for quite a while. And the studios are anxious to start on a picture with me."

By this time Lana had found a role she wanted. She was eager to play Maggie in *Cat on a Hot Tin Roof.* Metro owned the property, and Lana asked for the part. It must have been a cruel disappointment when the role went to Elizabeth Taylor.

The miscarriage and not working had unnerved her. The marriage to Lex was in its final months. It had lasted far longer than anyone had predicted. But the final blow of losing the child, Lex's reported disillusionment with the married life they had led, the conflict of their careers (for the first time in her adult life, she wasn't secure professionally), had paved the way for the breakup.

Even before the marriage, Lana had said, "It's next to impossible to find anyone with whom you can have sincerity linked with complete understanding. There are innumerable difficulties when you're both in the profession.

"You're needled from all sides with questions about how things are working out, and whether you don't think you've made a mistake. These questions build and build until they rock the very foundations of a marriage."

Later, when the divorce came in 1958, Lana told the judge that Lex had "an uncontrollable temper, which he showed too many times." She implied that Lex belonged back in the trees like the character he portrayed on the screen. "Once, during breakfast," she asserted, "he slapped my face," and she added that he used profane language.

"I was very upset and agitated, and it was very difficult for me to

168

look after the home and fulfill my professional obligations," she told the judge.

At the time they separated in 1957, there was no mention of Cheryl. Later, however, in an Italian magazine interview, Lex blamed Cheryl for the split-up.

"The girl told a story to her mother," he was reported as saying. "I denied it was true. But Lana always had one great fault—to believe her daughter first, although knowing she was full of complexes and accustomed to lie. The next morning I left the house."

Cheryl, the magazine quoted him as saying, was not a bad girl— "but certainly very strange." And he said he had warned Lana that her daughter "would end up involved in great trouble."

"You'll never get rid of me!"
JOHNNY STOMPANATO, 1958

10

Handsome hangers-on have always been part of the Hollywood scene. Many clever young men, with no visible talents, travel in Hollywood's highest circles, entertaining the lonely, vain, bored women who find excitement and diversion in them as they would with a new toy.

Some few of these men succeed. Most of them fade quietly into oblivion and are forgotten, as they are replaced by the newer, younger breed. Like most, pseudo-swashbuckler John Stompanato was certain that *he* could never be replaced and forgotten.

On Good Friday, April 4, 1958, Johnny Stompanato achieved the fame he sought. His name was splashed across headlines of every major newspaper in the world, his photograph appeared on television and in national magazines, his name blared over radio—he became part of Hollywood Legend. He was the catalyst for a best-selling novel. Johnny Stompanato's name would be forever linked with the famous movie star he sought to marry.

He had sworn he was hers until death. And so he was. For on that night he was fatally stabbed by her teen-age daughter, Cheryl Crane. Many people—especially Lana Turner—will never forget Johnny Stompanato.

Lana Turner met Johnny Stompanato in the spring of 1957. She had separated from Lex in February and was now thirty-seven years old. After five marriages and headlined romances with the most eligible bachelors in the world, her new love affair was a decided comedown. During her many years in Hollywood Lana observed similar situations—older women, younger men, glamour careers fading away. It could never happen to her. But she had succumbed to the charms of a second-rate gigolo.

Lana always found excitement, as did many stars, running occasionally with the hoodlum crowd that achieved semi-respectability in Hollywood after the war. Gambling Kingpin Mickey Cohen was a favorite in this social set, and it was indirectly through Cohen that Lana met Johnny Stompanato.

Stompanato, five-feet-eleven and 180 pounds, had flashing brown eyes and black wavy hair. He was a sharp dresser and had the kind of physique that could be displayed to great advantage in both bathing suit and tuxedo. He often frequented night clubs to meet wealthy women. He had been a $300-a-week bodyguard to Cohen before the mobster's gambling empire collapsed and Cohen did time on a federal tax rap.

Stompanato, cunning and cocksure, was just a small-time racketeer when he obtained Lana Turner's telephone number from Cohen and, via a series of persistent calls, finally arranged a date which he subsequently parlayed into a torrid trans-Atlantic love affair.

("I didn't know him, but we had mutual friends," Lana later told police. "We went on a blind date. He kept calling me after that, and would come over for a drink or a chat.")

Husky, swarthy, and not exactly shy, Stompanato was a man who made his living by courting thrill-seeking wealthy women, borrowing their money, and rarely paying it back.

At this time, the man from Woodstock, Illinois, who had been educated in midwestern military academies, had already been married three times and had a ten-year-old son. From his first appearance on the Hollywood scene in 1948, there was an aura of mystery about Stompanato. The ex-marine said that he had come from China, where he had run a string of night clubs after the war.

The truth was that he had been born in Woodstock on October 19, 1925. His mother died while he was a child and his father remarried soon after. Johnny spent a year at Woodstock High School and was then enrolled at Kemper Military Academy in Booneville, Missouri, but left in 1943 to enlist in the marine corps.

In China in 1946 he married Sarah Utish, a Turkish girl, and took her home to Illinois, where they had a son, John III. Sarah soon left him, remarried and was living in Hammond, Illinois, at the time Johnny was dating Lana.

After Sarah left him, Stompanato went west, where he married an actress, Helen Gilbert. They were divorced in 1949. In 1953 he married another actress, Helene Stanley, and they were divorced two years later.

In Hollywood, he had various jobs and businesses, ranging from auto salesman to proprietor of a pet shop and a furniture shop.

Prior to meeting Lana, Stompanato had traveled extensively. His passport issued in 1956 showed that from late October of that year to mid-January, 1957, he was in northern Europe, apparently based in Copenhagen. He made frequent trips to Sweden and at least one trip to Brussels. The story was that he was hoping to secure a sales franchise from a Danish manufacturer of dairy equipment. But the deal fell through. Other stories said that he was actually on a special mission for "the mob."

In February and March of 1957 Stompanato went to Uruguay and Brazil. No reason for these trips was ever unearthed.

Stompanato was operating a gift shop in west Los Angeles at the time he met Lana, but immediately he turned all his attention to her, forgetting business.

He filled the void in her life and gave her the lavish affection she craved. Her friends later said, "Lana was incapable of leading a manless existence for any length of time. But," they understated, "she unfortunately often chooses men who lack her kindness, charm and financial success."

As Ava Gardner has said, "When it comes to men, Lana and I are the world's lousiest pickers."

Stompanato appeared to be wildly in love with Lana, and apparently she returned the affection. She gave him a gold charm bracelet on which she had engraved: "For Johnny . . . Sweet Love . . . When you wear this, remember it is a tiny piece of my heart . . . and also remember, be careful . . . With all my soul, Lanita." Stompanato also carried a lock of her blonde hair and wore Lana's picture suspended from a gold chain around his neck. On it she had written in Spanish: "For Johnny, My Love and My Life. Lanita."

Beverly Hills Police Chief Clinton H. Anderson was familiar with Stompanato long before his liaison with Lana. At one point Anderson had thrown Stompanato out of a prominent Beverly Hills hotel when Stompanato became abusive during a police investigation. The police suspected he was at the hotel to extort money from a guest.

Police records show that Stompanato had been arrested six times, on charges ranging from vagrancy to suspicion of robbery, but he had only one minor conviction. Many people thought he was a payroll man for the mob—that he carried large sums of money which he transferred from one racketeer to another.

Whatever work he did, it was obvious that it was dangerous. Lana was later quoted as having told him many times to "Be careful." The danger, no doubt, added to the attraction she felt for Stompanato.

All seemed blissful for them during the spring and summer of 1957. He was encouraged when her divorce from Barker became final in July. But then his jealousy and social aspirations started to get out of hand.

("*I was dating other men during these months,*" *she subsequently told police,* "*but about September John began to assert his possessiveness.*")

Lana, always career-oriented, realized the place that Stompanato occupied in her life. It must be remembered that in 1957 the moral standards of the country were considerably more conventional and staid than today. Even members of the entertainment industry—always associated with the vanguard of changing morality—were expected to conform to certain codes of behavior.

There was no nudity on stage or in films, no swear words were permitted in movies or on television, and stars' images were kept free of scandal.

Only seven years earlier, Swedish-born Ingrid Bergman, who had reached the apex of cinema stardom, created an international scandal by having a child by Italian film director Roberto Rossellini before they were married. The American public and press branded her an "adulteress" and a "harlot," and her Hollywood film career came to an abrupt halt. (By the late 1960s, however, the country's standards of morality had changed so drastically that there was little reaction to disclosures by singer Connie Stevens and actresses Mia Farrow, Vanessa Redgrave and Catherine Deneuve that they were bearing children out of wedlock.)

174

But in 1957, morality clauses still were standard parts of contracts, drugs were not openly used or widely accepted publicly, and some press agents were on salary to keep clients' private lives out of print.

Lana's years with MGM had taught her the importance of her "image," and she wanted her relationship with the handsome gangland Romeo kept private.

Lana's career was about to enter a new phase. She had consented to play the mother of an adolescent girl in 20th Century-Fox's film version of the sensational best-seller, *Peyton Place*. Producer Jerry Wald convinced her to take the part over the objections of her friends, who felt that she was still too young to play a mother. But Wald pointed out to her that he had persuaded Joan Crawford to play a mother in *Mildred Pierce*, with spectacular results. That 1945 film not only launched a second career for Crawford, but won her the Academy Award as Best Actress.

In *Peyton Place*, Lana played Constance MacKenzie, the mother of a confused and unhappy young girl. In real life, Lana was indeed the mother of a troubled teen-ager. Cheryl was thirteen now, and finding it more difficult than ever to adjust to her mother's way of life.

She was an intelligent girl, too old now for a nanny. She had spent years in boarding schools, out of the public eye—except for an occasional mother-daughter photograph. Lana's goldfish-bowl position as a glamorous superstar made it virtually impossible for Lana and Cheryl to enjoy a normal parent-child relationship. Although Lana had kept Cheryl with her a great deal of the time (at least by movie-star standards) the child's rearing had in large part been entrusted to others. Even when they were together, Lana's shifting romantic attachments left the child feeling insecure. Whether Lana knew it or not, Cheryl was unhappy and disturbed.

The tragic events ahead were not without a prelude. One night in the spring of 1957, when Cheryl was supposed to be in boarding school, she was found wandering around the skid row area of Los Angeles at midnight.

Cheryl had been visiting with Lana, and was returning that night to the Sacred Heart School in Flintridge. According to friends, Lana had enrolled her daughter there because she felt the girl needed discipline. Cheryl was sharing a taxi back to school with Maggie Douglas, daughter of actor Paul Douglas, when she told the taxi driver to stop. Cheryl told Maggie she was going into the drugstore to make a phone call, and, after some time when she hadn't returned, Maggie continued on to school.

The Mother Superior at Sacred Heart called Lana to report that Cheryl hadn't returned. Lana informed Steve Crane and Crane called the police. A citywide police search was instituted. Reporters called Lana, and she told them, almost hysterically, "I haven't the foggiest idea why she ran away. She never did this before. All I can do is pray she comes home safely."

Down at Skid Row, Cheryl was wandering around carrying a suitcase. She was frightened and lonely. A young man, Manuel Acosta, began talking with her. She asked him if he knew where she could find a cheap hotel. "I only have about twelve dollars," she told him. Acosta said later, "She looked seventeen or eighteen but she was nervous and scared so I knew something was wrong. I didn't tell her I was taking her to the police station but she didn't object when I went in and got the police."

Crane, Cheryl and Lana had a tearful reunion at the police station, and Cheryl's official explanation for her action was that she didn't want to return to school. However, Acosta told reporters that Cheryl had told him she ran away partly because she had had a misunderstanding and partly because her home had broken up. (Presumably she referred to her mother's splitting with Lex Barker.)

The story made national headlines, and for the first time it was publicly indicated that Cheryl had emotional difficulties.

Like many daughters of glamorous women—both in and out of

show business—Cheryl had special problems. She was a plain-look-ing girl who had to cope with constant comparisons with a glitter-ing mother. Cheryl was insecure, and usually her mother wasn't around when she needed her. Searching for an emotional identity, Cheryl found it almost impossible to relate to Lana, who herself seemed little more than a teen-ager emotionally.

At the police station, bewildered and weeping, Lana held Cheryl, and sobbed, "Why did you do this to me?" Cheryl comforted her and told her everything would be all right.

If Cheryl's running away was a ploy to get out of going back to Sacred Heart Academy, it worked. Lana told Cheryl she didn't have to return to the school.

That summer, in Estes Park, Colorado, Cheryl had a serious acci-dent. She fell from a horse and broke her back. Again, both her par-ents flew to her side, and within a month Cheryl was out of the hos-pital and back in Beverly Hills. She shuttled between her mother, father and grandmother, and Lana enrolled her in a new school, The Happy Valley School in Ojai, about sixty miles from home. That way Cheryl could spend the weekends in Beverly Hills.

By fall, Lana's affair with Stompanato was in full swing. Then she left for London to film *Another Time, Another Place*, the story of a woman in love with a married man. The actor who would portray Lana's love interest in the film was not yet chosen. Many were screen-tested, and Lana herself selected a virile, young, unknown, Scottish-brogued actor for the part—Sean Connery. Lana's new production company, Lanturn Productions, was co-producing the film with Paramount.

Stompanato, wary of losing Lana to European competition, sensed his position in her affections was weakening. Although he had an expensive apartment and was driving a new Cadillac, that September he had to borrow pocket money from Mickey Cohen to fly to England to join Lana.

(*Lana told police, "I went to London to make a film. A few days later John called me at my London hotel. I guess he followed me from Hollywood. We quarreled, and for the first time he got violent." The police contradicted several of Lana's early statements, including this one, saying they had evidence that she had paid his way to London. They conceded, however, that Stompanato was a "tough guy" who never hit another man but wouldn't think twice before slapping a girl friend around.)*

The facts were that Lana left Los Angeles for Europe on September 18, and Johnny saw her off. She arrived in Copenhagen the next day, where she mailed a letter to him. Then she flew on to London.

After receiving her letter, Johnny went to the same travel agent Lana had used and he asked for an airplane ticket "on the cuff." He told the travel agent that he didn't like asking for the favor and he didn't really want to go to Europe but Lana was pressuring him to come. The agent was obviously not convinced and refused Stompanato the ticket.

Johnny then supposedly borrowed the money from Mickey Cohen and went back and bought the ticket from the same agent, paying cash. Following the same route as Lana, he arrived in Copenhagen, where he picked up a telegram of welcome from her, which had been sent to the Copenhagen airport. Then he continued on to London the same day.

Stompanato wanted to be with Lana, and he probably had cause to be wary of a long separation. He realized that Lana might easily forget him, and he was too tough and determined to let himself be thrown over. Naturally, Stompanato wanted to legitimize his liaison with Lana, but nothing could have been farther from her mind. It was a backstairs romance as far as she was concerned, though she was emotionally involved enough that his presence in London disrupted her work.

Friends said that their quarrels began in London when Lana refused to risk either her name or her money to help Johnny become

178

a producer. Men like Stompanato often used female stars to wangle business deals. Judy Garland, sometimes described as filmdom's only exploited brunette, had been manipulated careerwise. But Lana, unlike Judy and others, did not allow her lovers to interfere in choosing her material, controlling her career or finances. She might pick up a tab, but she wasn't about to jeopardize her professional future.

Stompanato had demanded that Lana put up $1,000 for an option on *The Bartered Bride*, a story by Robert Carson which Stompanato wanted to produce with Lana as the star. (The story leaked to the press, and Louella Parsons said the property might co-star Lana with Frank Sinatra.)

Benton Cole, Lana's former business agent, was now acting on Stompanato's behalf and had exchanged a series of letters with Ben Benjamin, who was representing writer Carson. In December, Benjamin wrote Cole, "I am a little stunned about the $1,000 payment, which was always an integral part of the deal when you and I discussed it.

"If Lana is really as interested in this as she seemed to be, I should think Morgan Maree [then Lana's business agent] could advance the money."

The deal did not appeal to Morgan Maree. A talent agent, an old friend of Lana's, says he was in Maree's office one day when there was a call from Lana in London. The agent, whom Stompanato had approached years earlier in an abortive bid to become an actor, remembers the conversation vividly. It seems Lana was imploring Maree to get her off the hook, not to advance Stompanato any money and not to option any properties.

Sean Connery felt his big break had come when he was cast in *Another Time, Another Place*, and all went well between him and Lana until Stompanato's arrival. Stompanato had heard of Connery's reputation as a lover, and, waving a revolver for emphasis, warned him to "keep away from the kid."

179

Obviously Connery was not impressed, since he immediately punched Stompanato in the nose. Stompanato, unable to make his point with the burly Scotsman, then turned his ire on Lana, and for the next several weeks he went about making life miserable for her and undermining the film by making her previously warm relationship with Connery turn coldly formal.

During this period, while Stompanato kept badgering Lana for money, it was rumored that the actress once quipped on the set: "I wonder if the screwing I'm getting is worth the screwing I'm getting."

A British journalist, who met Lana with Stompanato, described her as a woman "very much in love." He quoted Lana, "I am not getting married again but I need someone by me all the time. Am I so different from other women in wishing that?"

Lana later revealed that in London she was frightened, not only for her career and image, but for her life. She and Stompanato fought bitterly, and reportedly on one occasion he practically strangled her and threatened to scar her face with a razor.

"Once, in my hotel room," she has recounted, "he choked me into insensibility. 'You've got your life to lead, and I have mine,' I said. 'I can do without all this quarreling. Why don't you leave me alone? Don't bother me.' "

It was then, Lana said, that Stompanato went into the first of his many rages and told her something he was to say again and again:

"You'll never get away from me. You'll never get rid of me."

And Lana recalled he also threatened her for the first time with death or disfigurement, saying, according to her statements to police: "If I can't do it myself, I'll have it done. There are not enough policemen in the world to stop me."

Lana appeared to be a nervous wreck. Late one December night she telephoned her temporary secretary, Gary Thorne, pleading for help. "She said she was terrified of him," Thorne later reported, "that he had threatened her and was beating her up. She was almost hysterical and asked me to do something."

Thorne informed the studio, which used its influence with Scotland Yard and had Stompanato ejected from the country. Although Lana confided to many friends that she was "terrified" of Stompanato and his threats, it did not stop her from continuing the affair. Stompanato left England just after Cheryl came to join her mother for the Christmas holidays. Presumably the three of them spent time together in London.

At Christmastime, *Peyton Place* was released in the United States. It opened to good reviews and, more importantly, to sensational business. Universal, editing *The Lady Takes a Flyer*, an old-fashioned Lana Turner vehicle (co-starring Jeff Chandler) which she had made for them that year, readied the film for January release.

Peyton Place re-established Lana Turner as a big box-office attraction, and, soon after, she was nominated for the Academy Award as "Best Actress" for her performance. Wald's prediction about her success in the role had come true. Most critics agreed it was Lana's best work since *The Bad and the Beautiful*. As is often the case with the Motion Picture Academy, Lana was being recognized not alone for her current film but for previous, overlooked performances.

Stompanato was more than aware of Lana's new success. He wanted to cash in on it. After his return from Europe, he had taken a $125-a-month apartment at the Malibu Sands Hotel on the Pacific Coast Highway, where he stayed for about four weeks. He was driving a late-model Lincoln and also a white 1957 Thunderbird, and he seemingly led a quiet life while there. He had few visitors, all male, as far as sources knew.

It is a fact that he called Lana in London at least once and she called him at least three times.

By January 15, Stompanato was insisting that he rejoin Lana in London. She successfully dissuaded him, but agreed to meet him later in Amsterdam and then go to Mexico for a holiday.

(In her early statements to police, Lana said, ". . . after the picture was finished, I went to Paris and later took a KLM plane from Amsterdam to Mexico City. The next thing I knew—I was never more surprised in my life—John was on the plane." Police said they had reason to believe he was invited.)

Asked again, Lana conceded that Stompanato hadn't been entirely unwanted, according to Beverly Hills Police Chief Anderson. Then she gave a new statement. Lana said that she had encouraged Stompanato's courtship—and paid for it. She gave him thousands of dollars, police quoted her as saying, "not counting the tabs I picked up for him."

If Lana gave him large sums of money, she was not the first woman to do so. Rosemary Trimble, the wife of a doctor, had supposedly given money to Stompanato—$2,500 at one point and $25,000 at another. There was even some mystery as to whether this woman had at one point become Stompanato's fourth wife, but this was never proven. In addition, a widow, Doris Jean Cornell, told police that she had given Stompanato $8,150 to open his pet shop.

Stompanato checked out of his hotel on January 18, and two days later he met Lana in Amsterdam and they left for Mexico. This second trip to Europe was probably financed by Lana, since Mickey Cohen had told Stompanato that he wouldn't lend him money for the second trip. The travel agent who sold Stompanato the first ticket recalls that the hoodlum did not book his second flight through him. This leads to speculation that Lana sent Stompanato his ticket.

However, Lana had sent Stompanato a letter, postmarked January 13, in which she indicated that she had changed her mind about the trip and didn't want him to come. But the letter arrived too late and he was already on his way to Amsterdam. The letter was forwarded to Acapulco, indicating that the Mexican sojourn had been planned for some time.

With the Acapulco vacation Stompanato obviously thought he had scored a coup, but it proved humiliating to him to find that while in Acapulco he was housed in the servants' quarters of Ted Stauffer's Via Vera Hotel. (Lana, of course, had a suite.) But despite this housing discrimination, he and Lana were seen together at bullfights, on the beach and boating.

Jerry Wald telephoned Lana constantly in Acapulco, trying to convince her to play the fading southern belle in his production of *The Sound and the Fury*. While Lana had just successfully portrayed a mother, the Constance MacKenzie role had been one which enabled her to be youthful, attractive and chic. She had no intention then—or even today—of playing older-women, fading-beauty parts.

Jess Morgan, one of Lana's business agents, was in Acapulco when she and Johnny were there. He said at the time that Lana had not planned to rendezvous with Johnny in Mexico. "He forced his way into the party," Morgan said, and claimed that the *Bartered Bride* deal had never been taken up with his firm. If it had been, he said, "We should certainly have told Lana not to risk her money or her professional standing on such a deal."

Asked if it were true that Lana had given Johnny thousands of dollars, Morgan said: "It certainly is not. We write Lana's checks for any large sums, and no such sums to Stompanato have passed through our hands. If she gave him small sums we would not know about it."

He also said he did not know who paid the couple's hotel bills in Mexico. He wrote no checks for the hotel for Lana to sign, he said.

Later, among Stompanato's effects, were letters which showed he was being badgered by creditors. One of several bar checks bearing his name, Morgan's name and Lana's name, was for $900.

Lana told friends in London she was playing "the battered sweetheart instead of the bartered bride."

Lana's friends later testified that even during this Acapulco "idyll" (which lasted for eight weeks) she was frightened of Stompanato. Frightened or not, Lana was incapable of ending the affair.

Cheryl got a day off from the Happy Valley School in March to meet her mother at the airport and welcome her home. When Lana and Stompanato, both deeply tanned, arrived, the three of them were photographed together.

(In another early statement to police, Lana said, "They were not posed pictures. John just came up and grabbed me. I was so embarrassed. I didn't know what to do."

After Stompanato's death, these pictures appeared in every major newspaper and magazine. In many cases, the photos were cropped, cutting out Lana and showing Stompanato smiling at Cheryl, with captions to the effect: "Stompanato ogling his lover's daughter." The press often failed to report that it was entirely logical for Stompanato to be particularly attentive to Cheryl. He recognized the importance the child held in her mother's affections.

"He used to take me on little trips, to market, ice cream parlors and shops," Cheryl later reported. "He tried to use me to promote marriage between him and my mother.")

Back in Hollywood, Lana and Johnny continued their explosive relationship. She wanted to end it, and there was much violent quarreling.

(Police Chief Anderson later said that, exactly one week before the slaying, Mildred Turner telephoned to tell him that Lana was terribly frightened of Stompanato. Mildred wanted advice, wanted to know what could be done. The police advised her that Lana would have to come in personally to report the hoodlum's threats. But Lana never did.)

Events were rushing toward a tragic conclusion. It is important to note that it was Cheryl, and not Stompanato, who accompanied Lana to the Academy Awards ceremonies on March 24. Lana Turner represented in that spring of 1958 the durability and glamour of a Hollywood Star.

Academy audiences are notorious for being faithful to Hollywood-based productions and personalities. Although the Oscar for Best Actress went that year to Joanne Woodward for *Three Faces of Eve*, Lana's nomination was at last official recognition of her being an actress as well as a star. When James Stewart introduced her on the coast-to-coast Oscarcast, Lana looked radiant, still sporting her Acapulco tan, and received a rousing ovation.

The strain of her relationship with Stompanato certainly wasn't evident that evening. Only a few people in the industry—and certainly none of the public—knew of the torrid year-long Turner-Stompanato affair, which, in two weeks, would end in murder and scandal.

(Four years later, in October, 1962, novelist Harold Robbins, who has a penchant for writing fictionalized accounts of recognizable people and incidents, wrote a novel, Where Love Has Gone, *vehemently denying it was the story of Lana Turner, Johnny Stompanato and Cheryl Crane. In Robbins's book, a gigolo named Tony Riccio is fatally stabbed in the stomach in the house of his mistress, Nora Hayden, a glamourous sculptress. Nora is presented as an in-control but sex-oriented woman who had her first sexual experience at thirteen, her first abortion at fifteen. Nora's fourteen-year-old daughter Danielle is charged with the killing of Riccio.*

Robbins says he did research for the book at Juvenile Hall in San Francisco, where there were at least thirteen cases similar to this one.

Indeed, the events of the fatal night, as recounted in court testimony and newspapers, do read like the script of a second-rate soap opera.)

Lana had rented a mansion in Beverly Hills, and in early April Cheryl was home from boarding school for Easter vacation. According to testimony given at the inquest, the events and dialogue on the fatal evening went something like this:

It was Good Friday, April 4. Lana and Johnny had been arguing all day, and were an hour late meeting some of her friends at 3:30 p.m. for impromptu cocktails at her home.

Cheryl, out with a girl friend, was visiting her father and came home at about 5:30 p.m.

Soon after, Stompanato left the group. "I'll call you about 7 or 7:30," he told Lana.

Cheryl went up to her room. Lana declined a dinner invitation from her friends, explaining that since the maid didn't live in she couldn't leave Cheryl alone.

"She's never been left alone. I either arrange for my mother to come here or for Cheryl to go to her grandmother's."

Stompanato returned to the mansion shortly after 8:00 p.m. He and Lana continued the argument they had been having all day. Not helping matters was the fact that he was now furious with her because she had let her friends stay on for an hour after he had left.

Lana confided to Cheryl that it looked as if she was in for a bad night.

"Why don't you just tell him to go? You're a coward, mother."

"You don't understand. I'm deathly afraid of him."

"Don't worry, mother, I won't be far away. I won't leave you."

Later, Lana, tired and anxious to end the argument, told Stompanato to leave and began going upstairs. He followed right behind.

They passed Cheryl's room. Lana looked in. The girl was watching television. Stompanato continued to argue and berate Lana.

She whirled. "I told you. I told you I didn't want to argue in front of the baby!" (Cheryl was fourteen, but Lana still referred to her as "the baby.")

"Why not?" he demanded.

"Well, we're not going to," she said, and turned to Cheryl. "I'm going downstairs, Cheryl, and coming right back up, and I'm going to my room."

"Yes, mother," she answered.

186

Stompanato followed Lana downstairs. The quarrel was becoming more violent. She was discovering too many lies. Not the least of these was his lying to her about his age. He had told her he was forty-two; he was thirty-two. She was thirty-eight.

Speculations are that they also argued about money. Although she had been picking up the tabs during their fourteen-month affair, she apparently hadn't given him large sums of cash, as had most of the other women he had known. He was a gambler, and reputedly needed $3,500 to pay back gambling debts. A friend said, "Every time they went into a clinch there seemed to be a money tag on the kisses."

Another bone of contention between them was her not allowing him to escort her to the Academy Awards. For him it was the final straw in her refusal to be seen with him at important industry events.

Her attempts to get rid of him failed. The argument raged on. She stormed back upstairs to her pink-satin bedroom. Both were yelling at once.

"There's no use talking any further," she said. "I can't go on like this and I want you to leave me alone."

The young gigolo was not to be deterred. He had finally made the big leagues and had every intention of staying there. He grabbed Lana and began shaking her.

"I've told you before," he growled, "no matter what you do or how you try to get away, I'll never let you go. If I tell you to jump, you'll jump, and if I tell you to hop, you'll hop!"

The tough guy threatened, as he had in London, to cut her beautiful face, even to cripple her. Lana was petrified. There was no director to yell "Cut". The cliché dialogue wasn't coming from any script.

As if these personal threats hadn't convinced her that he was determined not to let her go, he also threatened to harm her mother and daughter.

Lana broke away and discovered Cheryl standing in the doorway.

"Please, Cheryl," she pleaded, "don't listen to this." The stunned young girl backed up and Lana closed the door.

Lana screamed at Stompanato, "That's just great! The child had to hear all that! I can't go through anything more!" He kept on swearing and threatening her.

On the other side of the door, Cheryl listened and heard him say, "I'll get you if it takes a day, a week or a year. I'll cut your face up and if I can't do it myself I'll find someone who will. That's my business."

The distraught fourteen-year-old, not knowing where to turn, ran downstairs. She found herself in the kitchen and saw a large butcher knife on the drainboard. She grabbed it and ran upstairs, with garbled thoughts of defending her mother and frightening Stompanato. Again she stood outside the bedroom door, listening.

The marathon brawl raged on. Stompanato went to the closet where he kept his clothes and grabbed a hanger. Lana kept insisting, "Don't ever touch me again. I'm absolutely finished. I want you to get out!"

Lana whipped open the bedroom door and once again found Cheryl standing there. In the heat of the argument, neither Lana nor Johnny noticed the knife in the child's hand.

"You don't have to take that, mother," Cheryl said. Before Lana and Johnny realized what was happening, the girl pushed the eight-inch blade into Stompanato's stomach.

(*"I saw them come together and I thought, 'Oh my God, she's hitting him in the stomach,'* " Lana later said.)

The husky ex-marine crumbled, making horrible noises in his throat and gasping.

Cheryl began sobbing and ran from the room. Lana still didn't realize what had happened. She later testified she didn't see the blood or the wound because of the way Stompanato had fallen. She ran over to him and then realized he had been stabbed. Horrified, she lifted up his sweater, saw the wound, and rushed to the

188

bathroom to get a towel. She called for Cheryl to come and help her. Lana put the towel on Stompanato's stomach. He was still gasping for breath. Lana rushed to the phone. She couldn't remember her long-time doctor's phone number. So she telephoned her mother.

"Mother, quick, call Dr. McDonald!"

"What's the matter?"

"I can't explain. Just tell him it's an emergency and to get here fast!" She hung up and again screamed for Cheryl.

"Cheryl, Cheryl, help me! I don't know what to do. Maybe some wet cloths would help!" Cheryl brought two wet washcloths, and Lana put one on Stompanato's forehead.

"Mommy, I didn't mean to do it. I didn't mean to do it." The terrified Lana tried to calm the youngster. The unreal scene continued.

"It will be all right," Lana reassured her. "The doctor will be here any minute."

But the doctor wasn't the first to arrive. It was Steve Crane. Cheryl had telephoned him.

Lana was on the floor, trying to talk to—call to—Stompanato. Crane appeared and took Cheryl into the next room. Then Lana heard her mother calling from downstairs. As Mildred came into the room, Lana got up and ran to her. "Mother, please don't look. It's John."

"What happened?"

"He's been hurt. Badly."

Mildred broke away from Lana and knelt beside Stompanato. She lifted the towel. She gasped when she saw the wound. She tried to talk to him.

Then she asked her daughter, "Has the doctor come yet?"

He hadn't.

Although it seemed like hours, it was only minutes later that Dr. McDonald arrived. Mildred had gone to check on Cheryl.

Dr. McDonald immediately began preparing a shot of adrenalin. "Lana, you'll have to call the ambulance," he told her.

She ran over and grabbed the phone. He had to tell her how to dial "O" and ask for "Emergency." It seemed to take forever.

There were all kinds of questions. Who was at the house? Who was the person involved? An exasperated and desperate Lana finally thrust the phone at Dr. McDonald, who gave his name, the address, and told them to rush a resuscitator to the scene.

While he was giving Stompanato the injection, McDonald told Lana to call another doctor, Doctor Webber. He also tried artificial respiration on the wounded man.

Frantically, Lana took over the artificial respiration as Dr. McDonald went to talk on the phone with Dr. Webber. Mrs. Turner came back into the room and tried to help by breathing into Stompanato's mouth. Lana, too, tried mouth-to-mouth resuscitation.

Off the phone now, Dr. McDonald prepared another shot. But then, "Lana, I can't get a heartbeat," he told her.

For a few frantic moments more he kept up the artificial respiration. And then he saw it was over.

(When Carmine Stompanato, the dead man's brother, went to Los Angeles to claim the body, he criticized the police investigation of the murder.

"Lana called her mother, her ex-husband and her press agent before calling the doctor," Carmine claimed. "And she never called the police.

"And Johnny was dying all the time.

"She should have called the police first. They might have called an ambulance and Johnny might have been saved."

Beverly Hills police reported that there was a lapse of at least two hours between the time of the slaying and their arrival on the scene.

But an autopsy showed that the victim was killed by a single *gash. The stab wound penetrated the liver, portal vein and aorta. Death came in a matter of minutes.)*

It was Dr. McDonald who suggested to Lana that she call attorney Jerry Geisler. Lana realized then that Stompanato was dead.

She had known Geisler, Hollywood's most famous lawyer, for years, but only on a social level. This was the first time that she required his professional help.

(Geisler [which he pronounced Geese-ler], was a short, plump man with a high nasal voice. He had successfully defended Charlie Chaplin, Errol Flynn, a host of other show-business personalities and underworld figures Bugsy Siegel and Mickey Cohen. He took cases ranging from marital discord to murder and was particularly successful in the defense of persons caught up in crimes of passion.

He was so successful at defending celebrities that the phrase "Get me Geisler!" became a Hollywood cliché.

His reputation was nationwide. Stompanato's brother later said, "They must have something to hide, or they wouldn't have gotten Geisler to defend them.")

Lana reached Geisler on the telephone almost immediately.

"This is Lana Turner. Something terrible has happened. Could you please come to my house?" she implored.

"Can you tell me what's happened?" he asked.

"Well, all I know is it's very dreadful. It's John Stompanato."

"Yes, I'll come."

Within the next few minutes, the house was overrun with people. The ambulance and the men with the resuscitator were there. Doctor Webber had arrived. So had Jerry Geisler. And shortly after, the police.

Police Chief Anderson was the first to question Lana officially. He later remembered that Lana was, under the circumstances, remarkably composed. When the police interrogated Cheryl in an adjacent room of the house, the girl's story was essentially the same as her mother's.

191

Anderson later testified that Lana wanted to take the blame. "Please," she had begged, "can't I say that I did it?" Chief Anderson convinced her that Cheryl's best interests would be served only if the truth were told.

(Taking his cue from much of the gossip after the killing, Harold Robbins, in Where Love Has Gone, *ends the book with the disclosure that Danielle [who might have been Cheryl's counterpart if the book hadn't been fiction] had taken the blame to protect her mother, who was the actual killer.)*

According to Anderson, the police established the facts of the killing beyond any question of a doubt. The department had been especially thorough, he said, since they knew, from long experience, that Jerry Geisler would uncover any errors in their report.

Lana, Crane and Geisler took Cheryl to the Beverly Hills police station to surrender her. There, where Cheryl had to remain until the juvenile court hearing, the famous blonde actress sobbed uncontrollably, while Cheryl seemed strangely calm.

The girl remarked, "I'm pretty strong—stronger than mother is." But she added, "I wish I could be like my mother. I wish I could cry."

"There is no such thing as justifiable homicide."
JOHNNY STOMPANATO'S STEPMOTHER

11

Cheryl was booked on a holding charge, a law peculiar to the state of California at that time, called suspicion of murder. As a juvenile, she faced a maximum penalty of life imprisonment, since minors cannot be executed under California law. But from the beginning, Geisler claimed, "This was a justifiable homicide. There is no justification for a trial."

Cheryl had to remain in custody because District Attorney William B. McKesson opposed bail. At Juvenile Hall, the girl was first kept in the infirmary because she had a mild temperature. A pre-detention hearing was originally set for Tuesday, April 8, but attorneys arranged to have it upped to Monday.

Over the Easter Sunday weekend, while Cheryl was kept in custody, Lana and Steve Crane made headlines when they received special permission to make an early visit to Juvenile Hall. United

Press International said, "Their party of two Cadillacs drove through the electrically-controlled gates while other parents waited outside in the rain until the regular visiting hour at 1 p.m.

"After the half-hour visit, Miss Turner and Mr. Crane whisked out the gates in their separate Cadillacs under the glowering gaze of still-waiting parents who stood under a ledge of the building to avoid the rain."

A Juvenile Hall spokesman said that Cheryl was "receiving no special treatment." But he added that it was felt that allowing her parents to visit her at special hours "would avoid having confusion arise during the regular time when other parents are here to see their children."

Lana returned home after visiting Cheryl and, as the rainy Easter Sunday wore on, the curious began driving by in an almost steady stream to gawk at the house where the murder took place. According to some reports, Frank Sinatra was the first person to visit Lana after the tragedy. Supposedly he visited her for fifteen minutes to offer his condolences and help. This surprised Hollywood insiders, since they assumed Frank and Lana had not been on good terms since the Ava Gardner-Palm Springs incident.

One of Lana's representatives told the press Lana had "been receiving literally hundreds of wires from all over the world and from a great many motion picture people expressing sympathy and prayers for her and Cheryl."

Much of the time during this period Lana was in a state of shock and at first required heavy sedation. Her long-time friend, make-upman Del Armstrong, along with her mother, stayed by her side.

On that Easter Sunday afternoon, Carmine Stompanato, brother of the slain man, visited Chief Anderson at police headquarters. With him were Max Tannenbaum of Brooklyn, and Ellis Mandel, later described by Anderson as "two known police characters." The men were concerned with locating some of Stompanato's missing property. Obviously, others had been interested in the mysterious property, since Stompanato's apartment at the Del Capri Hotel in west Los Angeles had been ransacked only a few hours after his death was made public.

Via the news media, millions of people throughout the world were now learning every detail of the Lana Turner-Johnny Stompanato affair. From the approach taken by the press, it was impossible to tell whether it was Cheryl who was on trial for stabbing the man who threatened her mother, or if Lana Turner was on trial for her moral character. Even the staid *New York Times* carried the story on page 1.

Unprecedented publicity followed. Some papers even ran a diagram of Lana Turner's bedroom, showing the stairway, the path Cheryl took, the exact spot where Stompanato was stabbed to death, the position of the wardrobe, the bed, the fireplace, the bathroom, and so on.

It was the biggest scandal to hit Hollywood since the 1920s, when another lurid murder trial ended the career of silent screen star Fatty Arbuckle (even though he was exonerated).

Moments after news of the Stompanato slaying broke, reporters for every major publication were assigned to dredge up all the details they could about the Sweater Girl and the ill-fated gangland figure.

In Los Angeles, shrewd Aggie Underwood, city editor of the *Los Angeles Herald-Examiner* (and the only woman city editor of a major U.S. metropolitan newspaper at that time) cleverly surmised that there must be some love letters. She was right. And she knew where to find them.

Mickey Cohen had maintained his ties with Stompanato. After a phone call from Aggie Underwood, the mobster and Stompanato's brother Carmine supplied the letters.

Cohen was sore at Lana. He had said his first reaction was that he felt sorry for her. But later, when he gave—or sold—the love letters to Miss Underwood, he claimed it was because he was angry that Lana had told police that she needed protection in case "the mob" tried to get revenge for her hoodlum lover's death. He was also angered that Lana had not tried to get in touch with the Stompanato family to offer to pay for the funeral expenses.

Cohen later claimed, "Normally, I'm a mild-mannered guy. A little rough, yes, but mild mannered. But when I saw what they were doing to Johnny after he was murdered I just blew sky-high. I lost my temper and wanted to do something to get even.

"Take the events as they happened and I'll show you what I mean. First, Johnny's older brother Carmine came out to the coast to claim the body. I suggested to Lana and Steve Crane through her attorney Jerry Geisler that they sit down with him and talk the whole thing out. Carmine, a fine man and an elder of his church, wasn't hot on anybody at this time. He just wanted to talk to somebody who would give him the real story of his brother's death.

"Geisler told me, 'A wonderful idea. I'll recommend that to Lana and Steve.' But that's the last I ever heard of it. Then I suggested to Crane's lawyer, Arthur Crowley, that Steve and Lana should pay for the funeral. It would have been a fine gesture under the circumstances because Johnny's family doesn't have a cent.

"Crowley told me, 'A wonderful idea. I'll recommend it.' I never heard from him either. I finally laid out the money—$2,300—myself, and believe me, with the government on my neck for back income taxes I don't have that kind of cash on me anymore.

"Then Lana made a statement that she fears mob violence. What kind of mob? Me? And," Cohen claimed, and this may be what angered him most, "the story broke just in time to influence a jury that was hearing my case with a waiter who claimed I slugged him. That was enough for the jury to return a guilty verdict.

"Well, with all these things happening I just got so mad that I decided to give the letters to Aggie Underwood."

Four days after the killing, Miss Underwood, with these letters, splashed Lana and Johnny's affair over the front pages of the world for a second performance. Interest in the case was so intense that even the *Washington Post* ran a banner headline:

IKE BIDS REDS JOIN IN A PACT

under which in only slightly smaller type, another banner head read:

LANA TURNER'S LOVE LETTERS REVEALED

The twelve letters were published for two days—April 8 and 9—and recounted the torrid romance. Some of the letters were actually photostated and reproduced in the newspapers in Lana's own handwriting.

Not since the Mary Astor diary of the 1930s was the public treated to such candid revelations of a star's love life. Ironically, the letters as published revealed Lana to be not the "wanton woman" she was being painted, but rather a naïve romantic.

In the letters she referred to herself as "Mommy," calling John "Daddy," "Papito," "Juanito." (Through the years she had often referred to herself as "Mama" and to the man or husband of the moment as "Daddy.")

The letters were sprinkled with affectionate phrases in Spanish and Italian, as well as English. Most were signed "Lanita" (using the affectionate Spanish diminutive meaning "Little Lana"). In the letters, she often cautioned him, "*Cuidado*" [Be careful].

But still, out of a dozen letters, the wildest phrase the newspapers could find to exploit was: "I'm your woman, and I need you, my man."

(*If* Where Love Has Gone *is based on the thirteen similar cases Robbins researched in juvenile court, then coincidences certainly aid his plot outlines. For the plot of his book included love letters in the possession of a mobster written to the gigolo Tony Riccio by both mother and daughter.*

Interestingly enough, Mickey Cohen told reporters that he had in his possession letters Cheryl had written to Stompanato. But he never produced these letters.)

However, a letter from Cheryl to Stompanato was subsequently discovered "nestled among the love letters from Lana to Stompanato" and printed first by the *Los Angeles Evening Herald Express* and later by Associated Press.

Mailed by Cheryl to Stompanato at Acapulco where he was vacationing with her mother, Cheryl's letter, misspellings included, read:

Dear Johnny:

First of all please excuse this paper but it's really all I have right now.

I just got your letter this morning because I was home for the weekend.

How have you been and how is mother?

Rowena [a mare Cheryl owned] is just fine. I'm not afraid of her anymore and she acts just the way she use to last summer. Yes I still want to take her to estes Park this summer. I thought for awhile I would't be able to handle her but I know now that I can.

School is just fine but not getting any easier.

I went to see Johnny Mathis at the Crescendo Sunday night he was terrific.

Have you been doing any waterskiing lately? Please do think of me. I love it.

When are you all coming back? soon I hope.

Mother and I really had a wonderful time in Europe. I can't remember when we've been that close.

My hair is way past my shoulders now and I have been wearing it in a french-roll in back with pixie bangs in front which are all the rage now.

Peter [a boy her age] and I had a big fight over another guy and he made me so mad by being so jelius that I broke up with him but I really regret it now. Oh well something has to happen.

I am writing this in study hall as I have finished my work. I thought I'd better write now before I forget and put it off. This writing is very mesy I know. But the bell is going to ring and I am in a hurry.

Guess what. I'm a member of the student council. Pretty good, huh!!!

Well the bell just rang so I've got to get now—I'll write again real soon I promise but now it's your turn.

Lova ya and miss ya loads.

CHERIE

P.S. Give my love to mother. Write soon and be good.

This letter, attributed to Cheryl, certainly indicated a happy relationship between Cheryl and her mother's lover.

Even Lana's letters to Stompanato were the kind that a 1958 high-school sophomore might have written to a college boyfriend. By today's standards, they are mild indeed. But in the spring of 1958, with the public supplying its own interpretation, the letters were sizzling material for locker room jokes and beauty parlor gossip.

> My dearest darling love . . . all I want to write and say is I love you! . . .
>
> Oh Pappy, Pappy . . . you've got to break this for us—I'm so stuck here, but I need you—now. I'm going to try and be calm and a good little girl and not torment each of us with my aching heart—at least try not to put too much of it on paper.

One letter, written to Stompanato after his forced exit from England, expressed Lana's tender concern for Cheryl:

> Christmas is finally over for Cherie and me. I must say it was wonderful and full of love and understanding . . . But even more important—and she said it—it was our being together that really made it —oh, so great.

Even though she was "terrified" after he attempted to strangle her, Lana still wrote:

> . . . So many previous things you told me, described to me, each beautiful and intimate detail of our love, our hopes, our dreams, our sex and longings. . . . My God, how you could write and when near me make most of those dreams come to life with the realness of you and me and us. . . .

Another letter, in late January, discussed the phonograph records which Stompanato had sent her:

> . . . darling . . . they bring back happy aches, if there is such a thing—only, I don't want to hurt and feel pain like this . . . I'll close now—the pills seem to be taking over! If only I could cuddle so very close to you—you know how it would be!

Lana's enemies said that the torrid love letters had been "plenty edited by the time they were published in the papers." Reportedly even veteran newspapermen were shocked by what was really written. Supposedly whole paragraphs had to be dropped in order for the "hot" letters to be printed in family newspapers.

This seems unlikely. If there were more passionate paragraphs they could have been included with blanks instead of unprintable words, or at the very least the newspapers could have alluded to paragraphs which had to be omitted.

Months later, Oxie Reichler, editor of a paper in Yonkers, New York, spoke before the New England Associated Press News Executives Association and used the publication of these letters as an example of the misuse of the press.

"Let's take a look at Lana Turner and the pack of letters that she wrote in such colorful language," said Reichler. "These were what is known in our shops as 'juicy.' Perhaps too juicy, I suspect, for family dinner table discussions. These letters offered a most fascinating example of how the press allows itself to be misused. Here were documents that made no contribution to the information of readers nor did they throw valuable light on a situation that already was shabby and ugly. What they did was to invade a personal and private area for the basic purpose of sensationalism." He told the editors that it was their shame that they played up to this particular aspect.

The Stompanato affair and the subsequent publication of the love letters (as innocuous as they were and despite Mr. Reichler's opinion that they did not contribute to the information of the readers) crystallized for the public Lana Turner's fabled search for sexual adventure.

Before that fatal Good Friday, the Lana Turner legend—born in a sweater, nurtured in femme-fatale roles and kept alive by her off-screen playgirl image—was still primarily a Hollywood story. But after the slaying of Johnny Stompanato, the Legend of Lana Turner, all myths shattered, gained a permanent (if to some, questionable) place in American folklore.

Stompanato was buried April 8 in his small hometown. An American flag was draped across the coffin, to mark his service in the marines.

Mickey Cohen, who footed the bill, helped Carmine select the coffin. Johnny was dressed in a tuxedo, embroidered white linen shirt, black tie and black pocket handkerchief initialed JRS. Cohen ordered everything, and said, "I want my friend to go as he used to dress in life—nothing but the best."

Although he hadn't achieved the fortune and fame he sought in life, Johnny Stompanato did not return to Woodstock an unknown.

The newspaper articles dragged on, especially in the tabloids. Each day, a new fact came to light—and each day a little more gossip was relayed, adding to the conflicting and contradicting tales of all parties concerned. The public speculated endlessly. Everyone had his own version of what "really" happened.

Police discovered that Johnny, who had introduced himself to Lana over the telephone, had a selection of phone numbers in his little black book. Although Johnny's black book was brown, it included the numbers of such celebrities as Zsa Zsa Gabor, Anita Ekberg, June Allyson, Mari Blanchard, Beverly Tyler, Pat Westmore and Arleen Whelan. Peggy Connolly, a singer, was also listed. Movie tough guy George Raft, screenwriter Sy Bartlett and bistro operator Mac Krim were among the men in the book.

However, the authorities were quick to state that there was no evidence proving that Stompanato knew or had contact with any of the people listed in the book.

Leading columnists devoted entire daily columns to the scandal —to Cheryl, to Lana's past love affairs and marriages. Even nonentertainment columnists and feature editors gave ample space to Lana Turner and the relationships between stars and their children as developed by the Hollywood social system. It was an ideal opportunity for the self-righteous to preach, and, of course, it made great copy and sold millions of magazines and newspapers.

From the beginning, Cohen and Stompanato's family were vehement about the black picture the police and press painted of Johnny. After all, they claimed, he *was* killed in cold blood. He was not an interloper or an unexpected burglar. He had been living with Lana Turner by invitation.

And from the beginning, it was true that, for the most part, the press was sympathetic toward Lana and Cheryl. However, *Time* magazine had branded Lana "a wanton woman," and many people were advocating that Cheryl be taken from her.

Paramount Pictures capitalized on the notoriety by rushing *Another Time, Another Place* for release even before the end of April, four months ahead of schedule.

Peyton Place was still drawing well at the box office. In many theatres, managers reported that Lana's entrance on screen was greeted by applause and shouts of, "We're with you, Lana!" Although *Time* said moviemen were confident that the Sweater Girl was "bigger box office than ever," many in the industry questioned whether her career would continue after these two films.

It was pointed out that Joan Bennett's movie career came to an abrupt halt in the early 1950s when a much less serious scandal erupted. Joan's husband, movie producer Walter Wanger, had attempted to kill her reputed lover with a revolver. The moral issue in that scandal was less explosive because it involved only adults. There was no question of unfit motherhood. And, of course, there was no actual murder.

It was true that Lana had usually played femme fatales, but the characters always possessed qualities to make the audience feel both empathy and sympathy. While this real-life crisis was consistent with the on-screen image she had projected for twenty years, the accusations of murder, illicit love and unfit motherhood could not be resolved in this case by a clever scriptwriter.

The notoriety and publicity Lana Turner received during the month of April, 1958, were staggering.

At the preliminary hearing on Monday the coroner's inquest was set for April 11, and a juvenile court hearing was set for April 25, to decide whether Cheryl Crane would be tried as an adult or a juvenile, if indeed she was indicted. Geisler and fellow attorney Arthur Crowley (Crowley, hired by Steve Crane, had been at one time the defense lawyer for *Confidential* magazine) made a petition for her release in the custody of her maternal grandmother. But at the pre-detention hearing April 7 it was ruled that in view of the tremendous notoriety of the case it would be better for Cheryl if she stayed in custody, far from outside influence and pressure.

But the pressures were just beginning.

Cheryl took the judge's decision without much show of emotion. When she was dismissed she threw her arms around her father's shoulders and walked with him to a side exit to the adjoining Juvenile Hall. Lana, in a tan polo coat, gold earrings and white gloves, was in tears. She followed them.

Naturally Lana had shied away from having her picture taken, and before the public was ordered from the courtroom for the closed juvenile session, Lana thanked the newsmen "for being so kind to me."

Later, immediately following the hearing, Crane held a press conference in Crowley's office. He answered a cryptic "No" when asked if he knew of Lana's long-time romance with Stompanato. He said he had no intention of seeking custody of Cheryl by having Lana declared an unfit mother. "Despite all this," he said, "I believe Lana is a loving, good mother."

By this time reporters had ferreted out Mrs. John Stompanato, Johnny's stepmother. According to her, Lana wasn't so averse to marriage with her stepson as she claimed. She also said that at one point Johnny and the actress planned to send Cheryl to public school in Stompanato's hometown.

203

"Last fall they wanted Cheryl to come to Woodstock and go to public school under an assumed name," Mrs. Stompanato said. "They wanted her to enter school here last September and stay a full year. They thought it would be good for her to be in a home and to be attending public school instead of private school."

The plans fell through, according to Mrs. Stompanato, because she refused to accept responsibility of caring for Cheryl. She concluded, "It's terrible the way my son's name is being slandered. I don't believe there is such a thing as justifiable homicide."

Mrs. Stompanato told reporters, "I destroyed most of the letters from Johnny. I didn't want anyone to see them. They were very damaging." When she was asked, "Damaging to whom?" she replied, "Lana Turner."

Before the inquest, it had been in the papers that the autopsy showed that Stompanato had an incurable ailment, which might have been fatal in just a few years anyway. Public sympathy was definitely with Cheryl.

On April 11, the day of the inquest, the curious started gathering at 6 a.m. Seats had been set aside in the courtroom for 40 people, and there were 120 seats for the press. All were filled.

Mildred arrived escorted by attorney Louis C. Blau, and Crane arrived with Crowley. Also on hand was Mickey Cohen. Cohen was asked to identify his slain friend.

"I refuse to identify him because I may be accused of his murder," he answered.

The hearing officer was astounded, but excused Cohen from further testimony. Later, Cohen told reporters that he refused to elaborate on the statement other than to say Beverly Hills Police Chief Anderson had led him to believe that he might be accused of the murder.

"He said that Johnny and Lana were going together to finance my operations. If he can say that, he can say anything and I'm not gonna testify about anything."

Cohen never explained what he meant by his "operations."

204

There had been rumors that Mickey had financed Stompanato's affair with Lana in the hope that Lana would eventually marry Johnny and pay him back, with interest.

The inquest opened at 9:00 a.m. Lana arrived on time, clinging to the arm of Jerry Geisler. She made her way through crowds of reporters. When a photographer asked her to remove her dark glasses, she said, "Will you wait just a minute, please?" She seemed to gather her strength, then took off her glasses, fighting back the tears.

Cheryl was not present at the hearing, but Lana had Mildred to give her moral support as well as to testify. Mrs. Turner appeared understandably weary. In thirty-eight years, she had been through a lot with her only child. And now she was on the witness stand.

Lana herself faced the ordeal in a severely tailored Italian gray-silk suit, her silver-blonde hair cropped short. Her posture was arrow-straight. Despite everything, she somehow remained elegant and majestic. She kept a white glove on her right hand but removed the glove from her left hand as she settled into the witness chair. She testified for a full sixty-two minutes, almost collapsing at times. Throughout the entire testimony she referred to Johnny as "Mr. Stompanato" and her voice trembled with emotion as she recounted the nightmare—sobbing, sagging, clutching her handkerchief.

The ten-man, two-woman coroner's jury brought in its verdict in twenty minutes: Justifiable Homicide. Newspaper headlines and columnists made melodramatic commentary such as: "Lana Turner, battling to save her teen-age daughter, played the most dramatic and effective role of her long screen career. The coroner's jury awarded her the Oscar."

After the verdict, District Attorney McKesson said: "After what I've heard today, and unless some new facts are uncovered, it would not be my inclination to prosecute her [meaning Cheryl] on criminal charges."

By the time the jury announced its verdict, Lana was already at home. When she heard the news, she sighed, "Thanks to God." When Crane was told, he wept and said: "No one will ever know how grateful I am."

The inquest had been recorded by ABC on a pool basis for radio broadcast by all the networks. CBS had filmed the inquest for TV on a pool basis. Unlike any previous scandal trial in history, the world was not only able to read Lana's testimony in newspapers, but also to see and hear her deliver it!

"Lana's desperation rang true," reported *Time*, "but even a Hollywood scenario might have missed the final touch that came when a man in the courtroom stood and shouted: 'This whole thing's a pack of lies. Johnny Stompanato was my friend! The daughter was in love with him and he was killed because of jealousy between mother and daughter!' "

Back in Woodstock, when he heard the justifiable homicide verdict, Carmine Stompanato said: "I can't imagine how they could reach a verdict like that." Carmine also stated that the inquest was "handled like they all had it figured out beforehand."

He also challenged Cheryl's statement that the final quarrel was precipitated when Lana discovered that Johnny was thirty-two instead of forty-two. Carmine claimed, "There wasn't a single person in Los Angeles or Hollywood, not even Mickey Cohen, who knew Johnny was thirty-two. I'm sure he never told his right age to Miss Turner. No one knew Johnny's age until I got to Hollywood the day after he was killed and told the police about it. That's just one of the things that has to be cleared up.

"I want to know if the police told someone about Johnny being thirty-two *after* he was killed. I'll bet everyone thought he was forty-two as Lana believed he was."

Carmine told reporters he had wired Los Angeles authorities asking that Lana and Cheryl be given lie detector tests. But the verdict was in. Despite the dozens of conflicting theories of what happened, despite the subsequent screaming headlines of stories differing, discrepancies found in stories of the principals, the verdict would stand.

After the verdict, the Stompanato family instituted a suit against Lana and Crane for $752,500. The petition was filed by one Jack Harris, who admitted he never knew Stompanato but had been asked by lawyer William Jerome Pollack to serve as guardian for Stompanato's son. The suit charged Lana and Steve with parental negligence and said that Lana "was negligent in that she falsely advised that Stompanato had threatened to disfigure or cripple her. Lana Turner," the suit charged, "otherwise incited Cheryl to inflict the wound."

An imaginative photo editor at *Life* ran a series of pictures of Lana on the real-life witness stand alongside of pictures of Lana on the witness stand in three of her movies: as the murderer of her husband in *The Postman Always Rings Twice*, as a witness in *Cass Timberlaine* and on the witness stand in *Peyton Place*. In that film, she had played a scene where she listened in horror as a young girl, her screen daughter's friend, recounted the brutal murder of her stepfather. Once again, scenes from Lana's real life and film life seemed interchangeable.

Despite all the snide innuendos concerning Lana's "performance" at the inquest, it is unfeeling, unthinkable, to believe that she was unaffected by this tragedy. Every mother in the world could surely identify with Lana's plight—a child, through little fault of its own, had committed an irrevocable deed, and the blame must surely fall on the failings of the parents.

Just as Lana had to some represented the gullible, trusting, believing, perhaps even stupid young woman who had been stepped upon, pushed around and used by men, now she represented the mother who had gone wrong. The mother who had given too much of the wrong kind of love. Too much sporadic affection. Too many gifts. Too much indulgence. But little guidance, little self-sacrifice. The Stompanatos' suit against Lana would drag on for years.

The Stompanato chapter of Lana's life would be re-examined in newspapers and magazines for a hundred months. Every mention of Cheryl would include a synopsis of the slaying.

After the inquest but before the hearing it was reported that the juvenile court officials were launching an investigation into the life and loves of Lana Turner and the impact they had on her daughter. The investigation was conducted by the Santa Monica division of the juvenile probation department. They had already expressed doubts over Cheryl's home life or lack of it. The department had ten days to complete the report.

During this period it was revealed that it was not only Lana and Cheryl who were suffering emotional stress. Steve Crane had collapsed, the victim of complete exhaustion, and his friends said they feared he was on the verge of a nervous breakdown.

The *Los Angeles Times,* the west coast's most respected newspaper, ran a scathing editorial calling Lana the juvenile delinquent in the case against her daughter. The *Times* said that it presumed Lana would recover from her ordeal, for "she has always found the way to heal yesterday's hurts with tomorrow's diversions.

"In the turnover of husbands and wives, lovers and mistresses," the *Times* said, "the Cheryls are the misplaced baggage, lost and found and lost again. In the Turner case," the *Times* concluded, "Cheryl isn't the juvenile delinquent. Lana is."

Police Chief Anderson said that Cheryl's case was handled no differently from any other but, since she was the daughter of a celebrity, she received worldwide publicity and was pilloried by some. He pointed out that a San Fernando youth who was seventeen had killed his mother's lover when the man resorted to violence, and in that case public opinion was on the youth's side. Anderson later opined that Cheryl had done no more and no less. In the over-all view, according to the police chief, Cheryl had more defenders than critics and his office received hundreds of letters sympathetic to her.

It was also Anderson's opinion that surprise and accident were

208

the main reasons the child had been able to kill so easily the tough ex-marine. She caught him off guard and the knife took a freak slant. Still, according to Anderson, it was a damaging blow to the ego of the underworld that one of their best bodyguards had been so easily disposed of.

In a confidential memo from a reporter to the home office of *Time* magazine, the researcher quoted Mickey Cohen as saying, "It's the strangest case I ever saw. The first time in history a murdered corpse has been found guilty of murder. That's just what they did at the inquest."

What had Stompanato's underground cronies hoped to find when they ransacked his apartment after his death? They may have been seeking a little wooden box which was later turned over to the Beverly Hills police department. According to the police chief, Stompanato had entrusted this very valuable property to an innocent individual. The box contained a revolver, bankbooks, some personal papers and some roll-film negatives. When the negatives were printed and enlarged, they revealed pictures of nude women in compromising positions. Some of the photographs had been taken while the ladies were unaware they were being photographed, but the women were recognizable. Chief Anderson later made public the fact that this picture collection verified information he already had, but he conceded that the police decided not to pursue their investigation since it would have been a cruel embarrassment to the women and would have served no legal purpose now that Stompanato was dead. However, Anderson noted that the photographs would have been a gold mine for a blackmailer.

Cheryl Crane and Lana Turner are the only two people still alive who know exactly what happened on that Good Friday eve. Cheryl has never told her story publicly. Her only court appearance took place at a closed juvenile hearing on April 24. The result was that she was made a ward of the court and placed in her grandmother's custody. It was assumed that Crane and Lana agreed on this course if the court agreed. Crane had made no secret that he wanted full custody of his daughter. At the time he said, "Frankly, I had hoped she would not be made a ward of the juvenile court." He added that he was happy, however, that she was released and in her grandmother's care.

"She has been in the custody of Lana's mother while Lana was out of the country and she was very happy with her grandmother," noted Crane.

Later in the year Crane appealed Judge Allen T. Lynch's ruling which made Cheryl a ward of the court. Apparently Crane was afraid that the judge might decide to place Cheryl in a foster home rather than leaving her with Mildred under the direct supervision of a probation officer. When Crane made this appeal in July, the transcript of the original hearing was made public.

"I am very much interested in [Cheryl's] future," the transcript quotes the judge as saying. "She's now got to be placed some place, in my opinion, where this, all this publicity, isn't going to be just heaped on her head every time she walks out the door.

"I have in mind that probably some school could be worked out where she could be placed under another name when she goes to school. What would you think about that, Cheryl?"

The girl said: "No."

"You don't want that?" asked Judge Lynch.

"No."

"You'd rather stay here?"

"Yes, definitely."

"And fight it out?"

"Yes."

"That's courage," the judge said.

Later in the hearing the judge told the fourteen-year-old girl: "Don't let all this attention that has been devoted to you and your mother and father during this period disturb your balance. Understand that that is nothing that is going to help you at all. You can't live on that sort of thing. Just try and forget all this bother and publicity. Do you think you can do that?"

"I'll try," she replied.

Lana said at the hearing: "A great part of me would like very much not to continue [working]. I wish I could say that I had enough put away so that I wouldn't have to work. I don't. I must continue working.

"The fact is that it's the only thing I know and that I have been the sole support of my daughter and my mother."

". . . what's past is past and I can't let it destroy me. . . ."

LANA TURNER, 1959

12

Lana had to go back to work. For emotional as well as financial reasons. But could she get a job? Of course she could easily work in a cheap exploitation vehicle—there was no doubt of that—but could she get a leading lady role in an "A" picture?

In that spring of 1958 Lana's worries were suddenly no longer confined to her career or to Cheryl. A couple of days after the hearing, police had to place several patrols around her house, her mother's house and the home of Jerry Geisler. Geisler had reported that death threats were made against Lana and against him. He said that he had received four anonymous phone calls with warnings such as, "We're going to get Geisler for getting Lana's daughter off. This is no kidding. Stompanato had a lot of friends. One of them is coming out from the east to get Geisler and Turner."

The attorney also disclosed that he had received an anonymous phone call from a sobbing woman who cautioned him on the death threats. He told police, "She was sympathetic and apparently just wanted to warn me that the gang was out to get me. She was crying. She begged us to pull the curtains down and keep the house dark."

Geisler conceded that all the calls might have come from cranks. Nevertheless, Beverly Hills police worked in special details watching the three residences.

As for *Another Time, Another Place*, the film proved to be a box-office disaster. Even with a big advertising campaign screaming LANA'S LATEST! THE STORY OF A WOMAN WHO LOVED WITH HER WHOLE BEING! to capitalize on the scandal, the film bombed, leading insiders to the conclusion that Lana's big-time box-office days were over. *Peyton Place* was a hit, but they reasoned it was because of the success of the controversial, sex-filled book and not Lana's drawing power.

While Lana pondered her future, publicity continued. There was still speculation that Crane wanted custody of Cheryl, and in May Geisler announced that Crane would be "surprised" if he engaged in a custody fight over Cheryl because "after all, she's been with her mother all these years."

It was also disclosed that Crane had been dropped as codefendant in the civil suit that the Stompanatos had brought against him and Lana.

Louella Parsons, far less influential now but still syndicated on the Hearst circuit and writing for the fan magazines, came to Lana's aid. She printed pro-and-con letters from her readers. Naturally, most were from women. One said, "Cheryl Crane is the innocent indictment of every broken marriage in the world." Another noted, "There's hardly a woman alive who at one time or another hasn't loved an unworthy man. Only Lana got caught."

Walter Winchell ran entire columns in Lana's defense. His influence had waned too, but he was still widely read. According to him, all the recently published love letters were in his possession and in a safety deposit box awaiting word as to whether Lana

213

wanted them back or burned. The columnist also said that Stompanato had had Lana's passport in his possession. "Authorities assume
he held it to keep his meal ticket from leaving the country without
him," Winchell stated.

Winchell printed a letter, supposedly from Gloria Swanson, de-
nouncing him for his defense of Lana. He quoted the letter as
saying: "Lana Turner has made every mistake in the books with
every advantage possible. After the first surging smash of mob sympathy, she will be nothing." But a few days later he printed another
letter from Miss Swanson denying she wrote the initial letter and
calling it "a forgery." It seems incredible that Winchell would have
printed the first letter without authenticating it.

But despite all the adverse publicity there was still hope for
Lana's career. At the Screen Producers Guild dinner, a primary
question was: "Would you hire Lana Turner?"

"I wouldn't hesitate to cast her in a picture if I had the right
property," said Buddy Adler, then head of production at 20th Century-Fox.

"Certainly I would cast Lana if I had the right part for her,"
stated David O. Selznick, who had turned her down for a contract
thirty years earlier. "Church authorities have said they would not
censure performers because of their private lives," he noted.

"I not only would cast her," remarked Jerry Wald, producer of
Peyton Place, "but I am actively seeking her for *The Sound and
the Fury*." He added, "We had a spot check around the country
about the audience reaction to Lana in *Peyton Place* and it has
been warm and sympathetic."

Producer Byron Foy prophesied, "Lana will be bigger than ever.
The tide of public opinion is going in her direction."

Everyone seemed willing to hire her, but she was still unemployed. Even needing the money, she had no intention of playing
the fading belle in *The Sound and the Fury*.

"Lana was really scared," some friends of that era recall. "She
didn't think the public would accept her."

Her career seemed over. Looking back on the Stompanato crisis, Lana once said that it made her realize how alone people actually are. "They say that no one is an island unto himself, and that's true," she commented. "But there are moments when we are completely alone even if other people are around us. That's when we have to find the deeper something we all have within us, if we are to continue living."

After the court inquest and hearing, Lana went into seclusion. The police twice received reports that she had committed suicide, and Lana later stated, "I wouldn't go anyplace. I dreaded meeting people. Not that I was afraid . . . but maybe a feeling of shame was mixed in with it."

It appeared that her luck finally had run out. Amazingly, it hadn't.

Producer Ross Hunter offered Lana the opportunity to return to work during the summer of 1958. Hunter wanted her for a film at Universal—a "woman's picture" with a starring role perfectly suited to Lana's talents and image.

Hunter, a former schoolteacher-turned-actor-turned-producer, had the Midas touch when it came to producing expensive-looking but low-budget "women's pictures" which returned huge profits. Up to that point his biggest success had been a re-make of *Magnificent Obsession*.

Hunter wanted to re-make another old Universal hit, *Imitation of Life*. Lana was perfect for the lead. The role in the updated version was that of an ambitious stage actress who sacrifices the man she loves and the bringing up of her daughter for her career. The theme—that of the conflict between a daughter and her actress mother—had a striking parallel with the Lana-Cheryl story.

There was even a scene in the film between the actress and her daughter when the daughter, who has fallen in love with the same man as her mother, accuses her mother of being selfish and neglectful.

215

The subplot was controversial as well, about the actress's Black companion-friend who has a daughter trying to pass for white.

Hunter's instinct told him the public would accept Lana in a role that required a great deal of sympathy. "It was a brave move on his part, since no one in Hollywood wanted to employ her at that point," confirm those who were on the scene. It was also a financially shrewd move, since he convinced Lana to take a percentage of the profits in lieu of a large salary. The risk would be minimal because the picture would be budgeted at a modest $1.2 million. There would be guaranteed tremendous publicity coverage for the film during shooting. If the picture flopped, Lana would have worked for practically nothing.

Producer Hunter went to see Lana personally, acting out the *Imitation* script and persuading her to take the role. Although she would play a mother, Hunter was offering her a glamourous role, complete with movie star wardrobe, dazzling jewels and winning the leading man by the final fadeout. The script contained certain other elements hitting close to Lana's private life, such as the use of various men to attain her career goals (implied subtly, 1958-style) and leaving the raising of her daughter to other women. But this did not deter Lana from accepting the part.

Later, proving she had no illusions about "a great comeback," Lana said she agreed to make the film because, "I was in debt and needed money. And besides, I had to do something to keep my sanity."

A clever public-relations decision was to have the set open to the press at almost all times. "Lana needed all the friends she could get," remembers a studio PR man. "I had worked with her before, and she was always a lot of fun and cooperative. But this time she was really concerned with what interviewers would write, so she was doubly cooperative."

Lana had been living on movie lots for over twenty years. She had been dealing with the press for just as long. The cast and crew of *Imitation* were trying to make her return as warm and uncomplicated as possible. Hundreds of well-wishers had sent flowers, and Hunter arranged for a trailer outside her dressing room to hold the overflow.

Despite her years of experience, Lana has remembered that the thought of the first day's shooting sent her into a panic. "I was terrified," she said. "I knew there was no going back—I couldn't run away. And I wanted to get it over with, even meeting the press. Usually a set is closed on the first days of shooting so the company can get to know one another. But we decided to throw ours wide open. It would be rough, but it seemed the best way to do it."

During that first day of shooting a number of reporters visited, and Lana met with them all individually. Most seemed kind and avoided the obvious questions on her recent ordeals. "But then," Lana has remembered, "one woman asked a few. I felt as though I'd been kicked in the stomach. But I smiled at her and said, 'I don't believe we'll discuss that, thank you.' Right afterward she said goodbye and walked out. In a way I was grateful for the experience. I knew I could stand up.

"You know those wonderful toys for kids," Lana then said laughingly, "—the kind that bounce back whenever you knock them down? I've felt like that so often!"

Bounce back she did. Under Hunter's careful eye the film was brought in on time and even under budget. The performances were excellent and the production was beautifully mounted. As predicted the picture received more in-production publicity than any other film that year, and the industry waited to see how the public would react.

Lana was living quietly. Cheryl was living with Mildred and, after having private tutors for a while, she was enrolled in Beverly Hills High School in September, 1958. Outwardly, things at home seemed fine.

Rumors were rampant throughout Hollywood and New York that "the Mob" was out to avenge Stompanato's death and Lana was petrified of leaving the house. This seems an exaggeration,

217

since access to the set of Universal was relatively easy and Stompanato had been, at most, a small-time operator who surely wouldn't necessitate big-time reprisals.

"Lana at this point was concerned with respectability," recalls a friend. "That Night Club Queen-Playgirl reputation of hers had to be supplanted by a new image of quiet respectability and dedication to her family and career."

Lana, Mildred and Cheryl spent a lot of time together. They saw each other almost every day, and Cheryl and Mildred were frequent visitors on the set of *Imitation of Life*. About this time, Lana said of her mother, "My mother and I have been close friends for a long time. In the early years, though, it was strained. I knew she loved me, and she was a warm and giving mother, but I never felt close to her. And yet today I find it easy to talk to her, and to shift roles too. She seems to know instinctively when I want her to talk as my mother and when I want to talk with her as a friend."

The previous Christmas Cheryl had spent with her mother in London. This Christmas she spent with her father and his fianceé, Helen DeMaree, who was in her middle twenties. Crane eventually married Helen and subsequently divorced her and married another woman much younger than he. Although Lana has gotten the brunt of adverse publicity about being Cheryl's much-married parent, Crane too has been to the altar a number of times.

Concerning Cheryl, Lana said in 1959 that she and Crane were cognizant of the fact that they had to develop the girl's sense of monetary values. They had compromised and decided that Cheryl would receive a $10-a-week allowance, half of which she had to save. However, Lana was still Lana, intrinsically extravagant and free spending, and Cheryl had always been financially indulged. All of her life Cheryl had faced the not-uncommon problems of her parents living by their set of rules but wanting her to live differently.

It must have been particularly difficult for Cheryl, especially liv-

218

ing in fantasy-turned-nightmare land. She was her mother's escort to the Hollywood premiere of *Imitation of Life*. The throngs outside the theatre applauded wildly when the Turner women appeared. Lana's fears had apparently been overly pessimistic. The public still loved her—perhaps now more than ever. To them, Lana was still "a nice girl, you can tell she's a nice person" who had gotten caught up in events beyond her control.

Lana was very candid during this period. She admitted then, "There was a time when tangible things were very important to make me happy. I enjoyed my big home and my furniture, my jewels and my paintings and Tiffany silver. But my possessions finally possessed me."

She had divested herself of many of them and placed her jewels in a vault to cut insurance costs. "I have a sense of freedom today, and it's priceless." Lana confessed that putting her jewels in the vault had been difficult for her. She said at the time, "It seems so childish, but I wanted the jewels at home because sometimes I liked to go in and just look at them, or pick up a few and try them on. When I finally decided on my own to place everything in the vault downtown I knew it was a victory for my will power. But for a long while afterwards I was miserable. Many times I'd go into my room and open one drawer after another, as though I were frantically searching for the jewels."

Though her personal life may have temporarily assumed ascetic overtones, on screen her fans found Lana bedecked in Jean Louis gowns and David Webb jewels and "suffering" in the lush surroundings that had always been associated with Lana Turner.

Imitation of Life, which was directed by Douglas Sirk, was a huge commercial success, despite poor critical response. It was, in fact, the biggest-grossing movie Lana had—and has—ever made and is the film most closely associated with her. Most importantly, her percentage of the profits not only lifted her from debt but gave her the financial security which she still enjoys today. While her deal guaranteed her only $2,500 weekly during production, it also guaranteed her 50 percent of the film's net profits. Her share came to over $1 million.

Lana Turner *was* bigger box office than ever. Otto Preminger announced her as the lead opposite James Stewart and Ben Gazarra in *Anatomy of a Murder.* That Lana would agree to star in a film with that title only a year after the Stompanato affair caused some surprise. It illustrated to some that she was an astute businesswoman (the hit book would undoubtedly be a hit movie). It illustrated to others that Lana was superhumanly capable of blotting out the past.

"I find that my reactions to life are very much different from what they were a year ago," she said. "I wish I could have learned these things another way, but what's past is past and I can't let it destroy me. . . ."

In *Anatomy of a Murder,* the wife of the army officer was an older woman. But Lana knew a good script when she saw one and overlooked this. She had respected Preminger since the 1946 days when he wanted her for *Forever Amber.*

However, a few weeks later Lana and Otto had a run-in. Headlines screamed LANA WALKS OUT ON "MURDER" (the headline writers, like movie advertising copywriters, were not averse to using Lana's recent past for eye-catching purposes). She "walked out" of the picture because of what she termed "complete disagreement" with Preminger, saying they couldn't see eye to eye on most phases of the picture.

Preminger said the argument (described as "heated") was over what costumes she should wear in the picture, but Lana countered that Preminger's temper, famed in the movie industry, was the cause.

"We had a conflict because I selected a pair of slacks and she didn't want to wear them," said Preminger. "She wanted to have her costumes designed by Jean Louis. I felt that the wife of a second lieutenant couldn't afford Jean Louis."

"Mr. Preminger is a very difficult and unreasonable man," countered Lana. "I would not walk out of a picture for anything as trivial as a costume.

"It was simply impossible to deal with Mr. Preminger's unpredictable temper," she said. "We just weren't suited to work well together. I can't work on a set where people go glaring about at you, making some people feel they're not quite as good as other people. But it's a terrific script and should be a fine movie."

Preminger told Sheilah Graham that Lana had been an hour and a half late for wardrobe fittings and then said she wouldn't wear the costume. "I explained that I treat extras and stars, everyone, the same."

Obviously, this was the bone of contention. Lana was used to receiving the Ross Hunter-Jerry Wald star treatment. Some insiders characterized Lana as "spoiled." Preminger said Lana had told Wald a week before starting *Peyton Place* that she wouldn't go on location. "Jerry said, 'All right. We'll send a double instead.' *I* would never have allowed that," declared Otto.

Preminger told Lana's agent she could drop out of the picture. "He thought I was bluffing, but I wasn't."

At the time, Preminger told newspapers, "I'll get an unknown and make her a new Lana Turner." But he signed Lee Remick (not yet a star but hardly an unknown) and changed the character from an older woman to a younger woman. The picture was both a critical and box-office hit and Lana's career would have been enhanced had she done it.

Instead of going to Ishpeming, Michigan, to film *Anatomy of a Murder*, Lana agreed to tour with Ross Hunter to promote *Imitation of Life*, which was becoming one of the biggest hits in Universal's history. Publicity man Frank Little, then with MacFadden, Strauss, Eddy and Irwin Public Relations Agency (Lana's PR agency then and now), traveled with Hunter and Lana.

Little remembers his first meeting with Lana, when he went up to her hotel suite in Chicago to introduce himself. "I knocked on the door," says Little. "She opened it and I said, 'Hi, my name is Frank Little.' She gave me the once-over, letting her gaze linger on my crotch. She smiled and said, 'Is it?' We became fast friends."

According to Little, the tour was far from dull. In every hotel, threatening notes awaited Lana. Obviously her reported fears of retaliation for Stompanato's death were not totally unfounded.

Whether these were crank letters or not, they had their effect. Little remembers two incidents. "Lana had dressed for the evening and was meeting me in the lobby of the Sheraton-Cadillac in Detroit. As always she was dressed to the teeth and carried herself majestically.

"Suddenly, there was a loud explosion outside the hotel, and in the blink of an eye Lana had disappeared. It took me several seconds to realize that she had dived behind one of the elaborate Regency couches in the lobby. But she picked herself up and we continued on with the same majesty.

"In Chicago," recalls Little, "we were all a bit tense. Lana, a producer and I were driving in a limousine to keep a publicity appointment, when a truck behind us backfired. An instant later the three of us found ourselves on the floor of the limo, like in a Hitchcock movie. The producer hissed to Lana, 'I'm not getting my ass shot off for you, honey!'

"Later, when we thought about it, it was actually quite a funny scene."

Little also remembers when Lana was the guest of honor at an Easter egg hunt for the benefit of crippled children, as part of the publicity schedule for one of *Imitation*'s local openings. She arrived hours late, and, while signing eggs, her eyes darted about searching for potential snipers. Almost from the moment she arrived she kept whispering to Little, "When can we leave? When can we get out of here?"

Whatever fears she may have had, she completed an extensive and remarkably successful tour for the picture. She was back on top. She appeared on the cover of the color-roto section of the Sun-

222

day New York *Daily News*. The paper stated what everyone in the world already knew: "For sheer drama, a script of Lana Turner's real life would outdo many of the story lines of movies she had played in."

It was announced that Lana would star for Allied Artists in a multimillion-dollar production of *The Streets of Montmartre*, in which she'd portray free-spirited Suzanne Valadon, mother of painter Maurice Utrillo. Louis Jourdan was supposed to co-star as her love interest, and *Imitation of Life* director Douglas Sirk was signed to direct. Illness caused Sirk to withdraw, and the entire project was abandoned.

But at Universal, the thinking was: If one soap-opera film starring Lana Turner could achieve such success, why not another? Lana and Hunter reteamed [for Universal] to film *Portrait in Black*, a script that had been around for over twenty years. In the forties it had been announced as a vehicle for Joan Crawford.

Although the script was rusty, Hunter gave the project polish with a lavish production and an all-star cast, including Lana, Anthony Quinn, Sandra Dee, John Saxon, Lloyd Nolan, Anna May Wong and Richard Basehart.

Universal mounted a mammoth publicity-promotion campaign and *Portrait* was another success, despite horrendous reviews. In July, 1960, Lana was again the cover girl of the Sunday *News* color roto magazine. The copy was almost exactly the same as the previous year, only this time it pointed out that "Lana Turner is in the midst of the highly successful second phase of her movie career."

At the time, to squelch a lot of speculation concerning Cheryl's future, Lana stated: "The public has the wrong impression. I have complete and legal custody of my daughter. I see her a great deal. The only thing is my mother has physical custody."

While Lana's professional life was flowing nicely, her personal life was in for a few new shocks.

Cheryl was dating a drive-in waiter, Martin Gunn, whose age was variously reported as nineteen, twenty, twenty-one and twenty-two. Cheryl was now sixteen, attending Beverly Hills High School and living with her grandmother. Friends said that Cheryl was in the habit of going to bed at the same time as Mildred. But, they added, Cheryl, who was still at this time a ward of the court, did not stay in bed. She sneaked out to her car and headed for the Wilshire Boulevard drive-in where Gunn worked. Her probation officer finally discovered this arrangement and reported it to Lana, Crane and the court.

Soon after, Judge Allen T. Lynch, who had made Cheryl a ward of the court after the Stompanato slaying, signed a committing order to have Cheryl put into El Retiro, a county school for problem girls. Lynch said he issued the order at the recommendation of the county probation officer.

El Retiro, a school in the San Fernando Valley, housed forty girls and was regarded as a home for delinquent girls, according to juvenile authorities. Authorities at the time said the school had no bars on the windows, offered a regular high school program, an athletic program and counseling.

Questioned by the press, Lana described El Retiro as an institution for "helping girls who need that extra bit of help. It was agreed by the authorities, her father and myself that this school is what Cheryl needs at the present time. How long Cheryl remains there is up to her as an individual."

Lana vehemently denied reports that the reason she and Crane had the girl committed was to stop her from eloping with Gunn. "There is absolutely no truth that she intends to get married," Lana said at the time, "not one word of truth. She did date a carhop, but she also dated many others. There was never any talk of marriage. He was just one of Cheryl's dates. He is a nice boy."

Newspapers reported that Cheryl had been sent to El Retiro for "psychiatric therapy." Obviously sophisticated for her age, the girl had developed into a tall, slender brunette. She was striking and attractive but, like her grandmother Mildred, her looks were not in the same league with Lana's.

Reporters, of course, ferreted out Gunn. "I'm not in any position to marry anyone," he told them. Obviously a bright boy, he refused to discuss his family or other background. He said the court decision to send Cheryl to El Retiro was a complete surprise to him, but added, "I'm not saying anything about it. I've been told not to."

Although Cheryl had been committed on March 11, the public didn't find out about it until five days later when the news of Cheryl's commitment leaked out. One correspondent said, "It is no compliment for a girl to be sent there, but gallantly Lana Turner made it sound almost that way."

According to some members of the press, every employee at El Retiro had been threatened with dismissal if one word concerning Cheryl's commitment leaked to the press.

"We felt that perhaps this, at last," Lana said at the time, "is a place where Cheryl can get away from it all—away from Hollywood, away from the publicity. It's a place we hope where Cheryl can be just that—just Cheryl. A place where she can find herself."

Cheryl did not find herself at El Retiro—not at first—although life at El Retiro was not really harsh. For girls from poor Mexican or Black backgrounds, it might even have seemed luxurious. There were only two girls per room, the girls didn't have to wear uniforms, and they had to do only a small amount of housework. There was a swimming pool and each girl had a regular session with the school psychiatrist. But for Cheryl it was a far cry from the life of luxury that she was accustomed to.

She was placed in the institution on March 11, but on April 29, with two other girls, she escaped. Headlines blared out: LANA TURNER'S DAUGHTER ESCAPEE FROM HOME FOR WAYWARD GIRLS.

Lana was in Palm Springs. She wept and said, "This is a terrible surprise. The reports on her from the school have been good."

Cheryl, along with two other girls—Donna Wilson, fifteen, and Cheryl Zumbrum, sixteen—fled the school by scaling the twelve-foot fence surrounding it, according to United Press International.

Immediately police were dispatched to watch the home of the carhop, Marty Gunn. Speculation that he was planning to meet Cheryl or at least trying to avoid reporters was spurred when Gunn didn't show up for work that night. A fellow employee said, "Marty phoned and said he was suddenly called out of town."

Several days went by, and the public eagerly followed the plight of Lana and her disturbed daughter. LANA NEAR COLLAPSE; NO CLUE TO CHERYL, they were informed. Lana was put through an emotional wringer when her daughter was reported found in Las Vegas and in police custody. But it was later discovered that the girl in question had hoaxed the police in Vegas. She was not Cheryl Crane.

On May 1, the girls narrowly escaped capture in Long Beach. The incident seemed like melodrama straight from a "B" movie. The police had gotten a tip that a Long Beach teen-age girl, a former inmate at the school, had heard from the three girls. They were watching the house where Cheryl and her two companions were supposed to rendezvous with the friend. Donna Wilson had telephoned this friend and said that she and the others would be "down tonight after dark." When the police learned this, they went to the house and waited. Donna telephoned again, and the police overheard her ask, "We're on the Pacific Coast Highway. How do we get to your place?" Her young friend described the route but, before the cops could stop her, she screamed out: "Don't show up or there'll be trouble."

Donna and the two Cheryls obviously heeded the warning, took off and avoided the police dragnet.

Crane said, "I understand that Lana's taking this very hard. She's in seclusion, won't see anyone and has been crying almost constantly, since she found out that the kid they have in Las Vegas really isn't Cheryl.

226

"I talked with her [Lana] and she's just wild. She cries and cries and says, 'Why doesn't our baby come home?'" Crane added, "God, I don't know why. I wish I did."

Distraught, Crane appealed to Cheryl through a letter in one of the Los Angeles newspapers. The letter in part said, "Dear Cheri: You have all of us who love you so much frantic with worry. I am sure you don't realize, Cheri, the danger of being out on your own —almost penniless, as you must be.

"Please call me. I haven't left the telephone since you ran away. Please call me, no matter where you are, and I will come and get you immediately." The letter was signed, "Daddy."

On May 2nd, Cheryl phoned her father and asked him to come for her and her two companions. Crane said, "They were scared, tired and hungry. They seemed like three kids who'd had it. You can't run away forever." Crane picked the girls up at a supermarket in Santa Monica and took them to his office, where they were met by a probation officer.

The girls were wearing the same Capri pants and sandals they had on when escaping El Retiro. They refused to reveal where they'd been, but said they'd spent the weekend with friends at a nearby house party.

"I've had nothing to eat but beans," Cheryl told her dad. "I'm so sick of beans I hope I never see another."

Headlines told the public: CHERYL GIVES UP. CALLS DAD AND SAYS, "I'M TIRED OF BEANS."

Lana was still in Palm Springs. Still weeping, she managed to murmur, "Thank God they're safe."

The three young girls were taken to the Los Angeles County Juvenile Hall for the night and then returned to El Retiro. Not for long, however.

About five weeks later, on June 3, Cheryl fled again. She and two other girls who were never specifically identified ran away. "We had no idea of running away," Cheryl said later. "It was just a spur-of-the-moment idea."

Evidence indicated the contrary. A reliable source told police and the press that a possible new escape attempt by Cheryl was discussed at a staff meeting of El Retiro officials a week prior to the second escape because of Cheryl's apparent "antagonism toward one of her parents." School officials had no comment on such a meeting, but most people felt they knew which parent was the object of Cheryl's "antagonism."

Cheryl and the others were found by police the morning after their escape, asleep in a Los Angeles city park rest room.

Up to this point Lana had, of course, received the brunt of all the adverse publicity concerning Cheryl's problems. But this time Cheryl's "image"—as well as Lana's—suffered a severe blow. Discussing Cheryl, Beverly Hills Police Chief Anderson told reporters, "This was a big change from the meek and mild little girl who came here on a homicide rap. She's very defiant, antisocial and nonconformist. It looks like *she* led the others out."

As Cheryl was being led out of the police station on her way to Juvenile Hall, news photographers crowded around her and Cheryl, according to reporters, shouted: "Get those ———— cameras out of here!" This was the first bad press Cheryl had received.

An unhappy Lana commented briefly on her daughter's latest escape: "I don't know what happened," she said wearily, "but I want Cheryl back where she belongs. I saw Cheryl two weeks ago and the girl seemed happy with her surroundings."

Cheryl remained at El Retiro and out of the public eye for the rest of the year.

Meanwhile, a new man had entered Lana's life. She was now dating sportsman-rancher Fred May. Handsome, square-jawed and soft-spoken, May was owner of the Circle MA, a fourteen-acre working ranch for thoroughbred horses. He was also part owner of the race horse, Solicitor.

May had been quietly dating Lana for months and had escorted her to the Bal Montmartre gala at which she had been guest of honor, after she had signed for *Streets of Montmartre*.

228

While Cheryl remained at El Retiro, the glamorous life for Lana went on. But it now seemed virtually impossible for her to avoid some kind of unfavorable headlines.

She attended the Hollywood premiere of *Portrait in Black* on June 29 with Fred May. She looked lovely and younger than her forty years. The event attracted many stars, and there was a lavish party afterward at Romanoff's. Among the guests were Robert Taylor, Loretta Young, Zsa Zsa Gabor, Robert Sterling and Anne Jeffreys, Jane Powell, Ricardo Montalban.

Also present were Hollywood's two leading trade-paper gossip columnists, the late Mike Connolly of *The Hollywood Reporter* and Army Archerd of *Daily Variety*. The premiere party would make headlines, but unhappily for Lana, not because of the film.

Connolly had written a column in which he criticized Lana's upbringing of Cheryl. When the columnist appeared at the party, Fred May grabbed him by his tuxedo, almost tearing the coat from his back. "I love this girl and the things you're writing about her personal life are unfair," said May, swinging at Connolly. Army Archerd stepped in to separate the two. Lana burst into tears as May and Connolly then exchanged verbal insults.

A number of the guests hastily departed.

"I don't know what it's all about," Lana cried. "I just don't want any trouble." She wiped the tears away with a handy napkin and sobbed to May, "Why did you do it?"

"Because I love you and I won't have anyone attacking your personal life," he answered.

Later May explained, "A man in love cannot stand by when his girl is insulted. Lana is a wonderful girl. She should not be persecuted by the press. It's all right to criticize her professional ability, but not her private life."

Despite May's opinion, it was her private life that was keeping Lana's name before the public.

The scathing editorials had petered out. Some writers now described Lana as a warm-hearted woman, a fond, impulsive mother

—and Cheryl as a sweet girl, not a brat. But they conceded that Lana was a very busy woman. They quoted her as saying, "Unfortunately, sometimes when Cheryl wanted me I wasn't there. You can't be in two places at once." And they noted that, to Lana, "her logic seems irrefutable."

Lana signed to star in *By Love Possessed* for United Artists. In the cast were Susan Kohner (Lana's agent's daughter, who had scored a big hit in *Imitation of Life*), George Hamilton, Efrem Zimbalist, Jr., and Jason Robards. It was Lana's second unsympathetic role in a row. In *Portrait* she had played a murderess, and now she was portraying a woman who was an alcoholic and an adulteress (albeit her character did have sympathetic reasons for her failings).

The script wasn't terribly good, but the property had been a bestselling novel, and Lana received $300,000 plus a percentage of the gross to do the film.

Toward the end of the summer Lana and Fred May took out a marriage license in Santa Ana as they were on their way to the Del Mar racetrack. May, forty-three, was described as a sportsman, a breeder of thoroughbreds, a rancher, a millionaire. Married once before and the father of two children, he had retired from the business world at thirty-eight.

Lana told friends, "He's a wonderful man and I only wish I had met him years ago. His advice to me is always good. He knows just what is best for me."

The license expiration date was November 28. On November 27, Lana Turner married for the fifth time. The surprise quiet ceremony took place at the Miramar Hotel in Santa Monica. Lana wore a light beige dress and carried a bouquet of yellow roses. It had been arranged for Cheryl to attend the wedding, along with Mildred, and Lana's secretary, Loorie Sherwood. Virginia Grey was Lana's matron of honor, and George Mann was May's best man.

Lana turned to May and told him: "I know it's going to be a very happy marriage." She had told friends, "I've always been physically attracted by a man's outward handsomeness, but with Fred I've learned to look past that to his mind, heart and stability."

Lana's friends were happy with her choice of May. Perhaps she had *finally* chosen well! May was handsome, cultured and seemed truly in love with *Lana*, not the glamour and success of an image named Lana Turner. He wasn't using her. His interests were far from the movie colony.

The wedding was a surprise (even though the couple had taken out the license months before) because one of Lana's representatives had previously announced a wedding postponement until she completed *By Love Possessed.*

Because the license was about to expire, May had proposed a quick wedding. After the ceremony, which was performed by the pastor of the Santa Monica First Methodist Church, the bridal couple drove Cheryl back to El Retiro, then continued up the coast where they spent a week's honeymoon with friends near Carmel.

Lana had achieved financial security on her own. At last it appeared that with May she had emotional security. She certainly now had the opportunity to work hard for emotional security.

There had been comment when May and Lana took out their marriage license that Lana was seeking a suitable marriage and future home to hasten Cheryl's release from El Retiro. But a close friend of Lana's at the time said, "Now I don't want you to think for one minute that Lana's getting married just so she can set up a home and get Cheryl out of that place. Lana and Fred are really very much in love. She can get Cheryl out of El Retiro any time. She could bring Cheryl back tomorrow if she wanted to—Cheryl's not confined there. As far as that's concerned, Cheryl's in that school because she needs it.

"Of course Lana wants to get Cheryl back from the court, but that's another thing. She's talked about several plans, but I really don't think she's going to do anything about it until the first of next year."

Lana and her new husband seemingly settled down to a happy family situation after she completed *By Love Possessed*. But her career was still important to her.

Variety carried a story that her Lanturn Productions was near to closing a deal with Frank Sinatra's Essex Productions for co-production tie-ups. The films would be released through United Artists, and were guaranteed a top male and top female star—Frank Sinatra and Lana Turner. Sinatra and Lana had never starred together on-screen and the industry found this item promising. But talks quickly died and nothing materialized.

In January, 1961, Lana and May managed to have Cheryl released from El Retiro and move in with them at the ranch in Chino. She was still a ward of the court, however.

It appeared that Lana was beginning life anew—as a housewife and a mother. "Fred and I lead a very quiet life at home," she said. "In the evenings we stay at home together. It's a life that agrees with me. It's as if I were beginning all over again. I won't be making any more films for a while," she said. "I'll be taking care of my husband and Cheryl."

Some felt there was a tinge of familiarity to her remarks. It was the kind of thing she had said when married to Topping.

Lana began talking of retiring or at least cutting down her work schedule. "She meant it when she said it," says a friend, "but Lana could no more stop working than a politician can stop talking. Working in movies is an integral part of her existence."

Lana said *By Love Possessed* would be her last film as "an employee" and she would "from now on" concentrate on her own production company. However, her next deal would bring her back as an employee to alma mater MGM, in a comedy opposite Bob Hope, *Bachelor in Paradise*. Hope had always wanted to work with Lana, and a comedy would be a welcome change of pace for her.

Although she was changing from drama to comedy on screen, the drama in her private life continued. On May 20, Lana settled out of court for about $20,000 in the $752,000 suit brought against her on behalf of Stompanato's son, who was by this time thirteen.

Some newspapers angled their coverage for sensational copy. "Staged at a cost of $20,000, the final action in 'The Killing Of Johnny Stompanato' will take place in a courtroom setting. . . . A short, undramatic scene will end—legally, at least—one of the most lurid scandals in Hollywood history," wrote Martha Martin in the New York *Daily News.* "But, in the real world that exists beyond the boundaries of this land of make-believe," continued Miss Martin, "a question mark still hovers over the story of how Johnny Stompanato, a small-time hoodlum and gigolo, was killed in the pink boudoir of Lana Turner."

Headlines shouted, "SUIT ASKS: DID CHERYL OR LANA PLUNGE KNIFE? . . . The suit charged that 'doubt' still existed over whether it was Lana or Cheryl who wielded the 8-inch butcher knife with which Stompanato was 'wilfully and intentionally stabbed in the stomach.' "

Newspapers said that, if the suit had gone to trial, facts about the "doubt" would have been bared. But the $20,000 settlement meant there would be no disclosure of any new facts in the case.

The Stompanato family lawyer, William Pollack, had interviewed Cheryl in 1958 and announced then that "certain discrepancies" had occurred between her story and Lana's.

Among other things, Pollack claimed that Stompanato was stabbed in bed and not standing up because, if he were standing up and were stabbed in the abdomen, he would have doubled up and fallen forward—and he supposedly fell backward.

Lana's lawyer, Louis C. Blau, said his client felt she could win if the case went to trial but she considered her daughter's welfare and privacy worth more than the settlement.

Attorney Melvyn Belli, now representing the Stompanatos, told the press he was turning down the offer of the settlement because of these statements attributed to Blau that Lana could win the case in court but was making the $20,000 offer to avoid publicity. However, the suit was eventually settled for that amount.

Cheryl bleached her hair a bright blonde for a while in 1961. "A phase all girls go through," sighed Lana, who had certainly had her own share of hair-color changes at Cheryl's age. Then Cheryl dyed her hair flaming red. The girl was now enrolled in Santa Monica High School.

News of the impending settlement of the Stompanato suit fostered another rash of articles about the slaying. To complicate matters, a few weeks later on June 11, Cheryl, now seventeen, was arrested along with two other girls at her grandmother's apartment. At about 2:00 a.m. a neighbor had called police and complained of a wild drinking party. Newspapers noted that one of the girls was dressed in mannish clothes and, months later, upon rehashing the incident again, the press didn't fail to mention that one of the girls involved in the arrest was picked up by police a couple of weeks later. They thought she was a boy until she explained she liked to dress in men's clothes.

Though arrested that night, Cheryl was allowed to return home. She was charged with lack of parental supervision and in danger of leading a lewd and immoral life. A hearing was set, and a return to El Retiro seemed very likely.

Then Cheryl vanished on June 12—or did she?—leaving a note saying she had gone away to think things over. Lana said Cheryl was in town "with friends," and was not a runaway. Newspapers said she had been in hiding for eleven days prior to her June 23rd hearing in Santa Monica Court. Whichever story is true, Cheryl was on hand for the hearing.

Lana, accompanied by May and Crane, attended the unofficial closing hearing. She was limping and leaning on Fred for support. She said she sustained the foot injury when a suitcase dropped on her during a scene with Bob Hope in *Bachelor in Paradise*.

Somehow the judge was convinced that things had appeared

234

worse than they really were. He allowed Cheryl to return to May's ranch in her mother's custody, with the provision that the girl be placed in a private school.

Probably after some long talks with her mother, May and Crane, Cheryl came to the realization that she was in need of professional help. A few days later she flew with her mother and May to Hartford, Connecticut, and signed herself in at the Institute of Living for Psychiatric Treatment. Dr. Gordon Edgren, assistant medical director of the institute, said Cheryl agreed to come "on her own." He added that the girl would be interviewed by staff personnel before undergoing treatment.

Cheryl, whose eighteenth birthday was just a few weeks off, was one of many celebrities and children of celebrities to enter the plush, exclusive psychiatric retreat. The institute, on thirty-five acres, has individual cottages, a nine-hole golf course and tennis courts. It is undoubtedly the kind of sanitarium that every mentally disturbed person should be entitled to go to. But it is extremely expensive (at that time about $300 a week), and the cost is far beyond the reach of the average person.

Usually information about the identities of patients is kept absolutely confidential. And information about patients' aberrations is always zealously guarded.

Since Cheryl's life had been covered so closely since the Stompanato slaying, it was inevitable that her commitment to the Institute would make headlines.

On the heels of the most recent publicity of Lana's plight with Cheryl, United Artists released *By Love Possessed*. (BEFORE YOU CONDEMN HER, SEE HER STORY! said the ads.) But it was not a good film and did not enjoy the box-office success of her two previous pictures.

Producer Jerry Wald chastised Lana and other stars for demanding huge salaries and ignoring other elements of a film. Wald had paid Lana a flat $125,000 for *Peyton Place*. "I explained to her it was the script that mattered," said Wald. "With the Mirisches [producers of *By Love Possessed*], the stars are taking money they cannot keep [Wald referred to taxes] and doing second-rate stories and wrecking their careers."

Lana's return to MGM was inauspicious. *Bachelor in Paradise* turned out to be "a routine comedy." But Lana had gone back to Metro and she did the film in order to pick up her pension. She'd started at the studio in 1938. It was now 1961. "Twenty-three years," she said. "I should be creaking."

When she'd left MGM in 1956 there had been a provision whereby Lana would make a picture a year for them at a very low figure for the next five years. But *Bachelor in Paradise* was the first and last picture under this pact. By finishing off the contract, Lana collected $92,000 from the MGM pension fund.

Bachelor was mediocre, but Lana proved that, although forty-one, she still looked beautiful and was able to be believable as a romantic leading lady. There was even a brief sequence where she displayed her dancing ability and performed a sexy hula.

In the fall of that year Lana flew to Hartford to visit Cheryl. (A patient at the clinic remembers that Lana brought her daughter pizzas.)

Questioned about Cheryl's progress, Lana told a reporter, "She likes it very much, and I think she'll be completely adjusted there."

As for her private life during this period, Lana said that she liked not working, enjoyed traveling and watching her husband's horses race.

That October, after a brief hearing, the $20,000 settlement to the Stompanato family became legally binding. Harold Robbins was working on his novel *Where Love Has Gone.* Lana joined an array of other celebrities and government officials on the dais for the Friars Club Testimonial dinner honoring Mervyn LeRoy and his thirty-five years in motion pictures.

Although Lana talked of slowing down, she signed with Paramount for *Who's Got the Action?* to co-star Dean Martin. She took second billing to Martin, enjoyed working with him and was pleased to be in another comedy. During the production the cast and crew decided to help Lana celebrate her forty-second birthday on February 8 with a small party at the end of the day's shooting. All seemed to be going well, but suddenly Lana collapsed.

Her co-stars, Eddie Albert and his wife Margo, rushed her to Hollywood Presbyerian Hospital, and officials at the hospital soon reported that her condition was not serious. A spokesman for Lana said she would probably return to work the following Monday.

"She's just exhausted," husband May explained. "She's been getting only four or five hours' sleep a night." Some felt these statements by May revealed that offscreen pressures were taking their toll on Lana's physical stamina.

Although *Who's Got the Action?* had top cameraman Joseph Ruttenberg in charge of photography (he had photographed her flatteringly in *Bachelor in Paradise*), for the first time Lana's on-screen appearance revealed her age.

Lana again talked about retiring. In April, Cheryl returned home from Hartford. She was of legal age now, and no longer a ward of the court.

Apparently the treatment at the Institute had been successful, and Lana said, "We are enjoying a new solid relationship. We've had lots of discussions, but have made no plans about Cheryl's future."

Cheryl said, "Some decisions are up in the air. All I want to do now is relax for a while. There are horses and animals and things here at the ranch. . . ."

By that summer, Cheryl had completed the transition from gangling teen-ager to graceful young lady, now five inches taller than her mother. She took a job with two other girls, Bobbie Gentry (who would later become a top pop-country singer) and Diane Lewis. The three were known as "The Summit Swingers" and they modeled nightgowns, bikinis and formals at a weekly cocktail fashion show at a night club on Sunset Strip.

Of course, newspapers, wire services and magazines picked up the story, with pictures.

Cheryl's parents weren't exactly pleased, and soon after Cheryl took a job as a hostess in one of her father's restaurants.

Meanwhile, unfortunately, Lana's marriage to Fred May was disintegrating. She denied a rift with him that June, but by August they had separated. Her friends were worried. Not only that she and May had split up—after all, there had been four previous marriages and divorces, not to mention the dozens of romances and affairs—but her friends were concerned that "the old flame and fire had left Lana." They said she was acting blasé about her current separation and divorce.

Lana was living at the couple's luxurious Malibu beachhouse. May had checked into a Hollywood hotel. "Actually," she said, "we've been more or less apart for quite some time. We have denied it before because we were hoping that Fred and I would work out our problems."

Friends were slightly startled at the tame announcement. "She used to kick up more fuss than that," they said. "She used to take a sour marriage harder. Maybe her troubles have taken the anger out of her."

In a confidential memo to *Time* magazine on September 27, 1962, one of its correspondents opined: "Lana has never been compatible with any man for one day longer than the moment she grew bored with him in bed." The correspondent had reached Fred May and quoted him as saying: " 'We're apart it's true. However, I have been going to the house two or three times a week. I can't even tell you for sure what caused the rift. It is too bad.'

"He has no plans to file for divorce," the memo continued. "That rumor is completely untrue. 'If there is a divorce I will not be filing for it. Nor will I file a cross complaint.'

"May heatedly denies another rumor that Cheryl had something to do with it. Lana's secretary, who says Lana ain't talking just yet, tells us Cheryl, who was modeling flimsy things at a jazz cafe here

238

recently, is currently out of school and unemployed. 'Just living here with some friends.' "

In October, Lana flew to Juarez, accompanied by her secretary, to obtain a quick Mexican divorce which May had agreed to. "I just couldn't say anything about this before because Fred and I wanted to work things out as quietly as we could," she told reporters.

May's only comment when he separated from Lana was dignified and simple and perhaps startlingly revealing of Lana's character: "Real life can't be lived as if it were a movie script," said May. "And husbands and wives can't exist happily every moment of the day as though a movie camera were turned on them."

When asked if Cheryl had anything to do with the breakup, May answered quickly, "No, no, no. I'm very fond of Cheryl and I think she looks on me as a second father. All the time she was ill in the East I wrote her three long letters weekly so she could keep in touch with our lives here. Hints to the contrary are very unfair."

That October, *Where Love Has Gone* hit the bookstores and was an immediate success. It was widely discussed, but Lana had "no comment." It was a best-seller for months. A film, much less successful than the novel, was eventually made starring Lana's contemporary, Susan Hayward, in the role of the glamorous sculptress and Bette Davis as her mother. Joey Heatherton played the teen-age daughter who took the blame for the murder her mother committed.

Who's Got the Action? was released at Christmas time, and was less than a hit. And by now, four years after the Stompanato slaying, film offers that Lana would consider acceptable weren't pouring in.

Some of those close to the actress contend that leaving Fred May was one of the biggest mistakes she ever made. Concerning her personal life, Lana once asserted: "Yes, people do learn from their mistakes. But their characters never essentially change."

"I started fucking when I was eleven . . .
All I know is that I get violent headaches
if I don't fuck every day."
    ROBERT EATON

13

Lana did not make marital headlines again until June, 1965, when, at forty-five, she married for the sixth time. It seemed she was on the road to equaling, perhaps surpassing, the marriage record set by her ex-husband Artie Shaw.

Lana's new groom was Robert Eaton, a startlingly handsome thirty-four-year-old described as a businessman and someone "associated with motion-picture production."

Still a sentimentalist, Lana said about the wedding, "Tears ran down my cheeks." It was incorrectly reported to be Eaton's first marriage. The wedding took place at the small, white-brick, Arlington, Virginia, home of his father, a retired navy captain. A local magistrate performed the ceremony.

Lana wore a street-length dress she described as "peach Italian lace over coral and China silk." A tier of pale peach carnations decorated her blonde hair. She wore a diamond necklace, bracelet and earrings and a simply designed wedding band of Florentine gold. She was slim, but her face appeared drawn in newspaper and magazine photographs.

It was a private, quiet wedding and the first of Lana's marriages after Steve Crane that Cheryl did not attend.

Again, as was the case with Crane, Lana had married an obscure man as far as the public was concerned. The newspapers were vague about his means of support. Who was Bob Eaton? Was he, as some said, a man paid when initially called on in a last-ditch attempt to keep Lana happy during the arduous days of shooting her last movie? Was he someone she had met on the Bel-Air party circuit? Or was he, as some newspapers and magazines implied, a socialite-businessman who was not interested in involvement with her career?

Her career was in a downswing and had been since her divorce from May. She had a lot of free time. While producers were always submitting scripts, the roles were no longer glamorous leading ladies but parts which might utilize her acting ability and deglamorize her appearance. Or they were not "A" vehicles. Lana wasn't interested.

But the two and a half years prior to her marriage to Bob Eaton hadn't been dull. In December, 1962, Lana had toured the Far East with Bob Hope and his troupe. It was her first out-of-the-country sojourn with Hope, and was filmed for NBC-TV and aired the following January.

She had trouble with her voice during the arduous twelve-day, 18,000-mile trek, and when it started to give out she had to use a special mike. Toward the end of the tour Lana was rushed to the naval hospital in Guam because of acute laryngitis. When she returned, she said: "Here I was, on stage for audiences ranging from 5,000 to 12,000 men. Their reaction was the only thing that kept me going. You could just feel the warmth rolling up onto the stage."

241

She conceded its hardships, however: "I hope Bob doesn't ask me again for a couple of years."

In 1963, Lana was reportedly discussing a television-series deal with Four Star Productions. She was also rumored about to play Ann-Margret's mother in a project titled *Not All Cats Are Grey*. Neither of these deals materialized.

She starred for Columbia in 1964 in *Love Has Many Faces*, which a reviewer described as "a sordid romantic tale of the beach boy set." It was filmed in her long-time playground, Acapulco, and Lana played a wealthy woman married to a younger man, Cliff Robertson. The script didn't offer much to anyone, but it gave Lana the opportunity to wear a fabulous wardrobe and jewels. Even the ads for the film—above the title—read: LANA TURNER IN A MILLION-DOLLAR EDITH HEAD WARDROBE. Undoubtedly it was the first time costumes received star billing along with actors. It didn't help—even with ad lines such as: THE BIG, BOLD, BLAZING STORY OF THE PRO BEACH BOYS . . . THE BIG DOUGH THEY GO FOR . . . AND THE WOMEN THEY GO AFTER!

"Everyone thought he was on a vacation during that movie," says one of the production personnel. "We had a great time but made a lousy film."

Lana was particularly photogenic in *Love Has Many Faces*. Helen Young says: "I can't say why she looked so good except she was at the right weight and I guess in the right frame of mind, too." Lana was happy to be back at work in a glamorous role.

However, reports were that Lana was advised to stay close to the lavish Acapulco estate Columbia Pictures had leased for her. It was predicted there might be some bad moments for her downtown where she had once cavorted with Stompanato. Night clubs and cocktail lounges were bringing out framed photos of Lana and Johnny at the beach, dining areas and at poolside.

Lana became ill during filming, contracting a mysterious virus common to the area. Then she suffered an attack of parathyroid and was ill in Acapulco for five days. She was not hospitalized, although her temperature ran as high as 104 degrees. After this bout she went to Mexico City to recuperate and started shooting the picture there, but had a relapse.

Columbia shot around her. Production ran way over schedule, and the film took over six months to complete. There were rumors that Lana was to be replaced by Susan Hayward or Joan Crawford. And, of course, due to all these delays, and her depression after the May divorce and the lack of a specific man in Lana's life at this time, many ugly reports popped up—even some that she was carousing with sixteen-year-old beach boys.

Back in Hollywood that July, Lana threw a gala twenty-first birthday party for her daughter at The Galaxy, one of the then current nightspots on the Sunset Strip. Most of the guests were Cheryl's contemporaries. There was also a sprinkling of Hollywood's young set—Elizabeth Ashley, Gardner McKay, Clint Eastwood, Doug McClure. Over a hundred and fifty guests came, and all were screened at the door by private detectives. Each table was decorated with red and pink daisies and carnations. Balloons covered the walls. Pink carnations spelled out HAPPY BIRTHDAY CHERYL over the bar.

Lana and Steve posed for pictures with Cheryl, as the girl cut the four-tiered cake with "21" at the top. Fred May was there too, and another old friend of the family—Frank Sinatra—dropped in.

Lana said, "For weeks I've been working on every detail—the flowers, buffet, entertainment. I took care of everything. I even invited every guest by telephone. I woke up this morning and wondered if I would finally live through it."

As usual she not only lived through it but did so in great style. She was chic in a beaded white lace dress, and she personally greeted each guest. Cheryl wore a low-back red formal and, when asked how it felt to be twenty-one, she replied: "Not a bit different."

Although she had been working as a receptionist, she was currently unemployed, and Lana half kidded: "She'd better get back to work pretty soon."

With *Love Has Many Faces*, Columbia Pictures was hoping to cash in on the vast women's audience that had paid to see Lana suffer in *Imitation of Life* and *Portrait in Black*. But when the film was released in February, 1965, it fell on its face, and Lana's second film career was in deep trouble.

She needed a box-office vehicle in a hurry. Again luck seemed to be with her when she re-teamed with Ross Hunter to do a re-make of the four-handkerchief soaper *Madame X*, an old-fashioned melodrama which had been made successfully several times before. It would allow Lana to take advantage of both her glamour and her acting ability in a tear-drenched tale of mother love. She would play a woman who ages in the film from thirty to fifty-five. In the early portion of the story she accidentally murders a man and later becomes an alcoholic and a tramp. Again, some people thought elements of her personal life were present in the screen story.

Though everything had run smoothly on her two previous films with Hunter, this time there was difficulty. One of the production people who had worked with Lana for almost twenty years notes, "I think it's one of Lana's greatest acting jobs. But the film had a tremendous psychological effect on her. While making it, she was her marvelous self when she was portraying the character as a younger person.

"But when she started the aging process, she became depressed. It was all but a closed set. She didn't want anyone but the crew there. Each day took longer and longer to shoot. She began living the part. She would procrastinate putting on the age make-up and would wear a veil to and from the set so the tour people at Universal wouldn't see her."

Even Lana said that, although she considered the film her "crowning achievement" as an actress, "I really go all the way. I

244

span twenty-four years. Do I look a wreck at the end? Honey, you'd better bring oxygen when you see me. It's a shock."

Referring to Del Armstrong, she admitted, "The make-up man and I almost ended a beautiful friendship over that. When I thought he'd make me look horrible enough, he said, 'You ain't seen nothing yet.' And he meant it. I mean, I've had some bad mornings in my time, but I've never looked like that. I got so self-conscious, I wore a gray veil over my head when I was off-camera."

Lana must have been horrified at the thought of being seen by someone who wouldn't realize that her *Madame X* age-transformaton was make-up. In addition, it must have been devastating for a glamour girl to be shown what she might look like in ten years.

However, when the film was in release and when she was married to Eaton, whom she met while filming *Madame X*, Lana told another interviewer: "Age to me is what I feel inside. I have no fear of growing old."

During production, Lana feuded with Ross Hunter. Ross would not tolerate costly delays, and although he is noted for treating stars with the adoration and respect they require, even he found it difficult to work with her during this period.

Lana later said there was no feud, but claimed, "I have five different hair colors in the picture, and he didn't realize that it took hours to change it. That led to a blow-up on the set. He called me everything under the sun. Then he stomped off, and we didn't speak for the rest of the picture. It was just a misunderstanding."

Hunter, however, is noted for dealing successfully with stars of Lana's temperament. He would not have made a fuss about hair styling or make-up. Observers felt that Ross was upset because Lana was allowing her personal problems to interfere with her work. If in the old days at Metro she stayed out all night, drank a lot and lived up to her night-club-queen reputation, she always managed to show up on time in the morning and look beautiful for the cameras. Perhaps it was a hard realization that at forty-five most people cannot lead the life they led at twenty-five and expect to function at the same level.

Before the start of the picture, Ross had said, "She no longer registers doubt or worry when I suggest a film role because she knows I'll knock myself out to present her in the lush aura of glamour and in the rich garb of beauty. She trusts me. Her belief in me delights me more than anything I can think of."

According to Hunter, from her percentage of their two previous films Lana had set up a $150,000-a-year annuity for life. They both looked forward to making *Madame X*.

Ross had expected professionalism on Lana's part. However, as production progressed, he became disenchanted. After the picture was completed, he told columnist Earl Wilson, "I'm not talking about Lana calling up the press and claiming I was mean, that I wouldn't talk to her. I'm known for treating my leading ladies well. I made Lana a millionaire."

As for other producers who had had trouble with Lana, Ross said: "I used to say it's their fault. They can't control her. I can. I proved how wrong I was."

Despite her depression about aging for *Madame X*, Lana still had a sense of humor on the set. Helen Young remembers, "There was again a role of a hairdresser in the script and Lana said, 'Here you go again, Helen. A star part.' "

Helen recalls, "She conspired with the kids on the set and she told them to make sure I had flowers the way she did and a mirror outside my dressing-room door. Lana, of course, had flowers and Lana always keeps a full-length mirror right outside her dressing-room door so that she can take a last-minute look at herself before she walks on the set. This is part of her perfection. She just wants to make sure everything is perfect from her shoes to the top of her head. She doesn't miss a thing. Of course, for me the kids got dead flowers from a nearby graveyard and a mirror that was completely cracked and shattered."

But moments of humor during filming of *Madame X* were few.

Sheilah Graham did not endear herself to Lana when she wrote, after visiting the set, that Constance Bennett, then in her late fifties and portraying Lana's mother-in-law in the film, looked younger than Lana, who wasn't even in her age make-up that day.

The picture was eventually completed more or less on schedule and budget. Whatever her differences with Hunter, Lana owned a percentage of the picture and was excited by the final results. She agreed to do a publicity tour, including appearing at the world premiere in Miami Beach.

She hoped the film would be another turning point in her career. If it was a hit, it would revitalize her, as *Imitation of Life* had. If it wasn't a hit, her career, like the careers of the other glamour queens of her era, was in question. Still, even at forty-five, Lana had outlasted Rita Hayworth, Hedy Lamarr, and other "box-office" contemporaries who had long since toppled.

At the time, when asked to what she attributed her durability as a star, Lana honestly replied, "Luck has been with me, all right. I've been through a lot in my life and career but somehow I always seem to land on my feet. I know I find myself dipping into the past and pulling forward some moment, or the essence of it, to convey emotion. I couldn't have made *Madame X* ten years ago," she said in 1966, newly remarried.

"Not that I look back. But it's hard not to, especially with your old pictures rattling around on television. Still, in a way all that's happened to me has prepared me for what I'm doing now in pictures." But she also stated, "At the same time, it's a trick for a happy woman—that's me, with a happy home, a darling husband and a daughter I love—to convey sadness."

Lana had married Bob Eaton after completing *Madame X*. Just before their marriage a story appeared in which Eaton was described as thirty-nine (instead of thirty-four) and as a Los Angeles real-estate dealer who had been "romantically involved" with Ginger Rogers. Supposedly his brother-in-law was Abbott Van Nostrand, president of Samuel French, the drama publishing firm. Ginger described Eaton as coming from "a very prominent Virginia family." And Van Nostrand said, "I don't know if he's been married before or not."

The press incorrectly reported that Eaton *hadn't* been married before, and no one knew whether Lana knew if he had been or not. But his previous marriage would not go undiscovered much longer. A *Time* correspondent wired the following confidential memo to his home office on June 25: "Eaton has no credentials as a Hollywood producer. Although he possibly may become one now with Lana's financial backing. Although the AP report of the wedding said this was Eaton's first marriage, this is not true. He was married August 11, 1956, in Las Vegas, to actress Gloria Pall, then 26.

"Miss Pall, who is six feet tall, now operates a successful real-estate business in Beverly Hills. She was granted a divorce from Eaton November 8, 1957, after testifying he left her for another woman who had given him an automobile.

"Lists Eaton's birthdate as January 31, 1931. Miss Pall said when she picked up the paper Wednesday morning and read that Eaton's marriage to Lana was his first she wanted to call her mother and say, 'Hey look, Ma, no billing!'

"She said Eaton hoped to be an actor but never got beyond a few assignments in TV commercials. In court she said he didn't support her, that she had supported him.

" 'He's living with another woman in New York,' she testified at the 1957 trial. 'I saw him with this other woman. Her arm was around him and they were walking to the car she had given him.' She tells me the woman was actress Denise Darcel and the car was a Thunderbird. She said he later romanced Ginger Rogers. I asked her how come all this charm for women. 'Well, he rides with the top of his car down so he keeps a good tan. And he also plays a good game of tennis.' "

A few weeks after the wedding, while vacationing in Palm Springs, Lana was hospitalized. The Eatons were staying at La

248

Siesta Villa and at two o'clock one morning she suffered an attack and was rushed to Desert Hospital.

A hospital spokesman said she was in extreme discomfort when she arrived and there was speculation that Lana had suffered a heart attack brought on by the strain of trying to keep the pace set by her athletic new husband.

However, it was soon diagnosed that Lana was suffering from an allergic reaction. She had a body rash indicating a nervous reaction to something. Just what, nobody knew.

In Walter Scott's syndicated question-and-answer column, the following appeared in July, 1965:

Q. After her fight with Ross Hunter, is Lana Turner washed up in films?

A. No longer the box-office draw she once was, Lana of late has been investing her surplus funds in real estate and has confided to friends that insofar as films are concerned, she's just about had it.

That December, while *Madame X* was being readied for release, Lana and Eaton went on a belated honeymoon to Acapulco. They stayed at the Villa Vera, the hotel where she and Stompanato had vactioned the winter of 1958.

When they returned from Acapulco, Lana confided to some friends that her delayed honeymoon was not as much fun as other trips. The reason, especially coming from Lana, was a bit startling: "There's a group down there that's even wilder than the jet set."

In January, Eaton opened plush new offices in the elegant 9000 Sunset Building. The building, on the famed Sunset Strip, is surrounded by restaurants and night clubs. Agent Henry Willson and many famous show-business personalities maintain offices there. Concerning Eaton's new business home, Lana said: "It's so beautiful and comfortable up here. I told Bob it's going to be our home away from home."

Lana was now temporarily cast in the new role of "businesswoman." Photos of her were sent out to the wire services, with Lana posed in her husband's office, her shapely legs crossed pin-up girl style, Lana talking on the telephone à la Roz Russell in one of her "boss lady" roles.

The Eatons were reading scripts, and undoubtedly Bob intended to follow through on the hoped-for demands for Lana's services after the success of the upcoming *Madame X.*

In addition to setting up a new business, Lana became a race-horse owner for the first time. Since Eaton wanted to own a horse, Lana again resumed her interest in the sport.

Bob and Lana celebrated her forty-sixth birthday a day early so that he could fly to Atlanta, Georgia, for business meetings with Lana's long-time friend, Greg Bautzer. Shortly after Eaton's departure, Lana was checked into St. Johns Hospital "suffering from the flu." There was talk that she was despondent because Eaton was able to tear himself away from her. Whatever the reason for her hospitalization, she recovered quickly and, later in the month, along with Eaton, her mother and Cheryl, attended the preview showing of *Madame* X at the Screen Directors Guild.

Conspicuously absent from the preview was producer Hunter. Columnists said he was "home with the flu." But it seemed the rift between Lana and Hunter was not going to be easily overcome. There was a heavy celebrity turnout at the screening, and Hunter had arranged for lace handkerchiefs to be distributed to the audience to point up the film's tear-jerking qualities. The screening was a success.

March, 1966, was a happy time for Lana. Although Eaton was more than ten years her junior, they made a striking couple. Few people knew that Eaton had a glass eye. "Lana paid for it," said a trusted friend.

Cheryl was working as a hostess at one of her father's restaurants. "Nine to five, six days a week," Lana said proudly. And, "learning real responsibility."

En route to Miami Beach for the premiere, Lana stopped off in

New York. Always the romantic, she gave an interview (with Eaton by her side) to Howard Thompson of the *New York Times*. "Love is the only security there is, isn't it?" she asked Thompson. "And you know something? I've got real roots now."

While in New York City, she consented to make a rare TV appearance and she was the Mystery Guest on "What's My Line?" Her appearance was met with an ovation from the studio audience. Lana's enthusiastic reception by the public in this and other appearances prior to the film's release seemed to indicate she would have another hit film.

Bill Peper, then a reporter on the New York *World-Telegram and Sun*, met with Lana at the Plaza. "She had a vodka martini in one hand, and that professional warmth for the press exuded on cue. But there was not the slightest sign of recognition of me in her eyes. How could she have forgotten that afternoon twelve years ago when we belted martinis together at '21'? I was a young reporter on my first movie star assignment," said Peper, "and she was relaying hilariously unprintable stories about some of her leading men. She didn't remember any of it, but she said, 'If you couldn't print any of it, we must have had a marvelous time.'"

Lana, Eaton and their twenty pieces of luggage flew to Miami, where it had been arranged for a crowd to meet them at the airport. Miami was a wise choice for the world premiere of *Madame X* because there was a predominance of glamour-oriented women in town, many of them Lana's age or older. Ross Hunter, who usually attends world premieres of his films, was absent, as he had been from the preview. But Lana's every whim and wish was attended to.

Upon her arrival, the suitcase containing her hairpieces and wigs couldn't be located. Lana was furious. She informed executives that, if it wasn't found, she would return to California. The suitcase was found.

Lana's entourage, in addition to husband Eaton, included Helen Young, Helen's husband, and Lana's personal press agent, Jimmy Sarno.

Lana's stay in Miami generated genuine excitement. Although she agreed to newspaper and radio interviews, she wouldn't do any television. She didn't like to face cameras unless she had total control of the circumstances.

At the premiere, she dazzled the crowd in a clinging white crepe gown. It was sexily slit up the sides and paved with ten pounds of beads. For the proper effect, a floor-length white mink coat was slung casually over her shoulders. The Miami police said that the crowds awaiting Lana's arrival at the theatre rivaled those for President John F. Kennedy several years earlier.

Lana made a personal appearance on the theatre stage after the film and received another ovation. Then she returned to her hotel "to relax," and was almost two hours late for the posh post-premiere party in her honor. Ed Sullivan and Danny Thomas were among those cooling their heels waiting to congratulate her. She and Eaton looked blissful as flashbulbs popped, but when things quieted down and they weren't being photographed, Lana appeared sullen. And more than a bit drunk. When an admirer approached the table where she and Eaton were sitting, her press agent waved him away and whispered: "Not now. There's tension between them now."

Many industry people talk of Lana's drinking, especially in the latter part of her career. Though she wasn't usually a problem during production, she certainly created headaches for publicity people. Publicists on many of her post-1958 films recall that Lana often drank heavily on publicity tours—that when drunk she became extremely depressed, "often went into crying jags that lasted for hours." And that extensive publicity schedules had to be scrapped at the last minute when Lana was "not able" to appear, even on taped radio shows—"She canceled and rescheduled some shows four and five times."

Madame X was a hit in Miami, but its success there was deceiving.

Prior to its other openings Lana did additional publicity, but in the rest of the country the film was not a financial success. Charles Champlin of the *Los Angeles Times* called Lana "a textbook case of success. She has been in a curious way all the Hollywood legends rolled into one—the original who gave rise to the typical."

In May, Lana's mother became ill and moved in with Lana. That same month, Lana and Eaton accompanied Cheryl and her date to the opening of Steve Crane's newest restaurant, The Scam, atop the 9000 Sunset Building. However, during the year, columnist Louis Sobol reported that Lana and Cheryl were feuding—"They have reached a melancholy stage when they no longer speak to each other. Lana is reported to be extremely unhappy over the associates her daughter seems to prefer."

While *Madame X* was doing only mediocre business in America, it got a shot in the arm in Europe when Lana won the David di Donatello plaque at the Taormina Film Festival in Italy for her "Outstanding Performance." It was actually a lesser award than the "Best Actress" trophy, which went to Julie Andrews for *The Sound of Music.*

The Eatons departed for Sicily to accept the award after celebrating their first wedding anniversary. They stopped over in Rome, where they dined with Clint Eastwood.

Clint at that time was on the verge of movie stardom. Supposedly he and Eaton were business associates and planned film-production ventures. The projects never materialized.

The trip to Italy triggered a rash of rumors that Lana would star in foreign productions. She met with producer Carlo Ponti regarding a starring role opposite Marcello Mastroianni. She was even supposed to be discussing a film with Federico Fellini, which she would finance. But Lana returned to Hollywood without signing for a film.

That fall, Cheryl was stricken with a mysterious virus that affects the muscles. At first it was thought to be polio meningitis. Her blood pressure dropped extremely low and, when she wasn't able to retain food, she was given intravenous feedings. She had blinding

253

headaches and lost a great deal of weight during her four-week stay at St. Johns Hospital.

By October, she had recovered sufficiently from the ailment to return to work at her father's new restaurant. If there had been a rift between her and Lana, it quickly healed as both Lana and Steve Crane were deeply concerned with Cheryl's physical welfare.

Lana and Eaton, not working hard, made the social scene. Lana, of course, wanted to work. Sheilah Graham reported that Lana hoped to star with Gregory Peck in *The Stalking Moon*. It would be her first western. The role went to Eva Marie Saint.

The poor theatrical showing of *Madame X* seemed to herald an end to Lana Turner's film career. Times had changed since *Imitation of Life*. The "woman's-picture" audience was now a television audience, as proven by the success of *Peyton Place* and other female-oriented television offerings. And indeed when *Madame X* was shown on network television, it garnered one of the highest ratings of any film, proving that it *had* an audience but not a ticket-buying audience.

Parts were not being offered to Lana, at least not on her own terms. In Miami, woman producer Vivian Morgan Kent had "had the audacity" to approach Lana about starring in *The Candy Moessler Murder Case*. Candy, of course, had made almost as many headlines as Lana when she and her nephew were accused of having an affair and murdering her wealthy, elderly husband. Lana was repelled at the suggestion that she portray Candy, and she was upset that someone of her star stature should even be asked to consider a project that smacked of cheap exploitation.

"You must be kidding," she told newspaperman Herb Kelly. Kelly had relayed the offer from Mrs. Kent, who had told him that Lana was "number one on my list."

"It's disgusting even to think of it," said Lana. "Here's a woman on trial for her life and they're going to make a movie about her. I've read enough about the case to know how sensational it is. It's an insult to think I'd be interested in a terrible story like that."

Lana was financially secure. She didn't have to accept that kind of picture. The production company she had set up with Eaton was looking for scripts and properties. She said she hoped to act in movies for a few more years, but she planned to stay in the business indefinitely as a producer. She told reporters she'd like to develop new talent, which caused more than a few snickers in Hollywood. "She's been developing new talent for years," observed a friend.

Whatever ideas she and Eaton had for developing new talent obviously went by the wayside. Their marriage was in trouble. If Eaton had married Lana thinking that she would be used as his stepping stone into films, he was mistaken.

Her second comeback had fizzled. Hollywood talk, especially in late October, when Eaton was planning a trip to Europe, was that she and Eaton were splitting. Lana denied the rift, claiming that the trip was purely business. "Bob and Clint Eastwood have formed a co-production company with an Italian film executive," she said. According to Lana, "Bob will either produce or be associate producer." A columnist who tried to get the story direct from Bob couldn't reach him—he was off playing golf.

Early in December it was revealed that Lana and Eaton were parting. It was also announced that, in addition to his Clint Eastwood business affiliation, Eaton had formed another company, Forum Films. That company announced they had commitments not only from Clint but from Lana as well.

Columnist Harrison Carroll called Lana to check on developments in the Eaton separation and was surprised to find that Bob was right there at their Malibu home. "The word divorce hasn't been mentioned," Eaton told Carroll. "There is no reason to talk to attorneys."

Carroll asked him if there would be any change in his association with the company that would produce Lana's next picture in Europe. "None," he assured him. "We plan to produce this and many other pictures."

When Carroll asked Eaton why he came to see Lana, Eaton laughingly replied: "Just to have lunch."

Their marriage during December was an up-and-down affair. He bought her a thoroughbred race horse for Christmas. But AP announced on December 12, LANA'S SIXTH MOVES OUT.

She had no comment on whether the separation would lead to divorce. But by the end of the month they were officially separated and he took off for Italy where, in the words of Sheilah Graham, he hoped "to be luckier in his film-producing career than he was in Hollywood." Sheilah added, "While Lana has not yet consulted an attorney, she insists there is no chance of a reconciliation."

But Lana wanted no more embarrassing headlines. By February, the Eatons were reconciled. Lana was still vague when discussing the reconciliation but seemed less vague concerning their plans to make a film. She obviously wanted very much to return to work.

Although Lana was only forty-seven, the public considered her much older, since she had been in the limelight for so many years. Was Lana wrong in still insisting on leading lady roles? After all, Doris Day was still getting away with playing young virgins on screen, and she was only a couple of years younger than Lana.

"I don't want to be a character actress with a cane," Lana said during this period. "I think I'll only make a few more pictures as an actress and then I'll go into production. I've developed a philosophy of living," she went on, " 'to thine own self be true.' I know those things which are written about me aren't true and that's all that matters.

"And then I also live by this: 'This too shall pass away.' But how could I have any regrets?" she asked. "Movies have given me so much. The things I've been able to do, the places I've been able to travel to, the financial security I have for myself and my child, the way I can live—when I have all that how can I have any regrets?"

When she reconciled with Eaton, they discussed a film they planned to make in Rome. The project never got off the ground.

In June she made a ten-day "solo" tour for the USO in Vietnam.

Lana sprained her ankle during the tour, "jumping one trench too many," and the famous "Turner gams" were "fought over" by "medics of all ages" vying for the privilege of changing the bandage.

"You know what they wanted and I know what they wanted," Lana told *Life* magazine with a sigh. "They all wanted to hold L.T.'s foot."

For the first time, and probably the last, Lana made some political statements. A close associate remembers that during all the years at MGM she never knew whether Lana was a Republican or Democrat: "She never discussed politics." On her return from Vietnam, however, Lana told newsmen that the morale of the American fighting boys there was "absolutely fantastic. It is much higher than here in our country, I am sad to say.

"The men have a job to do and they know why they are there." How did she entertain the troops? Her only act, she said, was to laugh, joke, shake hands and "talk to the men in hospitals and in the fields."

Lana was the fifteenth star to do a solo tour up to that time. Her mission now, she said then, was to appeal to other actresses to go "with an open mind and full heart" to the troops in Southeast Asia. About the soldiers, Lana said: "When they asked how it was at home, they would ask about the weirdos and the demonstrators and I was happy to say they were still in the minority."

It was a very patriotic and good-public-relations approach to the touchy Vietnam question at the time. "She always says the right things at the right time because she's usually coached beforehand," observes Artie Shaw. "She's kept aware of what's 'in' and what isn't, so she always appears to be informed."

Returning from Vietnam, Lana filed for divorce from Eaton in Santa Monica. But again they reconciled.

Professionally, 1967 was the slackest year of Lana's career. The Vietnam tour had been the high point. She made no movies, and no Lana Turner movies were in theatrical release. It seemed she was finally joining the ranks of the other movie queens of the forties—unemployed and forgotten.

Jackie Gleason said he wanted Lana and Ava Gardner as his leading ladies for an upcoming film, *Let Me Count the Ways*. However, they'd be portraying middle-aged glamour girls. Neither was interested, and the roles went to Shelley Winters and Maureen O'Hara, and the less-than-mediocre picture was called *How Do I Love Thee?*

Lana agreed to make a guest appearance on the Smothers Brothers television show. Her agents made a good deal and she not only received the top fee but her contract reportedly included clauses guaranteeing her a limousine to take her to and from the studio, a special dressing room, and two dozen fresh flowers every day for the week of rehearsals and taping.

Lana rarely performed before a live audience. Only her 1957 Bob Hope TV appearance had been live, plus her few USO tours and of course, her appearances on the Oscarcasts. The Smothers Brothers program, though taped, was performed before a live audience. Lana seemed petrified, but Tommy Smothers clasped her hand and she immediately relaxed and more than ably performed several skits. She looked great on the small screen.

Lana was invited back on the show, and accepted. However, one of the skits she was to be involved in was supposed to burlesque her friend, then Senator George Murphy, and she backed out of the show.

In January, 1968, Bob Thomas asked her why a star of "her obvious voltage" wasn't making movies. She retorted, "Why aren't a lot of actresses making movies?"

It had been two years since *Madame X*, and Lana explained that she wasn't working "because they don't make pictures for women any more. Everything is directed toward the men. If a producer can get Steve McQueen or Paul Newman for a picture, he's got it made. He isn't interested in female stars."

Besides, she added, she wouldn't work in the lurid films that were beginning to dominate the movie market. "Look, I'm no prude," she remarked. "I think I know what's happening. But I see no reason to put raw sex on the screen. For what? What does it prove? That human beings are like animals? If that's what movies are coming to, then I want no part of it.

"You wouldn't believe the filth that I find in scripts sent to me nowadays. Absolute filth! It makes me physically ill to read such things. And yet I notice that those pictures get made, and producers find actresses to play the roles. I feel sorry for girls who feel they have to play such parts just to keep in front of the public.

"I'd like to work, too. I've got a figure that is all right, and I don't look so bad. I'm not ready to give up on an acting career yet. But I'm not so desperate that I would take these dirty pictures that they're making today. Thank God, I am in the financial position where I don't have to."

Lana Turner as a moralist placed her on unfamiliar terrain and brought chuckles to many. But it was true that, whatever her private life, Lana had chosen her screen roles with discretion. After all, hadn't MGM taught her about keeping her screen image tasteful no matter what lurid headlines her private life made? Although she had been a sex symbol for two generations, she never had to resort to any photograph or film role that she or her generation regarded as distasteful.

Discussing nudity in films in 1968, Lana said, "That's another thing I think is revolting—these actresses who think nothing of taking off their clothes." She remarked, "Why do they do it? Don't they know that it only cheapens them? Some things are better left to the imagination. A man's conception of what a girl really looks like is usually better than how she looks in the nude.

"And how many bare bosoms can you look at? There can't be much thrill left after you've seen a lot of them."

Since her film career seemed over, Lana and Eaton turned to a television series, a career move she had shunned up to this point.

Although she and Bob had talked of film production for years, Lana made only one film while married to him, *The Big Cube*, and that after signing for the television series.

The Big Cube was her worst film to date and the cheapest production she was ever involved with. Lana as usual was believable in her role—almost a personal triumph considering the obstacle of non-script she had to overcome. She played a glamorous actress secretly being given LSD by her stepdaughter, who was trying to drive her insane. Lana's wardrobe was expensive and flashy and she was very slim but her hair was unflatteringly coiffed, and the production itself, shot in Acapulco in the spring of 1968, looked cheap.

The Big Cube was an independent film financed by Mexican funds. The budget was under $1 million, and Lana had probably been lured by the glamorous role, the Acapulco setting and the $40,000 wardrobe.

Talk in Hollywood was that Lana had had her face lifted before making *The Big Cube*. Many people felt she certainly looked different in the film. Her features seemed subtly changed. Walter Scott carried the following in his syndicated question-and-answer column:

Q. I hear that Lana Turner has had her face lifted, her bosom siliconized, and her hips rounded. I understand, too, that she only weighs 80 pounds. Is all or any of this true?

A. Miss Turner is 50 and fighting it. Her face and bosom have been treated in an attempt to preserve the appearance of youth, but her hips remain unaltered by surgical hand. Currently a size 4, the film star of yesteryear weighs less than 100 pounds.

Although Lana had weight problems in the forties—she tended toward chubbiness—the problem had reversed itself by the late 1960s. Now it seemed difficult, virtually impossible, for her to gain weight. Some people theorized that the years of continuous drinking were to blame.

When signing for her television series, that amazing Turner ability to turn her back on the past again cropped up. The entertainment world was somewhat aghast when for her first television series Lana Turner agreed to star in *The Survivors*, a creation of none other than Harold Robbins, the man who had used the Stompanato-Turner affair as the basis for *Where Love Has Gone*.

Remembering the novel, a reporter asked Robbins: "How does Lana feel about it now?"

"Oh, she's all straightened out," he said. "I told her that during the six months I spent at Juvenile Hall in San Francisco, doing research for the book, there were thirteen cases just like this one. She'll be here this afternoon and you can ask her, if you want."

This afternoon meant a special barbecue to celebrate signing for *The Survivors*. Lana was escorted by Eaton. The select group included about twenty-five other guests. One of Robbins's friends recalled, "It was interesting to see the way Harold and Lana had acted after the book was published. At first, of course, they went out of their way to avoid each other, but eventually they got together like a couple of strange cats. One would make an overture and the other would back away and then the other would begin to get friendly and the first one would shy off, but now they're a couple of buddies."

Robbins announced Lana as the lead in *The Survivors* at a Hollywood bash at The Bistro. The invitations read:

> If you are interested in booze, broads and the better things in life, why not join Lana Turner and George Hamilton, stars of our new ABC-Universal Television show, *The Survivors*, at an old-fashioned drink-in upstairs at The Bistro.

Lana not only was guest of honor at The Bistro, she was the hit of the party. She wore a short black chiffon strapless dress, the entire bosom covered with black ostrich feathers, on which she had fastened an assortment of diamond pins and brooches. Her blonde hair was a short page-boy style with bangs. Her figure slim but curvy. She looked wonderful and radiated the old Turner glamour, as reporters were to point out in their columns the following day. It was a pleasant change for television reporters, who were used to interviewing the nonglamorous everyday "stars" of television.

A surprise guest at the Lana Turner-Harold Robbins party was Ross Hunter. When asked if he and Lana were still on the outs, Hunter said, "Hell, no. That was two years ago!"

Lana's new free-and-easy relationship with Robbins went beyond the social. The Harold Robbins Company now occupied the office suite at the 9000 Sunset Building which had been Bob Eaton's. Eaton still maintained a small office there.

Cheryl, about to turn twenty-five, seemed serious in pursuing a career in her father's restaurant business. Lana said, "They call her 'Miss Executive' now. She has a private office and two telephones. She respects me and is close to both of us despite our divorce.

"Now she has her own little house and works every day. She owns one third of her father's restaurants, so it behooves her to work hard and keep an eye on the business. When she first began working, I cut off her allowance and charge accounts. It was then that she realized she was on her own. The kids who make it big before they are ready have their whole sense of values twisted."

Although *The Survivors* was set in April, 1968, with William Frye signed to produce, the series was considered too prestigious—and too expensive—to debut in January as a "Second Season" entry. It was decided to postpone the debut until September, 1969.

At the beginning, Eaton was involved in production on the show as a co-producer. He, Lana and Helen Young went to the Riviera for location shooting. Helen recalled that Lana telephoned her, asking her to work on the series. Then Lana asked Helen's husband for his permission to let Helen travel. Lana said, "I know the importance of keeping a good marriage. It's much more important than working."

The Survivors location shooting may have been another vacation for Helen, but it was no picnic for Lana and Eaton. Their relationship was strained, and Eaton obviously felt he was being squeezed out of the picture. And he was.

While shooting *The Survivors* on the Riviera, Lana made headlines again when she had a run-in with producer Frye. There was a lot of name-calling and Lana hauled off and socked Frye when he called her a bitch. When he recovered his equilibrium, he slapped Lana back. The following day, Eaton ran into Frye at the Cannes Yacht Club, punched him and Frye punched back.

Variety said: "In the first week of shooting her first vid-pic series, Lana Turner was involved in a verbal and physical hassle with her producer, and he is no longer with the series."

With Frye out as producer, Grant Tinker, then a Universal executive (and husband of Mary Tyler Moore), became temporary producer. Universal and ABC were co-producing the show, and it was receiving more in-production publicity than any other show of the last decade.

Walter Doniger, who had piloted the *Peyton Place* TV series, was brought in to produce, and he was the man who received screen credit when the series debuted.

Robbins got an astronomical sum for selling his idea and writing the first script, which was never used. Reports were that the initial script was filled with blatant sex. Incredibly for TV, it supposedly had a scene with Lana in bed under the covers with a man, the camera concentrating on her facial expression while the man slid down and out of camera range.

Lana's top-billed co-star, George Hamilton, was being paid more than she. She was getting neither top billing nor top salary. But she was doing the series because she wanted to work and be active, not because she needed the money.

She seemed to have some insight into the person she had become when she told a writer, "You think you're beautiful. You think you're interesting. You then create the illusion of glamour in yourself, in the outer self that others see. Like I said, glamour is only an illusion."

But *The Survivors* offered no time for illusions. After shooting European location work on the show, the Eatons returned to Hollywood, and Lana and Eaton again separated. After they parted, Eaton wrote a book.

His novel, *The Body Brokers*, has a leading character named Marla Jordan. Eaton's book carried the statement that: "This is a work of fiction. All events and all characters are products of the author's imagination. Any resemblance to real events or real persons, living or dead, is purely coincidental."

Marla is described in the book as a forty-five-year-old movie queen who was discovered at seventeen, stuffed into a sweater and converted into a sophisticated woman. She freely used her body ("her tits and her cunt") to climb the Hollywood ladder. Marla Jordan and her teen-age daughter, an obviously disturbed girl who's the only thing Marla loves besides herself, push a young lover, who won't sleep with both of them at the same time, off a cliff. They get away with the murder. At the end of the book, Marla is appearing in a television series written by a successful pulp writer who wrote a thinly disguised book based on Marla and her daughter's scandal.

At the end of *The Body Brokers*, the character who resembles Eaton himself, the character who was actually responsible for the idea for the TV series, and the selling of it, has been squeezed out by Marla, the writer and the sharpies at the television network. But indeed he is a better man, walking into the sunset, having cleansed himself and freed himself of *The Body Brokers*.

Eaton paints his character Marla, the fading movie queen, as an alcoholic in constant competition with her daughter for the favors of young lovers. She is a woman who not only delights in fellatio but "switch hits" and was once found in bed with another Hollywood glamour queen.

When Marla has to make a personal appearance or a film, she is able to dry out, muster up her energies and, with cosmetic help, pull herself together to look "almost as good as ever."

The Body Brokers was not successful. In a brochure to the book trade, the publisher had advertised the author as "Lana Turner's ex-husband," but when the book was commercially advertised all mention of Lana was eliminated.

After the book was released, Eaton talked with Sheilah Graham. "I truly believe that there is not a man in the world who can handle marriage to a movie star—the old-world film star," he told her. "The mere fact of all the divorces substantiates this. While only one person ever referred to me as Mr. Turner—and he apologized immediately—marriage to an aging film star can be a humiliating experience.

"By the way, the man who introduced me as Mr. Turner was Fred May, the husband before me."

Eaton told Sheilah, "I introduced Lana to Robbins. She disliked him at first, but as soon as the almighty dollar was visible they became the greatest friends. We created *The Survivors* to star Lana. Robbins wrote it for Universal and our company. George Hamilton received $17,500 a week, Lana $12,000—and this irked her. Ralph Bellamy and Kevin McCarthy each were paid $10,000 a week. I was getting nothing.

"That's when I made up my mind to write *The Body Brokers*."

Eaton gave many interviews promoting his book. But the most unusual and insightful was granted to a writer of *The Advocate*, a gay-liberation newspaper published out of Los Angeles. Headlined: SUPER-STUD . . . HE GETS HEADACHES IF HE DOESN'T * DAILY, the interview explained that Eaton used the word "fucking" so often that in order to save space the writer would use an asterisk instead.

"I met Mr. Eaton for drinks and right away he was falling back in the chair making the most of his tight white trousers and even *more* of his no jockey shorts underneath," said the story.

"Yeah, man, I was saying to myself," the writer went on, "you may not be Henry James but you could sure as hell have lived your super-sex story."

The writer's opinion was that, "Even now, close to 40, Robert Eaton could command a very good price. Maybe not a Rolls-Royce

if he were being kept, but a Caddy perhaps, an Impala for sure."
(Did *The Advocate* interviewer know about Denise Darcel?)

"I wrote the book standing at the bar of '21' in New York,"
Eaton told the interviewer. Though Eaton wanted to discuss
women—"When I first saw Jacqueline Bisset on the screen I
grabbed Jim Aubrey by his fucking arm—" the interviewer changed
the subject to Harold Robbins.

"Eaton jutted out his jutting jaw: 'The most unworthy person I
ever tripped across. He's a * vegetable!' "

Eaton told *The Advocate* that he came to Hollywood when he
was twenty-five and gave himself until thirty to make it. "Obviously, I fucked up," he confided laughingly.

"I started fucking when I was eleven. My first orgy when I was
twelve. We had a baby sitter with beautiful big tits and I loved to
wear a sailor hat. She'd slide my sailor hat down her front and then
asked me to feel around down there for it. You could say she broke
me in."

When asked how he would define "stud," Eaton, without blink-
ing, said: "I never knew what the definition of stud is. All I know is
I get a violent headache if I don't fuck every day."

Lana kept completely mum about *The Body Brokers*, but she
was undoubtedly hurt and unhappy. Columnists, including Marilyn
Beck and Jack O'Brian, implied that the reason Lana resented the
book most of all was that the heroine was described as "not so hot"
in the "romance" department.

*"If they're clever and if they give
me the right story, I take the bait.
Then I get kicked in the teeth again."*
    LANA TURNER, 1969

14

"I found myself living under tremendous anxiety and nervous tension, which was really beginning to tell on me. It was affecting my work as an actress," Lana testified on April 1, 1969. She was granted a default decree and was officially divorced from Bob Eaton, husband number six.

Lana was tremendously unhappy with problems besetting her professionally. *The Survivors* had been in production for a year. Discussing the characters in the script, Lana said, "At first we all hated each other. Now we just dislike each other.

"I don't see how the series can begin because I don't think anybody knows where we're going. I hear scuttlebutt that my father in the series will die and I'm suspected of murder and there'll be a trial."

The Carlyles were Lana's banking family in the program: Ralph Bellamy played her father; George Hamilton, her brother; Kevin McCarthy, her husband; Louis Hayward, her uncle. An illegitimate son, Geoffrey, was one of the later twists to the show. "In the original version," said Lana, "I was something of a swinger. Now because of Geoffrey I keep my skirts clean."

When Bill Greely discussed *The Survivors* in weekly *Variety* later that year, he noted: "An ABC spokesman last spring was moaning about the $1.8 million that had gone into preparation and pilot for 'The Survivors' when violence and sex hit the Washington fan. Not a foot of film could be salvaged and a major star was talking of quitting. ('No sex, No star' was the threat.)"

Discussing her character while the series was in production, Lana said, "I don't really know who or what I am. Doing a film, you had a script with a beginning, middle and end. You could read it and find out what the character you were playing was. Here, you never know. She changes week to week, script to script. Sometimes she changes so completely I don't recognize her—and they rewrite it. But not until I object.

"They have to make my costumes each weekend because until Friday night they don't know what I'll be doing Monday."

She had a falling-out with her costume designer, noted fashion savant Luis Estevez, who told syndicated columnist Joyce Haber, "I've been super-kind to Lana for over a year. I deserve the Croix de Guerre for that."

What Luis got instead, noted Miss Haber, was a couple of printed interviews in which Lana announced she had Estevez fired because she decided his designs made her look matronly.

"Perhaps it was not my designs that made her look matronly," Luis said. "After all, nothing is forever. I wasn't fired. I quit three times. Twice I stayed because of my respect for producer Walter Doniger and head of costume Vince Dee, and out of the friendship I felt for Lana.

"Quitting then would have created an awkward situation for

Lana and the show, and both needed all the help they could get."

The third time he resigned, Estevez followed through: "It was after an unpleasant incident with Lana the day before we started shooting. I let Universal out of my contract.

"It's impossible to create a wardrobe for a TV series in 1969 as it was done in 1945," said Estevez. "Especially when you're given a week and you're working with the last of the studio-made stars, who wants to be fitted within an eighth of an inch of her body."

The Cuban-born designer noted that the script called for Lana to project a chic image associated with a young New York matron. "She just couldn't understand that elegance and a Hollywood sex-pot image simply aren't one and the same. I quit."

According to Miss Haber, word went around Universal after the initial episode, in which critics (who hated the show) liked Kevin McCarthy: "Miss Turner has ordered her bosses to cut McCarthy's part severely in future episodes."

In addition to the Bill Frye slapping incident and Estevez's quitting, there was the publicized "limousine episode." As Joan Barthel reported in *Life*, Lana explained: "Television provides cars for no one. No one! But since I've been in my position I've always had limousines. Now I'm the only one on the lot who has a limousine and it took quite a bit of doing. Not that I got into it myself . . . that's what I pay people for."

Lana continued, "First they said, all right, they'd pick me up in the morning and take me home at night. I said no, I want to know that that car is there outside that stage at every moment. I said I might just have to go to the ladies' room, and I won't use the one at the stage. I only go to my permanent dressing room. It's a block away, and I won't walk. Not that I *can't*, but just because I have gone into another medium doesn't mean that I'm going to change my way of living and working. So now that car is *there*." And Miss Barthel noted that the car was there "outside the house [Lana] has rented in Beverly Hills. It was there all day, beginning early in the morning, with the chauffeur sitting in the back seat, not even reading, just sitting there all day until after dark when Lana decided she wasn't going anyplace."

A question getting louder was: Where was *The Survivors* going? The European segments of the show were scrapped almost entirely. The weekly segments, now being filmed at Universal City, were running as high as $270,000 each.

In addition to hiring a new producer (Doniger), it was reported that the series was having complications scriptwise. Agnes Nixon, the "young princess" of daytime soapers (*Another World*), was hired to work out of Philadelphia guiding *The Survivors* scripts. A couple of seasons earlier the reigning queen of soap-opera scripts, Irna Phillips, had secretly guided the *Peyton Place* series from Chicago, for producer Doniger.

But there was no one to guide Lana's private life. She and Eaton had been separated for months before their divorce. She was insecure and lonely. But, at forty-nine and with six broken marriages behind her, she was still a romantic.

While yet in the throes of shooting *The Survivors* at Universal City, and only a month after the Eaton divorce was final, Lana Turner married husband number seven, Ronald Dante, a nightclub hypnotist. She thereby took the undisputed lead as Hollywood's most-married glamour girl. She later said, "If they're clever and if they give me the right story, I take the bait. Then I get kicked in the teeth again."

She had talked to syndicated columnist Shirley Eder about a month before marrying Dante and, when asked about a new romance in her life, Lana exclaimed: "Not in mine. I've had all that. And I just want to keep my freedom. No more marriages for me."

Miss Eder met the Dantes later on in the year and observed that Lana was very much in love with her new husband. "But then, Lana is always 'very much in love' with the man she marries," observed Miss Eder.

The Golden Girl had traveled a long way from Bob Topping and trips to Europe on the *Mauretania* to performer Dante, who would garner more sad, unfavorable headlines for Lana's scrapbook. (Actually, she doesn't keep a scrapbook; her mother does.)

The venture with Dante was Lana's shortest marriage (six months) since Artie Shaw. She married Artie when she was twenty, Dante twenty-nine years later. But she was the same girl emotionally, said friends.

The Dante marriage was preceded by one of Lana's shortest courtships—about three weeks. "It was love at first sight, although it was in a discotheque and it was so dark I didn't recognize her right away," Dante later said. "In fact it wasn't until we started to dance that I knew who she was, and even then I wasn't positive because she gave me her married name.

"I remembered," Dante continued, "that we talked about why she should give up smoking, and I told her I was a hypnotist. We exchanged phone numbers and started seeing each other a lot. I never had seen any of her movies until I saw *Madame X*, and she was crying so much in that picture that I couldn't conceive it was her."

This was also the first time Lana had married so soon after a divorce. For a short while Lana and Dante lived at the Sheraton-Universal, the hotel on the Universal lot. This was no doubt to make it convenient for Lana to be at the set on time. However, shortly after her marriage, the Dantes moved to a lavish Beverly Hills estate befitting Lana's movie-star image.

She granted *Life* magazine an in-depth interview to publicize *The Survivors*. The interview was at her new home, where on one wall she had framed stills from her movies. However, there was a drapery that could be drawn over the pictures for moments when Lana cared not to remember.

Lana and Dante posed lovingly together at the edge of her pool. She wore a billowing caftan, and cooed to her heavy-lidded, hippie-mod husband in her cuddly, little-girl voice, "People will think we're expecting. And we're not, you know."

"But we're working on it," he murmured, and leaned over in a

271

languid kiss. As *Life* pointed out, except for three press agents, a hairdresser, a make-up man, a wardrobe woman, a photographer and a reporter, they were alone.

The Little Girl side of Lana described her daily regimen: "When I leave in the morning for work, my darling is sleeping. I try to be so quiet getting my panties out of the drawer, getting my dress off the hanger. He opens his eyes and says, 'Goodbye dear, have a good day at the office.' That's our private kind of love joke.

"He brings me little gifts. He brought me these sunglasses [Christian Dior, says Dr. Dante]. When he buys me a candle it means more to me than diamonds. Diamonds I've got, in the vault, and I love them. I love everything money can buy, but I've got it; I mean, how many mink coats can you wear at one time?"

But the businesswoman Lana added, ". . . my mother and my daughter are beautifully taken care of; Cheryl's twenty-six now— *twenty-six* and very happy, working for her father with his restaurants. I have thoroughbred racing horses, and land, and money; I've got an awful lot of money. I'm not doing this TV series because I need the money. I'm doing it because I need activity—oh God, I need activity! It was approaching three years that I hadn't worked, and that's not healthy. I was getting into a very deep rut, I was becoming stale. I like to work; it's the only thing I know."

This was only a few months after her marriage to Dante, and there was, not surprisingly, already talk of divorce. But Lana insisted they were very much in love.

Dante roared around on his motorcycle while Lana continued working on the series, which would premiere on ABC in September. She told people Dante was writing a book on hypnotherapy, and delighted in calling him "Dr. Dante."

While married to Dante and again to promote *The Survivors*, Lana granted an interview to one of the nation's top journalists. When the writer showed up at Lana's home, Lana appeared so inebriated that she could hardly stand straight. She was friendly and candid in her statements but not particularly coherent. She couldn't remember many of her old pictures or leading men. She wore a hippie outfit. "It cost twelve bucks," she told the writer. "My husband got it for me. He likes this kind of thing. He threw out all my Jean Louis!"

The writer observed that dozens of Walter Keane-like paintings of pathetic, saucer-eyed little girls decorated the walls, and Lana's collection of porcelain mice—all sizes and shapes—abounded.

When the journalist saw Lana again on the set at Universal, she was another person—articulate but cold, formal, aloof. The interview was never written, the writer not wanting to tarnish the Turner image further. Also observed was the fact that Lana's relationship with Dante was less than idyllic. The correspondent felt it was reminiscent of a scene from *Sweet Bird of Youth.*

Like many of the men in Lana's life, Dante had a background which could not easily be deciphered. Gossip columnists used blurbs complicating matters by carrying faulty information such as: "Dating at the Luau, Lana Turner and millionaire hypnotist Ronald Dante. . . ." (It's interesting to note that Lana usually dines at one of Steve Crane's restaurants, where naturally the tab is taken care of.)

Dante, far from millionaire status, claimed he was forty-nine. Friends said he was thirty-nine but wanted to appear older since he was aware of Lana's desire to be married to someone her age or older. Her close associates said Lana now felt that she would be ridiculed if she continued to marry younger men.

Other friends theorized that Lana indeed wanted to be married to a younger man, at least a man that everyone *knew* was younger, because that made her appear to be still desired by youth. But it was necessary at the same time for the man to be chronologically her own age to avoid nasty gossip. Always the romantic, Lana, they said, yearned for the impossible.

Dante's age wasn't the only information about him that reporters discovered to be faulty. He claimed to have been born in Singapore, but his entertainer's working permit listed his birth date as 1930 and his birthplace as Chicago.

He also claims he has a Ph.D. in psychology from Singapore University and that he once served in the U.S. marines. But he has declined to elaborate on either point.

Soon after their marriage in May, Lana was in for a couple of unwelcome surprises. A *Hollywood Reporter* gossip column asked: "Is Lana Turner's 7th, Ronald Dante, the same hypnotist, real name Ronald Peller, who had such a messy annulment suit against him in Florida in 1963?" Dante was, it turned out, Peller. It was later printed that Dante supposedly had married a Mrs. Clair Kisiel, in Hollywood, Florida, and supposedly spent her life savings. She asked for an annulment of the marriage and to have her money (about $19,000) returned.

It was only the beginning. Shortly after he married Lana, Dante claimed he was shot at in a subterranean garage on Doheny Drive in West Hollywood by an unidentified gunman. He told police he was parking his car when the gunman leaped from behind another auto, firing a pistol. He said his assailant was blond, about five feet eleven and wore an Australian bush hat. Dante claimed he escaped serious injury by diving to the floor of the car. He received minor cuts from flying glass. Police deputies confirmed that five or six shots had broken the car's windshield.

The hypnotist could give no reason for the attack, and the gunman was never found or arrested. Except for the cuts from the shattered glass, Dante was otherwise unhurt.

When the police in Hollywood broadcast an alarm for the apprehension of the gunman, the Dante name obviously rang a bell with Santa Ana police, who began a search for Dante on a year-old grand theft felony warrant. He was arrested sixteen hours later and charged with an attempted theft of $18,000 worthy of motor boats. He had jumped bail the previous year.

274

It seems that Dante, according to Santa Ana police, had given the Marlin Boat Company in Santa Ana a check for $17,460 the previous May, which proved to be worthless. He promised to return with cash to pay for the boats he had purchased, and the company locked the boats up behind a chain fence. Allegedly, Dante returned that night with a trailer truck, broke the chains, and was about to make off with the boats when he was caught. He was arrested but released on bail.

He posted bail for $12,500, jumped bond and successfully eluded police for almost an entire year, even though he subsequently made national headlines by marrying Lana Turner.

According to Dante, after the boat incident he received a threatening telephone call and a man had said that: "If I did not pay him $5,000 by Tuesday he would make it so I'd never be able to walk again." Dante said the threat came from a man who identified himself as "the owner of a boat company."

Dante denied he trumped up the entire incident for attention. He claimed the shooting incident was observed by his personal manager, Art Newburger. Dante said he told his wife nothing about being shot at except that he had been in a little accident. "When the driver of our car turned on the radio news and she [Lana] heard about the shooting, she passed out," said Dante. "She fainted."

The theft charges against Dante were eventually dismissed, and during the year Lana reportedly went with him to Arizona to meet his parents.

In August, about a month before the scheduled debut of *The Survivors*, quite a stir was created when *Daily Variety* carried a quarter-page ad, handwritten and unsigned. It read:

> *Congratulations to ABC-TV*
> *for coming up with the new series,*
> *"The Survivors," starring*
> *$8 million and no sense.*

275

The ad caused consternation at both the New York and Hollywood offices of *Variety*, since it had slipped by the editorial department. It was later revealed that the ad had been placed by the socially conscious writer and Smothers Brothers cohort Mason Williams.

Before its debut, there was a great deal of speculation as to whether *The Survivors* would succeed. It certainly had more than its share of in-production problems and word was out that the show was a dud. But in the unpredictable world of television it is impossible to tell what shows will catch on. Lana's movies on television consistently registered top ratings, and the thought was that she might save the show from total disaster.

Helen Young worked on *The Survivors* only during the European location shooting. She recalls, "It was just awful. My heart would break for Lana when she had to go out there and try to do something with a scene and there was just nothing there to work with.

"When we got back they didn't use one inch of that footage. They threw everything away. The only thing they used were the background scenes—the Monte Carlo casino." Helen also remembers that Lana had ambivalent feelings about returning to work. She was both happy and unhappy. "She knew how demanding TV is," says Helen, "and she knew how fast it had to move. Not that she can't work fast. She can. But she has the feeling of not doing her best because she has the feeling of having to rush."

In TV there are only four days to shoot a script as opposed to six weeks for a feature film. And Helen makes the important point that, "In television there are different directors all the time." Each director has his own approach, and Lana wasn't accustomed to the constant changes of style with each director.

To make matters even more treacherous, *The Survivors* was scheduled opposite top-rated *Laugh-In* on NBC and *Gunsmoke* on CBS.

Cynthia Lowry, television feature writer for Associated Press, interviewed Lana before the show premiered. Miss Lowry described the star as very nervous about the reception that would greet *The Survivors*. Lana was particularly concerned that her thirty-year career could be obliterated if the show received a poor response.

The Survivors was launched on September 29, 1969, and was universally panned. Even the rating for the premiere episode was below expectations. Bill Greely, in his *Variety* review, noted that: "The meller about the jet set turned into an old-fashioned soap opera about a banking family. There was the taint of a novel in the machiavellian twists of character and plot in *The Survivors* but it finally boils down to suds with the gambits of daytime drama working overtime. That old debbil pregnancy, etc."

Greely thought Lana Turner "smooth" in her part, but said that she had become rather matronly, "except for the velvet sexy pipes of old." He went on to say that the direction was "obvious and trite, but ironically this along with the plush celluloid production values might be a plus with the Nielsen [ratings] vine-swingers." It wasn't, and word was out almost after the first episode that *The Survivors* wouldn't survive. And Lana's marriage wasn't surviving very well.

She went to San Francisco in November to do a benefit for a Presbyterian Hospital auxiliary. The gimmick was that Lana was going to be auctioned off to the highest bidder for a fabulous night on the town. People wondered why she was doing this, since she certainly didn't need publicity. Perhaps she had been talked into it because *The Survivors* was floundering. Or perhaps, as others say, she has a soft spot in her heart for San Francisco.

She was scheduled to fly in on a Saturday, and Phil Sinclair, the man in charge of coordinating Lana's activities, awaited her 2:00 p.m. arrival. She arrived at 5:15. The plane was cleared of other passengers before she disembarked.

Sinclair boarded the plane to meet her. "How thoughtful of you to dress for the party on the plane," he said. "We are running a little late." He was impressed with her red velvet floor-length gown trimmed with black fox. "My dear," Lana said straight-faced, "this is my traveling outfit."

Along with Lana, Sinclair encountered her hairdresser, male secretary, publicity man and husband Dante.

San Francisco Chronicle columnist and humorist Herb Caen covered the entire weekend for his paper, and later reported in a column titled "Hail to the Queen": "She may look all of her 49 or 50 years under closest scrutiny, but she's still every inch (or every other inch) the kind of movie goddess they don't make anymore—by turn regal and petulant, demanding and generous, temperamental and cuddly. At one moment, Gloria Swanson in *Sunset Boulevard*, eyes flashing, chin up, sweeping about in a perpetual spotlight. The next moment, Little Girl Lost, lips quivering and eyes flooding with tears. . . ."

Caen also observed that after her arrival, "Per her instructions (demands?), a black limousine and police escort were waiting. At the Mark Hopkins, autograph collectors clustered around with little yelps of love, and Lana was gracious. Then she went upstairs and reappeared in a red lace gown, white foxes and, by her estimate, $187,000 worth of diamonds. She had been drinking vodka on the rocks and was feeling no pain. . . . 'I always sleep with my diamonds on, darling,' she said gaily. 'That way, if they come to steal them, they have to steal me too.' "

Lana has a penchant for arriving late and leaving early. At the charity event, according to Caen, she continued with her vodka on the rocks, was "frosty" with the other so-called celebrities, but girlishly friendly with the musicians, her police escort and her chauffeur. Caen remarked, "The auctioneer, nervous about her ingestion of vodka, put her on the block first instead of last, and she was 'won' by a boy who looked to be in his teens. Lana covered him with motherly kisses while her husband, Mr. Dante, glowered. 'Let us be off!' cried Lana gaily as the party was only fairly getting under way."

The party went on to Finocchio's, one of San Francisco's tourist lures. There Lana continued drinking and even jumped up on the stage and sang, according to Caen. He noted that the transvestites eyeing her jewels, her furs and her red gown turned green with envy. The party moved to the Casa Madrid, where "Lana danced a crazy flamenco" and then moved on to another spot where "husband Dante, who obviously wasn't having a good time at all, just plain disappeared."

Caen summed up events with: "Next day, the sun was shining but it was Gloomy Sunday around Lana's suite at the Mark Hopkins. Her husband was still missing. Sympathetic Phil Sinclair tried to ease her pain by saying, 'Think how silly he must feel, wandering around on this beautiful day in his tuxedo.' That made Lana smile a little but the tears soon returned. She and her hangers-on went to A. Sabella's for an early dinner and she fell in love with waiter captain Scotty Cuthbert's tweed jacket. 'I must have that for Ronald!' she cried. 'But it's so old,' he protested. 'It's my father's—he had it made in 1925!' (True.) Still she bought it off his back for $80.

"When she boarded the plane for Los Angeles that evening, Husband No. 7 was still missing. 'Wonderful weekend!' she said bravely to Sinclair, smile on lips, tears in eyes, having left her heart and her husband in San Francisco."

That San Francisco weekend precipitated the split in the Dante-Turner marriage. Newspapers reported, "A week ago last Saturday Lana Turner and her husband went to San Francisco, where she was to appear at a charity benefit. After the festivities Lana said she was hungry and wanted to go to a restaurant. Dante said for her to go on in her limousine with some friends. He would take a cab back to the hotel because he wasn't hungry. Later, when Lana returned to their hotel suite, Dante was not there. He didn't come back that night. The next day, Sunday, Lana returned to her Beverly Hills home and discovered that her husband was cleared out, leaving a note saying that he was leaving to try his own thing, Lana said."

Lana must have been shaken. Back in Beverly Hills, she didn't show up for work at Universal that Monday. She discovered that $35,000 which she had recently deposited in their joint checking account had been withdrawn by her husband. However, she and Dante had formed a business corporation and, of course, he might be using that money for mutual business interests.

Dante's version of the split was, "We finally split up November 9. Lana was in San Francisco doing a benefit for some hospital. I was with her, both as her husband and her escort. She was supposed to auction some stuff and attend a couple of parties, but she didn't want to go out.

"This thing had been building up for some time, and the last straw was this misbehavior on her part when she refused to do what she was supposed to do. Although she has always been very shy at times, this was not one of the times she should have been."

November, 1969, was a bad month for Lana. *The Survivors* was already doomed. Her worst fears about its failure were realized. The Dante affair was a fiasco, and Lana went into seclusion in Palm Springs. The fan magazines ran stories claiming that she was recovering from the effects of a hushed-up overdose of barbiturates.

By December Lana had filed suit against Dante. She accused him of defrauding her of $34,000. She claimed that he converted $34,000 of the $35,000 to his own use. She said that on November 7 he had talked her into signing a personal check. The money was supposed to be for a joint business operation. They were going to incorporate Tower Funding Ltd., a real-estate firm of which Lana was to be sole stockholder. But Lana claimed the hypnotist used the money for his "personal desires." In the suit she asked for the return of the $34,000 and $10,000 more for exemplary damages.

After the breakup many publications quoted Lana as having said, "Each one has its own individual hurt. I'm not bitter, but you know to love and be loved are two very different things.

"I always thought I was being loved for myself. It was only later I found out I wasn't.

"I'm so gullible. I'm so goddamn gullible. And I'm so sick of being gullible."

It was a sad end to the shoddiest of Lana's seven marriages.

"How is the old bastard?"
 LANA TURNER, 1971

15

Lana gasped when, in October, 1970, she learned, supposedly for the first time, that her biography was being written. She immediately called her press agent, Frank MacFadden, to see what he could do about it. MacFadden said he knew nothing of the forthcoming biography but that he would check on it. When he hung up the phone, he was upset.

MacFadden's concern was understandable. It is reported by a former employee of MacFadden's agency that Lana Turner, one of their top clients, pays at least $1000 a month for their services, and MacFadden handles her account personally. As is the case with most celebrities, public relations people are hired not only to seek publicity but, when necessary, to suppress it or channel it. Lana Turner, like most stars, prefers not to be "involved" directly. After all, as she has said, "That's what I pay people for."

The next day, either via MacFadden, Lana or a leak in the MacFadden-Strauss-Irwin office, syndicated television columnist Rona Barrett reported that Lana Turner wanted it known that she had no intention of cooperating on the unauthorized biography. Within a few days, the same information appeared in a number of syndicated newspaper and trade paper columns. Although the news deterred a few people who had at first agreed to be interviewed in connection with the book, the majority of those interviewed were either unaware of or unconcerned with Lana's attitude—or they felt that their information would aid Lana by presenting the facts.

Although MacFadden denied any knowledge of the biography, it was he who personally answered a letter addressed to Lana Turner the previous year which informed her of the project and asked for her cooperation in the interests of accuracy. "Thank you very much," MacFadden wrote back, but "Miss Lana Turner" was not interested in cooperating. MacFadden undoubtedly thought the matter closed.

Some of Lana's friends think her objections stem from her feeling that when a biography is written it denotes the end of the subject's career. Other intimates feel that, with her survival philosophy of never looking back, Lana did not want her life revealed and reviewed for herself, her family or the public. And perhaps since the year hadn't been a very productive or happy one in Lana's life, more than ever she had no desire to look back.

The Survivors had been officially canceled in December, 1969. *Variety* noted that it was "one of the most expensive flops in television history." Although the outlook for Lana's career was bleak, her friends rallied to her side. A long-time admirer, columnist Sidney Skolsky, wrote, "Lana will survive *The Survivors*."

Marilyn Beck interviewed Lana, who told her, "Naturally I'm sorry the series came to an end, but as an actress I can't say that I was stunned when I got the news." Miss Beck said that Lana's plans were indefinite, but Lana added, "I know I'll be working in movies and, yes, television too when the right scripts come along."

However, ABC-TV reportedly turned Lana down as the lead for a feature-length motion picture for television because of the poor showing registered by *The Survivors.*

In the face of career disaster and marital failure number seven, Lana intensified her social activities. She dated a Las Vegas hotel man and Henry Berger, husband of the late Anita Louise. However, she was seen most frequently with her male secretary-companion, Taylor Pero. A handsome divorced man about thirty, he accompanied Lana to premieres and parties. He was her date for Harold Robbins' Christmas party.

Pero also took Lana out to restaurants and bars, including a bar in the San Fernando Valley frequented by homosexuals. And it was probably Pero that gossip columnists Igor and Oleg Cassini were referring to when in February 1970 they wrote: "Yes, Virginia, that was Lana Turner visiting a rather questionable bar in Palm Springs recently. Her escort was her hairdresser and only her hairdresser knows why."

Lana was still legally married to Ronald Dante, although they were separated. Talk was that he wanted a $250,000 settlement and Lana's lawyers advised her to play a waiting game. Dante threatened to write a book about his marriage to Lana, naming names and events. He also threatened to reveal in court the most intimate of details. He said the story of their six-month marriage read like "science fiction."

"I will tell why no man is able to live with her," Dante promised when he filed suit for divorce. "I will tell what her other husbands are afraid to reveal." Dante refused to list his specific complaints: "They will come out in court and will be provocative," he said. "I don't want to hurt anybody now or then." But he added that the matter of "what kind of sex life we had . . . undoubtedly will come out at the trial."

Both Lana and Dante were apparently playing a waiting game.

During the year the night club entertainer provided his wife with more unwanted and low-calibre publicity. The *National Enquirer*

284

published "an exclusive interview" with Dante. "She's settled and relaxed," he was quoted as saying. "However, it wasn't my way. I like a little more excitement. I like to get out. Talk to people. She didn't like to meet friends at all. She wanted basically to keep me at home, which was really a bad situation. But she's been having things her own way pretty much her whole life."

Movieland magazine published an alleged interview with Dante: "I married her on a bet," he said. "My friend, the manager of The Candy Store [a discotheque], said, 'I'll bet you a half a buck you can't get her to have dinner with you.' That was the first bet and the evening was just beginning. I knew he was playing with my mind. He was talking amateur talk with me. I'm a pro. So I said, 'You're on.'

"Lana is very shy. An uncannily shy person under normal conditions," Dante went on. "But I know what she does to transform into whatever she transforms into whenever she goes out.

"That certain something," he hinted, "the thing that will come out in court."

He said he then bet his friend a dollar that he would marry her within three months. He married her in two weeks, according to him. Dante said he had never been in love with Lana. "Lana has one hangup, as I've already said before in court," he stated. "She's a magnificent woman in every respect, but she has just one hangup that makes her not perfect. No one is perfect, but it's a hangup that I don't intend to live with."

Dante never, of course, disclosed that particular "hangup."

Soon after, it was reported that Dante was dating Nancy Sinatra, Jr., and Dante claimed that he began receiving mysterious telephone calls ordering him to "cool it" with her.

While the *Enquirer* and *Movieland* are not *New York Times*-calibre publications, they do reach an audience and create unfavorable publicity which even the most astute public relations man can't squelch.

In the past, Lana's career had always provided her with escape when her private life was in turmoil. But in 1970 this was not the case. She tried to keep busy by occasionally appearing on TV variety programs, such as the Carol Burnett Show and the Tim Conway Show. This was understandably not her forte, but there were no acceptable film offers.

A film industry spokesman noted at the time, "I know Lana could make a comeback if they again begin writing scripts for women."

Almost all of Lana Turner's past directors remark on how well she takes direction. George Sidney believes Lana didn't reach her peak as an actress because her personal life was so confused. But he regards her as a good actress and one who has always been underrated. "Anyone who is called a glamour girl would never be recognized by critics," says Sidney. He feels that this undoubtedly affects actresses who know they've done their best but can't hope for recognition.

Tay Garnett says: "I've always felt that Lana's love life has been so botched up that it's been a preoccupation which has infringed to a great extent on her development as an actress. I think if she had some sort of peace, an anchor of some sort, she might have reached unbelievable heights." Garnett's opinion is that Lana "was happier when working than during any other time. Even when she wasn't married there was always some romance cooking. I think she's been a completely frustrated gal all her life. She's always looked for a movie romance, a story book romance—a Prince Charming, the whole bit. And I don't think she's ever quite conceded the fact that it just isn't realistic. I don't think she's ever quite let go of that youthful thing she's been clinging to."

Mervyn LeRoy notes, "She's an all-round good actress. I think she's ruined her professional life in the last few years because she's picked the wrong scripts and the wrong things to do. But that's her business. When she worked for me she was never late, she was always a pro. But I hear now she's a little devil.

"In the beginning I think there was a need, a career drive," says LeRoy. "But I don't think it's there anymore."

Cheryl was back in the news in April 1970, when she was charged with possession of marijuana. Also charged was her roommate, twenty-six-year-old Maria Cebrario. They were living in Calibasas, a Los Angeles suburb, at the time. Cheryl and Maria were driving when they were stopped on suspicion of speeding. Police allegedly discovered potted marijuana plants and cigarettes inside the car, but the charges were later dismissed for insufficient evidence.

For almost a decade Cheryl had avoided adverse publicity. She had casually worked for her father for the past few years, and reports in Hollywood in 1970 were that she was working as an information gatherer for a syndicated Hollywood columnist, Kitty Tremell.

There has been a series of books, called *What Ever Became Of . . .*, which deals with once popular but now forgotten personalities. By the third book in the series the author had run so low on personalities that he included Cheryl Crane. The book sketchily rehashed the infamous Stompanato chapter in Cheryl's life and also made the comment that Cheryl, who has remained single, "when seen in public . . . is usually in the company of girls."

Lana has discussed her relationship with grown-up Cheryl: "We don't talk about the past—not a name, not a date, nothing. . . . If I knew then what I know now . . . yes, she was insecure, let's face it, with all the different changes in. . . . But she never called any of them 'Daddy.' Only her father. We would always find something for her to call her particular stepfather at the moment—nicknames, not sassy ones, maybe an abbreviation. And we never pulled the 'Uncle So-and-So'—I mean, who are we kidding?"

And discussing her marriages, Lana was candid. "You know why I've been married so many times? . . . Take the seven men. I could have lived with any of them, other than the father of my daughter,

287

without that piece of paper. But I want it right on the table. I want it legal. I gotta marry 'em. Better I shouldn't maybe, but I did."

Those that say that Lana's string of men through the years represent her search for a father image are, according to the actress, way off-base. Discussing a father complex, she has said, "Now look! I wish I had known my father better. He died when I was very young. But I didn't develop any complexes about it. I'm a very uncomplexed girl."

Lana moved to a lavish penthouse apartment in Malibu, in a building with full-time security, after her Bel-Air mansion was burglarized.

Although Taylor Pero maintained an apartment of his own in the San Fernando Valley, he spent most of his time at Lana's. The apartment had two large terraces filled with flowers and plants, and Lana hired a gardner to come in several times a week to tend the greenery.

As the year dragged on, the outlook for the future, personally and in her career, remained dismal. The settlement with Dante had not been made, and he commissioned a writer to work on an initial draft of his book.

Robert Kendall, a West Coast freelancer, said he had a contract as a ghostwriter for Dante and produced three drafts of a book. But, "Dante broke his contract with me," said Kendall. "He's not very reliable, to say the very, very least."

Robert Eaton's *The Body Brokers* was in bookstores and being discussed in gossip columns. Dante had literary aspirations. An unauthorized biography was on the horizon. Lana was, to say the least, unhappy and needed to keep busy.

Practically speaking, there was only one road left for her to follow in her career. But it was one which terrified her—the stage. "Live" performing. It was in this area of show business that Lana Turner could still wield Superstar power. She realized that the vehicle for her stage debut had to be exactly right. But she was shrewdly aware of her limitations. She has said the producers of *Applause* wanted her to replace Lauren Bacall in the Broadway production. "I politely turned it down," she remarked. "I am *not* Miss Bacall. She created the role. She's a very strong actress. It was Miss Bacall's baby. Lauren Bacall and Lana Turner are two different types. For me to go in and try to take over would be stupid on my part, leaving myself wide open for comparisons."

When, early in 1971, producers Lee Guber and Shelley Gross offered Lana the starring role in a summer stock package production of the romantic comedy *Forty Carats*, she showed more interest. Lana had seen and liked a West Coast production of the play starring Barbara Rush. ("Had anyone told me that I'd play it, I'd say 'You're out of your mother's skull,' " Lana later observed.) Julie Harris had created the role of the forty-year-old woman in love with a twenty-two-year-old man who wants to marry her. June Allyson and then Zsa Zsa Gabor subsequently replaced Miss Harris before the long-running show closed on Broadway.

"When my agent called for *Forty Carats* I thought he meant the picture," Lana told Earl Wilson. While actress Lana dreaded the prospect of doing a play, businesswoman Turner perked up and asked her agent, "What's the deal?"

The deal was spectacular. For the ten-week tour (originally eight weeks but advance response was so strong the producers added additional cities) she would earn close to two hundred thousand dollars. (Was it coincidence that this was about the same amount Dante was demanding as a settlement?) In addition, it was reported that the producers would pay for Lana's personal entourage: hairdresser, makeup man, chauffeur and limousine. The producers also agreed to Lana's requirement that her personal costume designer, Nolan Miller, the man who had replaced Luis Estevez on *The Survivors*, create her expensive *Forty Carats* wardrobe. It was decided, too, that for Miss Turner's benefit, rather than hiring different ac-

289

tors in each city for the minor roles, all cast members in the touring company would be permanent. The cast would have two weeks of rehearsals rather than one.

To overcome the problem of Lana's voice being too "small" for stage performing, it was decided that she and the rest of the cast would be equipped with invisible "body microphones."

The whole production would be a fitting showcase for a Hollywood Goddess, and Lana signed the contracts. Immediate reaction by West Coast insiders: "She'll never be able to do it. . . . She's too scared of performing in front of audiences. . . . She's used to being able to do re-takes. She'll never remember the lines. . . . She'll never last. . . . She doesn't have the stamina. . . . A dame who drinks like that won't be able to do eight shows a week. . . ."

Lana was in fact extremely nervous and didn't keep it a secret.

With her new venture she was back on the publicity circuit. However, interviews were to be conducted on her own terms: 1. No questions about Johnny Stompanato; 2. no questions about Cheryl Crane; 3. no questions about her last marriage or current romances.

Leroy Aarons, a syndicated writer, noted after interviewing her: "She speaks in an oddly high-pitched voice, unlike the sultry memories of *The Postman Always Rings Twice*, and it seems like she's straining to sound urbane and cultured. She is oblivious to frequent errors of syntax. Every once in a while, she lets loose with an earthy —even suggestive—throwaway line, and you speculate that this is the more honest, more likeable side of her personality."

"I don't like sitting around, I like to work," she told Aarons. Revealing her tough, earthy side, she added: "I still will not do crap."

Many new photographs accompanying articles about Lana's debut were unflattering to her. But these pictures were deceiving— in person she was still youthful and pretty. It was ironic that she no longer seemed to be photogenic.

In all her interviews she reiterated her fear of performing "live." At the same time, she went into training. She had no trepidations about the role itself. It was well within her range. But it would be a strenuous ten weeks. There would be over a dozen costume changes in the course of a performance. Many performances would be "theatre-in-the-round," which called for numerous ramp entrances and exits.

Barry Nelson, the Broadway and Hollywood actor-director, was signed to direct, but he soon dropped out of *Forty Carats*, and there was speculation that this was only the first of many problems that would beset the production. According to an informed source, Lana had to be treated "like a fragile figurine. She needed *confidence*. This was a big step for her, her stage debut, and she wanted to do it right. Everything had to be *just* right. And, let's face it, she was absolutely right in *caring* as much as she did. It was her last chance to stay in the big-time as a box-office attraction rather than a nostalgic relic."

Lana has said it was John Bowab who convinced her that she could do the play. People who know him say that Bowab did a lot of "convincing." When Barry Nelson left the production, Bowab took over as director. ("If you can get him, he'll pull you through the show," Lana's friends had told her.)

A handsome, sensual man about forty, Bowab is an expert at dealing with ladies of Lana's temperament. ("There's no bull about him," Lana later explained. "And if I do something wrong, he's the first to criticize. But hell, I can take that. I never claimed that I know everything.") As associate producer of Fryer-Carr-Harris' Broadway musicals *Sweet Charity* and *Mame*, it was Bowab who prepared the New York, London and Las Vegas productions of those shows, working closely with Ann Miller, Susan Hayward and Ginger Rogers.

Because of his involvement in getting *Forty Carats* on the boards, Bowab, a long-time close friend of the late, unmarried Lawrence Carr (of the Fryer-Carr-Harris team), drastically changed his off-beat life style to keep Lana happy.

At fifty-one, Lana's "romantic fantasies" were intense as ever. "She needed—demanded—full-time reassurance," said a friend.

"There suddenly seemed to be no time in Bowab's life for anyone but Lana."

The actress said that she and director Bowab "sat for hours over a card table just reading and rereading the script.

"That part was easy," according to Lana. "And then I had to get in shape. Three gals and I made up a dance class so that I could tone up and, believe me, I found muscles I didn't know I had.

"I also began taking long walks on the beach . . . long walks and long strides and singing marching songs as I went along." Her drinking tapered off. She took voice lessons.

It would not have surprised Hollywood and New York doubters if Lana had backed out of the *Forty Carats* commitment. As far as many were concerned, Lana Turner was over the hill.

By this time, Taylor Pero had become her personal manager. He had seen Lana through the difficult period following her separation from Dante. Pero knew Lana's habits and needs. He made sure "everything was handled correctly."

Before her stage debut on June 8, 1971, in Shady Grove, a Washington, D.C., suburb, Turner and entourage arrived in New York City for several days of rehearsals. She was enthroned at the Plaza Hotel and rehearsals were in a west 57th Street hall. Lana granted Earl Wilson an interview and was totally frank—not only about her fears concerning the play but about her past life. Nostalgia obviously held no magic for her.

Wilson asked, "Have you seen Artie?"

"Artie who?" She knew he meant Artie Shaw, her first husband. "How is the old bastard?" she smiled.

Wilson said, "Shaw doesn't believe marriage is the greatest invention. . . . He says you and he had nothing in common."

Lana retorted, "That's why it only lasted four months and three days. I knew it was over in three days but was too busy on a film to tell him."

Before leaving for Shady Grove, Lana spent a few days relaxing with friends on Fire Island.

Forty Carats opened on schedule, surprising a host of disbeliev-
ers. Lana was radiant and ecstatic after the opening night performance. "We got through it. We got through it," she kept saying
in the dressing room afterwards. Mildred Turner, dressed in black,
was on hand to share her daughter's triumph. While Lana held
court, Mildred patted Lana's forehead with a Kleenex.

"I was ready to take the gaspipe," Lana told *The New York
Times*. "I felt like a parade horse walking around that ring. . . .
That horrible first moment! I couldn't get air from my throat. I
couldn't speak. All I could think is 'Please, dear God, let me get
one good breath in me. Please God, don't let me fall on my face.
. . . I'm a blithering idiot at this point. I'm too up. After this, the
sky, baby, the sky."

Newsweek summed it up: "The play had ended and the audience
was on its feet. 'Oh, my God,' thought leading lady Lana Turner as
she came onstage for her curtain call, 'they're getting ready to leave
the theatre, and I haven't taken my bow.' Most actresses might
know better, but [Lana Turner] could be excused for failing to recognize a standing ovation. In addition to her rhinestone-studded
'bow gown,' she wore sixteen costumes and the critics seemed to
feel that they had seen more of a fashion show than a performance.
'That kind of threw me,' said Lana about her reviews. 'But I think
most people dig beauty, and if I'm capable of looking good in these
clothes, what's wrong with that? Thank God I'm not an old
frump.' "

Most of the critics were unfair in their reviews. Lana was actually
extremely believable and effective in the role, and created a character with color and dimension. Obviously the theory is correct that
no matter how good a performance she might give, Lana won't receive full recognition as an actress.

The critics did note that Lana was smart enough to play Lana.
She knew her audience and provided them with the kind of show
they wanted. And she must have been pleased when one critic, Emerson Beauchamp of the *Washington Star*, noted: "It's fairly easy

to believe that this particular middle-aged woman *could* take her pick of prospective twenty-two-year-old bridegrooms. . . . Lana Turner at fifty-one still looks like a dream walking and it's hard not to wonder what happened to all the men in her life."

Ronald Dante was still causing her problems. According to a story in *Women's Wear Daily* in July, Lana was "livid about the use of her name and testimonial in ads placed by her estranged husband Dr. R. Dante on behalf of his course in self-hypnosis. In an affidavit, Miss Turner notes, 'It has come to my attention that in publicity and advertising presumably issued by Dr. Dante, I am quoted as saying, "Lose weight permanently. Quit smoking forever. And gain more confidence effortlessly. As I have done in just one day through my husband Dr. R. Dante's instantly taught science of self-hypnosis." I have never made the statement quoted above or any statement similar thereto,' said Lana, who's pressing for a divorce from Dante."

There were conflicting reports as to whether they were officially divorced and whether or not she had given him a cash settlement. Columnist Jack O'Brian wrote that Lana was so irked by Dante's claims that he never got a penny from her that she planned a lawsuit to get back her alleged $250,000 settlement. Walter Scott, in his syndicated column, answered the question, "Can you tell me why Lana Turner gave her seventh husband $200,000 and now wants it back?," by saying: "Miss Turner insists that the document she signed turning $200,000 over to Dante for helping her through a trying emotional time is not valid because of the condition she was in when she made the grant."

This information raised a few eyebrows. Naturally Lana is keeping mum about the entire Dante debacle. Only her lawyers, and Dante's, know the intricate details of the mystery settlement and the status of the Dante-Turner divorce. However, as yet, there have been no "revelations" in court as Dante threatened.

Whether officially divorced or not, by late summer of 1971 Dante was in the past. Lana's future again looked bright.

She is in the midst of her successful summer tour as this book goes to press, although she has missed a few performances as a result of a knee injury complicated by bursitis.

With her stage debut, Lana Turner proved she is still box office. She remains in the minds of millions as Hollywood's truest example of a glamorous star.

Currently, Lana's personal life appears relatively tranquil. She is still close to her mother, as always, and she is on friendly terms with Cheryl.

While many people who know Lana find her to be shallow, they also note that this isn't meant in a derogatory sense. "Because of Lana's beauty, her image, and the characters she played, people expect Lana to be more than she actually is. It's *their* fault if they're disappointed, not hers. Lana has never pretended to be anything she isn't."

Those who know her intimately have strong, varying feelings about her, but almost all agree that she is basically honest, and likable, and that she has the ability to laugh at herself, often referring to herself in the third person, as "L.T." or "Mama."

"Look, let's not get mixed up about the *real* Lana Turner," says Adela Rogers St. Johns. "The *real* Lana Turner is Lana Turner. She was always a Movie Star and loved it. Her personal life and her Movie Star life *are one.*"

Lana Turner was a movie star *first.* Then she became an actress. Her secret is that she has contented herself with being Lana Turner. And her luck has been that the public reacts, just as her friends do, to a woman doing the best she can, although she sometimes falters, sometimes makes stupid mistakes, and is often indiscreet.

Lana still engenders a fervent kind of fan adoration. In New York City, for example, an affable young man, Lou Valentino, has devoted innumerable hours (and dollars) to his Lana Turner Collection. He has over 25,000 still photographs of her and corresponds with people all over the world in his search for additional Turnerabilia.

While the rest of America has not followed her life with Mr. Valentino's zeal, the name Lana Turner remains a household word. She is still capable of holding the public's interest and surprising them. Has her philosophy changed regarding her love life? "Absolutely!" she exclaimed to *Newsday*'s Jerry Parker. "No more paper work!" Did that mean no more husbands? "Let people figure that out for themselves," answered Lana. "Do you expect me to say I'll never fall in love again? Oh no, baby, I've got too many juices still flowing."

She recently told the New York *Daily News* that she believes in reincarnation. "I feel I was a member of an Egyptian royal family at one period," Lana said seriously. "Not any of that Cleopatra jazz, but royal. Also—and this may sound strange—I was once an American Indian."

Whatever else she is (or may have been), Lana Turner *is* uniquely American. She remains an indestructible symbol of her generation. In her own lifetime she has become part of American folklore: the teenage star discovered at a soda fountain; the Sweater Girl; and, most notoriously, the woman associated with the killing of Johnny Stompanato. The names Lana Turner and Johnny Stompanato will be forever linked like those of Frankie and Johnny.

When approached about writing an autobiography, Lana has told publishers: "Thank you so much, gentlemen, but the answer is NO. Why? Because I'm still living. God has other things in store for me."

Lana Turner's spirit is indefatigable. Although nothing is more out of date than last year's blonde or yesterday's sweater girl, Lana Turner has managed to make her world-famous sweater last well over three decades. Even if some threads are ragged, it's still quite an achievement.

Perhaps Helen Young best sums it up when she says, "No matter what it is . . . even today, and through all of her life, Lana has had that little girl quality about her. Life is always offering the unexpected and she's there ready to meet it. She can have just as much fun in the kitchen trying to roast a Thanksgiving turkey, it holds just as much intrigue for her, and she can be just as enthusiastic about it as she can about a new $2000 gown or anything else. . . ."

When confronted with memories of the past, Lana often laughs. "Doesn't it make you sick?" she once said, referring to some of her escapades. "Now you understand why my friends tell me I'm the hokiest broad in the world. Well at least I can laugh at myself. If I couldn't, I'd be in an asylum by now!"